SPIKE LEE

INTERVIEWS

CONVERSATIONS WITH FILMMAKERS SERIES
PETER BRUNETTE, GENERAL EDITOR

Courtesy of Photofest

SPIKE
LEE

INTERVIEWS

EDITED BY CYNTHIA FUCHS

UNIVERSITY PRESS OF MISSISSIPPI / JACKSON

www.upress.state.ms.us

Copyright © 2002 by University Press of Mississippi
All rights reserved
Manufactured in the United States of America

10   09   08   07   06   05   04   03   02   4   3   2   1
⊗
Library of Congress Cataloging-in-Publication Data

Lee, Spike.
   Spike Lee : interviews / edited by Cynthia Fuchs.
      p.   cm. — (Conversations with filmmakers series)
   Includes index.
   ISBN 1-57806-469-4 (cloth : alk. paper) — ISBN 1-57806-470-8 (pbk. : alk. paper)
     1. Lee, Spike—Interviews.   2. Motion picture producers and directors—
United States—Interviews. I. Fuchs, Cynthia. II. Title. III. Series.
PN1998.3.L44 A5   2002
791.43'0233'092—dc21   2001046941

British Library Cataloging-in-Publication Data available

CONTENTS

INTRODUCTION

''A Spike Lee Joint.'' The phrase means different things to different people. Some associate it with insightful social critique, others with contentious political activism, joyful cinematic creativity, self-conscious community-building, or skillful self-promotion. But no matter how you understand it, one thing is certain: when the young Lee began using the phrase to denote his self-produced films during the 1980s, he was also declaring the emergence of a provocative, influential artist and entrepreneur. Part entertainment and part treatise, part self-expression and part cultural analysis, a Spike Lee Joint comes out of a particular set of conditions, while articulating specific principles and aspirations.

When Lee's *She's Gotta Have It* was released in 1986, much was made of the facts that he completed his first full-length feature for $175,000 and that it then grossed over $8.5 million, opening wide the door for his subsequent contract with Columbia Pictures (for *School Daze*) and the longer-term affiliation with Universal (*Do the Right Thing, Mo' Better Blues, Jungle Fever, Malcolm X, Crooklyn,* and *Clockers*). Lee immediately understood the point: if your picture makes money, you can get funding for your next project. In particular, *She's Gotta Have It*'s remarkable profit margin was a function of its appeal to a "cross-over" audience, that is, an art-house (read: predominantly white) crowd as well as the expected "urban" (read: black) demographic. It was a lesson the twenty-nine-year-old filmmaker took to heart, not in the sense that he would always set his sights on a "white" audience, but in the sense that he would always be conscious of that audience, as well as its representation by white media.

She's Gotta Have It's critical and (relative) commercial success made Lee an "overnight" star, though in truth, he had been struggling to make movies for several years. On his graduation from New York University's Film Program, his thesis film, *Joe's Bed-Stuy Barbershop: We Cut Heads,* won the Motion Picture Arts and Sciences' Student Academy Award. His time at NYU was not always so copasetic. At the end of his first year, he made *The Answer,* a short film about a black screenwriter assigned to remake D. W. Griffith's *The Birth of a Nation.* As Lee recalls in *Best Seat in the House,* "Somehow the faculty did not like this film. They felt I was defaming the father of cinema, or whatever. They wanted to kick me out," he writes, but couldn't because he'd already been granted a teaching assistantship for the next year.

As this story suggests, Lee could not help but be conscious early on that by making the movies he wanted to make, he would be challenging established systems and values. And he has never shied away from such challenges, from his early declaration that African Americans could not be "racist" because they have historically lacked the power to dominate another group, to his more recent criticisms of Quentin Tarantino's overuse of "the n-word" in his scripts; the spurious "histories" offered by *Mississippi Burning, Amistad,* and *The Patriot;* the black characters whom Lee has called both "magical Negroes" and "spiritual mammies to white folk" in *The Legend of Bagger Vance* and *The Green Mile;* or the television sitcoms and rap videos that perpetuate minstrel conventions. Spike Lee has again and again shown that he is willing to rock the boat when the stakes are high. He puts it this way: "I've been blessed with the opportunity to express the views of black people who otherwise don't have access to power and the media. I have to take advantage of that while I'm still bankable." For Lee, the stakes of U.S. racism and hypocrisy are always high.

Throughout his prolific career—at this point, in mid-2001, he's directed nineteen films (that's about a film a year), dozens of music videos and commercials, and published seven books (with an eighth, co-authored by his wife Tonya, due out in 2002)—Lee has again and again taken on the entertainment/sports industries with indisputable passion. His music video collaborators include a wide range of artists, from Branford Marsalis, Miles Davis, and Anita Baker, to Steel Pulse, Public Enemy, Stevie Wonder, and Naughty by Nature (their "Hip Hop Hurray" became something of an anthem on its release in 1992), as well as Bruce Hornsby and Michael Jackson. Lee has often described himself as an independent filmmaker (he always has "final cut" in his contract, beginning with 1988's *School Daze*, a right rarely granted, especially to an artist making his second film). And yet he has, since *She's Gotta Have It*, regularly worked with studios to get his work financed and distributed. (Significant exceptions would include *Get on the Bus*, for which he put together funding from a one-off group called "15 Black Men"). Lee's fiercely autonomous thinking comes with a price, as he often draws criticism as much for the format he uses as for stories he tells and the charges he makes. For instance, he's been accused more than once of "selling out" by making commercials for Nike, the U.S. Navy, or most recently, Jaguar, who in 2000 commissioned an eight-minute short film, "The Harlem to Martha's Vineyard Special," designed to appeal to a "diverse" audience, as well as other spots to be produced by Lee's advertising company, Spike /DDB. Lee's response to such criticism is part practical and financial, part ideological and idealistic: he wants to widen the scope—the assumptions and the address—of so-called "minority" images and audiences. He wants to be able to compete, to represent, like any white corporate entity, to sell products and create art that are pitched to multiple "demographics."

Lee always knew his would be a hard row to hoe. As he tells Marlaine Glicksman, "When I was becoming a filmmaker, I knew it would be harder for me to be a black filmmaker—to be a filmmaker because I was black." And he credits his parents—and grandmother Zimmie Jackson Shelton, who funded much of his education and his first films—for his precocious political and aesthetic awareness. His mother Jacquelyn was an art and African American literature teacher, and his father Bill is a jazz bassist (who has written the scores for Lee's first four films). Lee remembers for the *New York Post*, "My mom made me read Dickens and Ralph Ellison and Zora Neale Hurston when I was thirteen." He adds, "When I was in college, she would send me back my letters, correcting my grammar in red ink. She gave me high standards, telling me 90 percent wasn't good enough. I had to be twice as good as my white classmates" (AP, September 10, 2000).

Hurston figures conspicuously in *She's Gotta Have It*, which includes an epigraph from *Their Eyes Were Watching God*. Lee was praised as well as disparaged for his efforts to represent a black woman's experience in his first feature. But he has always remembered that early criticism. As he told George Khoury in 1999, the only aspect of any of his films that he would like to "do over" is the scene where Nola Darling is raped. It's not every artist—or even every person—who can admit that his best intentions have gone wrong. But while he took seriously his responsibility in this case, he never stopped taking on complex, difficult, and troubling subject matter. The controversy ignited by *She's Gotta Have It* was only the first of many surrounding Lee's films. Indeed, whenever a new Spike Lee Joint arrives in theaters, a new debate usually flares.

At the same time, nothing about Lee or his work is predictable, and he need not have a film in theaters to make waves. Though he has, from the beginning of his career, asked that he not be considered a "spokesperson for the race," he has also stepped up to articulate and represent what he sees as pressing problems. Though most of these have to do with race and racism, and though he accepts being seen as a "black filmmaker," he has other interests, and counts among most important influences a range of artists and activists, including Ella Fitzgerald, Billie Holiday, Akira Kurosawa, Martin Scorsese, Budd Schulberg, Melvin Van Peebles, Muhammed Ali, and Malcolm X.

Lee's brilliance as a filmmaker was demonstrated beyond doubt with *Do the Right Thing* (1989), which revealed in one big bang his talent for combining groundbreaking art and overtly political content. The film earned him multiple awards and nominations, including Academy Award nominations for Best Original Screenplay and Director, Golden Globe nominations for Best Director–Motion Picture and Best Screenplay–Motion Picture, the Chicago Film Festival Critics Awards for Best Picture and Best Director, and the Los Angeles Film Critics Association's Awards for Best Film and Best Director. While some critics at the time worried that the film would "start riots" or that he had not "accurately" represented the Bedford Stuyvesant neighborhood where the film is set, because there were no "drug dealers" in sight, he sensibly and resolutely defended his vision, pointing out repeatedly that the film—and such reactions to it—exposed a culture that valued a white man's pizzeria over a black man's life.

Lee's passion is almost palpable in his work, despite the often-made observation that his films are rarely "personal" per se (1988's *School Daze,* a musical based on his time at Morehouse College, and 1994's *Crooklyn,* based on memories of his mother, including her death from liver cancer, and co-scripted by his siblings Joie and Cinqué, come closest). Nowhere are his passions clearer than in *Malcolm X,* the movie that he publicly fought to direct, claiming that the white director who was signed to do the job, Norman Jewison, would not be able to do justice to the slain leader's experiences and ideas.

This assessment in itself was controversial, as was the charge made against him by Amiri Baraka that his representation of Malcolm was "negative." Also upsetting was the dispute with Warner Bros. and the Completion Bond Company, when the film went over budget, during which Lee called out the companies as "racist." When an October 1992 *Esquire* magazine cover story declared that "Spike Lee Hates Your Cracker Ass," the fight was apparently on, and Lee made no bones about connecting his film to then current events, namely, the Rodney King beating and L.A. uprising. Again, Lee understood what he was doing and what the stakes were. As he told Gary Crowdus and Dan Georgakas at the time, "Racism is art of the fabric of American society, so why should the film industry be exempt? I think it's a racist assumption that white America will not go to see a black film that's not a comedy, or that doesn't have singing and dancing, or that doesn't star Eddie Murphy."

Lee's outspoken outrage has not, however, precluded his other interests or efforts in a variety of areas, particularly in film technology and business (of course, as he will be the first to point out, these areas are wholly connected to the workings of race and racism in the world economy). He shot his latest film, *Bamboozled* (2001), in relatively inexpensive digital video, not only making his project doable, but also with an eye toward making this technology commercially viable and further democratizing the process of filmmaking and distributing.

Lee has also worked closely and generously with fellow artists, understanding from jump the media's inclination to pit him against his own contemporaries, such as John Singleton and Matty Rich (Lee noted repeatedly that the industry was only ready for one "black filmmaker" at a time). He has always worked closely with his crew (most of whom are repeat hires over the years, constituting a kind of on-set family, and some of whom—Ernest Dickerson most notably, have gone on with their own directing careers), as well as actors (he has worked closely with—and even introduced to the world—many respected performers, including Ossie Davis, Ruby Dee, Laurence Fishburne, Samuel L. Jackson, Delroy Lindo, Jada Pinkett Smith, Wesley Snipes, John Turturro, Denzel Washington, and Alfre Woodard, among others), and musicians (in addition to his father, he has worked with Chuck D, Prince, Stevie Wonder, and Mos Def, to integrate visual imagery with contemporary and innovative soundtracks).

His work with and for the next generation is also worth noting: Lee has

consistently encouraged, mentored, and produced work by young filmmakers (for example, Gina Prince-Blythewood, Rusty Cundieff, Nick Gomez,
Lee Davis, and Lee's own cousin, Malcolm D. Lee), in order to ensure that
multiple voices and viewpoints are available to represent the "black community." He has served as a master teacher of film at the Tisch School of the
Arts and Harvard University, and has started a film program at Long Island
University. He regularly does college lectures, during which he tackles all
sorts of questions. So visible is he in so many ways that he has long since
become "Spike," recognizable to many filmgoers (and basketball fans) by his
first name only.

And yet, "Spike" has maintained a certain public reserve concerning his
personal life. While interviewers do ask him about that life (in particular,
Charlie Rose likes to ask, how has being married or being a father changed
him?), they are more likely to focus on his opinions concerning current
events and entertainment. While most interviewers will ask him point blank
about race and racism, and some about his attitudes toward "women," Alan
Frutkin reminds Lee of repeated accusations that his films offer homophobic
images, and more pointedly asks if he is himself homophobic (to which Lee
observes that the "black community" may be more homophobic than "others," but that he feels "people are free to pursue whatever they want to").
Moreover, Lee always has something to say about his "beloved Knicks" (as
most writers describe them in relation to Lee) and has no qualms about discussing sports management, journalism, and commerce (in fact, he grapples
with all of these problems in his 1998 film, *He Got Game*).

Emphatic and shrewd about the ways that entertainment affects attitudes
and behaviors, Lee takes his own responsibility on this issue seriously. He
made *4 Little Girls* (1997) with the idea that "our legacy"—not just that of
African Americans, but of all Americans—must be preserved and confronted.
Histories and legacies come in various forms, of course. And when he made
Summer of Sam (1999), he was asked about his decision to make a movie with
a non-black cast, as well as the sensationalism of the subject matter (New
York City's famous 1976 serial killer). As always, Lee made his case whenever
he was asked to do so.

Lee's generosity, enthusiasm, and dedication to his art and mission have
never wavered. Because he is yet so young, we may count ourselves fortunate
that he will be making films, television programs, commercials, and music
videos—as well as giving interviews about them—for a long time to come.

Spike Lee: Interviews follows the standards set by the University Press of Mississippi for its Conversations with Filmmakers series, meaning that it reprints interviews as they originally appeared, in hardcopy and online forms, and, in the case of the Charlie Rose interviews or the Independent Film Channel's "Delroy Lindo on Spike Lee," transcribed from a television program. This collection of interviews is designed to be useful to researchers as well as to aficionados of Spike Lee's work.

Because of this format, some interviews necessarily repeat information, particularly biographical and introductory information, as well as anecdotes or observations. Lee has, over time, been selective about giving interviews: when he finds people whom he believes understand, respect, and also challenge him, he welcomes the chance to speak with them again. And so, this collection includes a couple of interviews with the same interviewer, namely, Marlaine Glicksman of *Film Comment,* Charlie Rose (with whom Lee has appeared several times), Stephen Pizzello of *American Cinematographer,* and Gary Crowdus and Dan Georgakas of *Cineaste.* But such repetitions in themselves are informative, as his increasing sense of ease with particular writers becomes apparent in what he says and how he says it. It should be noted that Lee has also embraced online publications, for he sees in these venues a way to reach what he perceives as his audience, and some interviews here have been selected to reflect that perception.

While Lee is no doubt an industrious and dynamic artist, he has not always been comfortable speaking about his creative and thought processes; early interviews are harder to come by than those concerning his more recent work and life. He's also not the easiest person to interview. He's been described by more than one writer as "combative," "defensive," or "prickly." Over the past few years, his attitude has reportedly "mellowed," and writers have said as much (the two times I have spoken with him, for *Jungle Fever* and for *Bamboozled* have given me a similar impression). Still, because Lee began making films and attracted so much attention at such a young age, the interviews assembled here reveal changes in his public attitudes toward critics and interviewers, the many spotlights cast on him and his own relationship to his work and communities.

Thanks to the many interviewers and publications who have been generous enough to allow their work to be reprinted in this volume. Thanks also to Tobias Peterson and Dale Leech, for their help in researching this project; to Peter Brunette, my colleague and general editor of the series; and to my

editors Seetha Srinivasan and Anne Stascavage for their patience and generous direction, as well as to Judy Coleman and the other members of the
University Press of Mississippi crew.

And thank you especially to my angel, Jeffrey Corbett, for his guidance,
support, and inspiration.

CHRONOLOGY

1957 Born Shelton Jackson Lee, March 20, 1957, in Atlanta, Georgia, to Jacquelyn and Bill Lee; his siblings are Chris Lee (b. 1958), Joie Lee (b. 1960), Cinqué Lee (b. 1963), David Lee (b. 1968), and half-brother Arnold Lee (b. 1985).

1975 Graduates from John Dewey High School, in Brooklyn, New York.

1977 Jacquelyn dies, from liver cancer.
   Buys Super-8 camera and shoots his first film, *Last Hustle in Brooklyn.*

1978 Father remarries, to Susan Kaplan.

1979 Graduates from Morehouse College in Atlanta, with a major in mass communication; his tuition is provided by his grandmother, Zimmie Jackson Shelton, alumna of Spelman College (Class of 1929), affiliated with the all-male Morehouse.
   Summer internship with Columbia Pictures in Los Angeles.
   Begins three-year program at New York University's Tisch School of the Arts, again supported by his grandmother Zimmie. His first-year final project, a ten-minute short called *The Answer,* tells the story of a black screenwriter assigned to remake D. W. Griffith's *The Birth of a Nation.*

1982 Graduates from NYU, with a master of fine arts degree in film production. His forty-five-minute thesis film, *Joe's Bed-Stuy Barbershop: We Cut Heads,* is showcased at Lincoln Center and the Museum of Modern Art, and wins the Motion Picture Arts and Sciences' Student Academy Award, and Lee gets an agent.

1983   Unable to find filmmaking work, Lee works part-time at First Run Features, then a small film distribution company.

1984   He is forced to abandon a semi-autobiographical story about a young bicycle messenger, *Messenger,* due to lack of funding. His grandmother loses $20,000 on the project.

1985   Founds 40 Acres & a Mule Filmworks (and some time later, a record label, 40 Acres & a Mule Musicworks), and makes *She's Gotta Have It* for $175,000, again backed by his grandmother, Zimmie Shelton.

1986   Island Pictures distributes *She's Gotta Have It,* which wins the Prix de Jeunesse Award at the Cannes Film Festival, the Los Angeles Film Critics Association's New Generation Award, and the Independent Spirit Award for Best First Feature; it earns over $8.5 million.
        Directs his first music videos, for Branford Marsalis, "Royal Gardens," and Miles Davis, "Tutu Melody."

1988   Publishes *Spike Lee's Gotta Have It: Inside Guerrilla Filmmaking,* with photos by David Lee.
        Directs first commercial, for Nike Air Jordan campaign (seven commercials), featuring his *She's Gotta Have It* character Mars Blackmon and Michael Jordan.
        Releases *School Daze,* a musical made for an over-budget $4 million, under a one-picture deal with Columbia Pictures.

1989   Publishes *Uplift the Race: The Construction of School Daze,* written with Lisa Jones.
        Releases *Do the Right Thing* to critical accolades and controversy (media declare the film will "cause riots"), inspiring a now-famous press conference at Cannes, where he is asked to explain how he can portray a Bed-Stuy neighborhood without showing drug dealers (this press conference is included on the DVD released in 2001). The film wins an Academy Award nomination for Best Original Screenplay; Golden Globe nominations for Best Director–Motion Picture and Best Screenplay–Motion Picture; Chicago Film Festival Critics Awards for Best Pic-

ture and Best Director; and the Los Angeles Film Critics Association's Awards for Best Film and Best Director.

Creates two retail companies, Spike's Joint, based in the Fort Greene section of Brooklyn, where he has resided since childhood, and Spike's Joint West in Los Angeles (these close in 1997).

1990   Publishes *Do the Right Thing: A Spike Lee Joint,* written with Lisa Jones, photography by David Lee.

Releases *Mo' Better Blues,* made for $10 million, Lee's largest budget to date. The protagonist, Bleek Gilliam, is inspired by Lee's father, Bill, who writes the score, as he has for Lee's previous three films.

1991   Publishes *Mo' Better Blues,* written with Lisa Jones, photography by David Lee.

Publishes *Five for Five: The Films of Spike Lee,* with photographs by David Lee, and five essays on his films by five writers.

Inspired by the 1989 murder of Yusuf Hawkins, *Jungle Fever* is released.

Appears in a film directed by his longtime editor, Barry Alexander Brown, *Lonely in America.*

1992   Releases *Malcolm X,* a film Lee had fought publicly to direct, replacing original director Norman Jewison. He completes filming only by patching together funding from friends and supporters, including Bill Cosby, Oprah Winfrey, Michael Jordan, Magic Johnson, Prince, Janet Jackson, and Tracy Chapman. Controversy attends its opening, including an open letter published by a focus group called the "United Front to Preserve the Memory of Malcolm X and the Cultural Revolution," led by Amiri Baraka. The film also wins the Chicago Film Critics Association's Award for Best Picture.

1993   Marries corporate attorney Tonya Linette Lewis, October 2.

Publishes *By Any Means Necessary: The Trials and Tribulations of Making Malcolm X,* written with Ralph Wiley.

Appears in two documentaries, *Seven Songs for Malcolm X* and *The Last Party.*

1994   Daughter Satchel Paige born.

Releases *Crooklyn,* based on memories of Jacquelyn Lee, coscripted by siblings Joie and Cinqué.

Appears as interviewee in *Hoop Dreams.*

1995   Releases *Clockers,* based on co-screenwriter Richard Price's novel.
Executive produces two feature films, Nick Gomez's *New Jersey Drive*
and Rusty Cundieff's *Tales from the Hood.*

1996   Releases two films: *Girl 6,* scripted by Suzan-Lori Parks (the first film
Lee has directed that he has not also written), and *Get on the Bus,* about
the Million Man March, scripted by Reggie Rock Blythewood, and
funded in part by 15 Black Men, a group Lee puts together that includes
Will Smith, Robert Guillaume, Johnnie Cochran, and Wesley Snipes.
Directs a piece of Albert Belle for HBO's *Real Sports* (for which he later
receives an Emmy); helps to organize a Forum on Racism in Sports
Journalism.
Appears as interviewee in *When We Were Kings,* documentary about
the Ali-Frazier fight in Zaire.
Establishes advertising company called Spike/DDB, in association with
DDB Needham, where he will direct commercials aimed at "urban
markets."

1997   Son Jackson born.
Publishes *Best Seat in the House: A Basketball Memoir* (New York: Three
Rivers Press), written with Ralph Wiley, chronicling his lifelong devo-
tion to the New York Knicks. Releases *4 Little Girls,* a documentary on
the church bombing in Birmingham, Alabama, in September 1963. The
film is nominated for an Academy Award for Best Feature Documentary, losing to the Holocaust documentary, *The Long Way Home,*
directed by Rabbi Marvin Hier and Richard Trank; it wins the Broadcast Film Critics Association's Award for Best Documentary, and the
Golden Satellite for Best Documentary.

1998   Releases *He Got Game,* starring real NBA star Ray Allen, exposing the
exploitative strategies of the professional sports/entertainment
industry.
Directs HBO's *Freak,* a "concert" film of John Leguizamo's one-man
off-Broadway show.

1999   Releases *Summer of Sam* to public controversy over the subject, David
Berkowitz, the famous serial killer who menaced New York City during
1976.

Executive produces *The Best Man,* for his cousin, writer-director Malcolm D. Lee.

2000   Produces *Love & Basketball,* for Gina Prince-Blythewood, and *3 A.M.,* for Lee Davis.

Releases *The Original Kings of Comedy,* "concert" film of stand-up comedy by Steve Harvey, D. L. Hughley, Cedric the Entertainer, and Bernie Mac.

Releases *Bamboozled,* which critiques black representations in media, focused on television. Controversy ensues.

Signs with Barry Diller's Studios USA to produce an hour-long television drama.

2001   Directs *A Huey P. Newton Story,* based on star Roger Guenveur Smith's play.

Wins Cinequest's Maverick Spirit Award.

2002   Publishes *Please, Baby, Please,* written with his wife Tonya Lewis Lee, illustrated by Michael Ray Charles.

FILMOGRAPHY

As Director

Student Films

LAST HUSTLE IN BROOKLYN (1977)
THE ANSWER (New York University, 1980)
SARAH (New York University, 1981)

Short Films

SATURDAY NIGHT LIVE: Horn of Plenty, with Branford Marsalis and Diahane Abbott (1986)
MTV: Five One Minute "Art Spots" (1989)
HBO: "Iron Mike Tyson" (1991)
HBO's REAL SPORTS: "John Thompson" Coach (1995)
HBO's REAL SPORTS: "Albert Belle" (1996)

Feature Films

1983
JOE'S BED-STUY BARBERSHOP: WE CUT HEADS (40 Acres & a Mule Filmworks/New York University)
Producer: **Spike Lee**, Zimmie Shelton
Director: **Spike Lee**
Screenplay: **Spike Lee**

Cinematography: Ernest R. Dickerson
Editing: **Spike Lee**
Art Direction: Felix De Rooy
Music: Bill Lee
Cast: Monty Ross (Zachariah), Donna Bailey (Ruth), Stuart Smith (Thaddeus/ Teapot), Tommy Redmond Hicks (Nicholas), Horace Long (Joe), LaVerne Summer (Esquire), Africanus Rocius (Spinks)
16 mm, B&W
60 minutes

1986
SHE'S GOTTA HAVE IT (40 Acres & a Mule Filmworks)
Producer: **Spike Lee** (as Shelton J. Lee) and Pamm R. Jackson (associate producer)
Director: **Spike Lee**
Screenplay: **Spike Lee**
Cinematography: Ernest Dickerson
Production Design: Wynn Thomas
Editing: **Spike Lee**
Music: Bill Lee
Cast: Tracy Camilla Johns (Nola Darling), Tommy Redmond Hicks (Jamie Overstreet), John Canada Terrell (Greer Childs), **Spike Lee** (Mars Blackmon), Raye Dowell (Opal Gilstrap), Joie Lee (Clorinda Bradford), S. Epatha Merkerson (Doctor Jamison), Bill Lee (Sonny Darling), Monty Ross (Dog 1), Lewis Jordan (Dog 2), Erik Dellums (Dog 3), Reginald Hudlin (Dog 4), Eric Payne (Dog 5)
16 mm, B&W, with color ballet scene
84 minutes

1988
SCHOOL DAZE (40 Acres & a Mule Filmworks/Columbia Pictures Corporation)
Producer: **Spike Lee**
Director: **Spike Lee**
Screenplay: **Spike Lee**
Cinematography: Ernest Dickerson
Production Design: Wynn Thomas

Editing: Barry Alexander Brown
Music: Bill Lee and Stevie Wonder (song: "I Can Only Be Me")
Cast: Laurence Fishburne (Dap), Giancarlo Esposito (Julian), Tisha Campbell (Jane Touissant), Kyme (Rachel Meadows), Joe Seneca (President McPherson), Art Evans (Cedar Cloud), Ossie Davis (Coach Odom), Bill Nunn (Grady), Branford Marsalis (Jordam), **Spike Lee** (Half-Pint), Kadeem Hardison (Edge), Eric Payne (as Eric A. Payne, Booker T.), Roger Guenveur Smith (as Roger Smith, Yoda), Rusty Cundieff (Big Brother Chucky), Joie Lee (Lizzie Life), Cinqué Lee (Buckwheat), Tyra Ferrell (Tasha), Jasmine Guy (Dina), Kasi Lemmons (Perry), Samuel L. Jackson (Leeds)
35 mm, color
120 minutes

1989
DO THE RIGHT THING (40 Acres & a Mule Filmworks/Universal Pictures)
Producers: **Spike Lee**, Jon Kilik (line producer), Monty Ross (co-producer)
Director: **Spike Lee**
Screenplay: **Spike Lee**
Cinematography: Ernest Dickerson
Production Design: Wynn Thomas
Editing: Barry Alexander Brown
Music: Bill Lee, Chuck D. (songs), Flavor Flav (songs), Mervyn Warren (songs)
Cast: Danny Aiello (Sal), Ossie Davis (Da Mayor), Ruby Dee (Mother Sister), Richard Edson (Vito), Giancarlo Esposito (Buggin' Out), **Spike Lee** (Mookie), Bill Nunn (Radio Raheem), John Turturro (Pino), Joie Lee (Jade), Rosie Perez (Tina), Paul Benjamin (ML), Frankie Faison (Coconut Sid), Robin Harris (Sweet Dick Willie), Samuel L. Jackson (Mister Señor Love Daddy), Roger Guenveur Smith (Smiley), John Savage (Clifton), Steve White (Ahmad), Martin Lawrence (Cee), Leonard Thomas (Punchy), Christa Rivers (Ella), Steve Park (Sonny)
35mm, color
119 minutes

1990
MO' BETTER BLUES (40 Acres & a Mule Filmworks/Universal Pictures)
Producer: **Spike Lee**, Jon Kilik (line producer), Monty Ross (co-producer)
Director: **Spike Lee**

Screenplay: **Spike Lee**
Cinematography: Ernest Dickerson
Production Design: Wynn Thomas
Editing: Sam Pollard
Music: Bill Lee, Terence Blanchard (special music, uncredited)
Cast: Denzel Washington (Bleek Gilliam), **Spike Lee** (Giant), Wesley Snipes (Shadow Henderson), Giancarlo Esposito (Left Hand Lacey), Robin Harris (Butterbean Jones), Joie Lee (Indigo Downes), Bill Nunn (Bottom Hammer), John Turturro (Moe Flatbush), Dick Anthony Williams (Big Stop Williams), Cynda Williams (Clarke Bentancourt), Nicholas Turturro (Josh Flatbush), Samuel L. Jackson (Madlock), Leonard L. Thomas (Rod), Steve White (Born Knowledge), Ruben Bladés (Petey), Abbey Lincoln (Lilliam Gilliam)
35mm, color
129 minutes

1991
JUNGLE FEVER (40 Acres & a Mule Filmworks/Universal Pictures)
Producers: **Spike Lee** (producer), Jon Kilik (line producer), Monty Ross (co-producer)
Director: **Spike Lee**
Screenplay: **Spike Lee**
Cinematography: Ernest Dickerson
Production Design: Wynn Thomas
Editing: Sam Pollard
Music: Terence Blanchard and Stevie Wonder
Cast: Wesley Snipes (Flipper Purify), Annabella Sciorra (Angie Tucci), Lonette McKee (Drew), **Spike Lee** (Cyrus), Ossie Davis (The Good Reverend Doctor Purify), Ruby Dee (Lucinda Purify), Samuel L. Jackson (Gator Purify), John Turturro (Paulie Carbone), Halle Berry (Vivian), Tyra Ferrell (Orin Goode), Anthony Quinn (Lou Carbone), Michael Imperioli (James Tucci), Brad Dourif (Leslie), Theresa Randle (Inez)
35mm, color
132 minutes

1992
MALCOLM X (40 Acres & a Mule Filmworks/Universal Pictures)
Producers: Preston L. Holmes (co-producer), Jon Kilik (co-producer), **Spike**

Lee (producer), Ahmed Murad (producer: Saudi Arabia), Monty Ross (co-producer), Fernando Sulichin (associate producer), Marvin Worth (producer)
Director: **Spike Lee**
Screenplay: **Spike Lee** and Arnold Perl, based on Alex Haley and Malcolm X's *The Autobiography of Malcolm X* (1972)
Cinematography: Ernest Dickerson
Production Design: Wynn Thomas
Editing: Barry Alexander Brown
Music: Terence Blanchard
Cast: Denzel Washington (Malcolm Little/Detroit Red/Malcolm X), Angela Bassett (Betty Shabazz), Albert Hall (Baines), Al Freeman, Jr. (Elijah Muhammad), Delroy Lindo (West Indian Archie), **Spike Lee** (Shorty), Theresa Randle (Laura), Kate Vernon (Sophia), Lonette McKee (Louise Little), James McDaniel (Brother Earl), Debi Mazar (Peg), Giancarlo Esposito (Thomas Hayer), Roger Guenveur Smith (Rudy), John Sayles (FBI Agent), Mary Alice (School Teacher), Elise Neal (Hooker), Monty Ross (MC, Roseland), Peter Boyle (Captain Green)
35mm, color
194 minutes

1994
CROOKLYN (40 Acres & a Mule Filmworks/Childhood Pictures/Universal Pictures)
Producers: Jon Kilik (executive producer), Cinqué Lee (associate producer), Joie Lee (associate producer), **Spike Lee** (producer), Monty Ross (co-producer)
Director: **Spike Lee**
Screenplay: Cinqué Lee, Joie Lee (also story), **Spike Lee**
Cinematography: Arthur Jaffa
Production Design: Wynn Thomas
Editing: Barry Alexander Brown
Music: Terence Blanchard
Cast: Alfre Woodard (Carolyn Carmichael), Delroy Lindo (Woody Carmichael), David Patrick Kelly (Tony Eyes/Jim), Zelda Harris (Troy), Carlton Williams (Clinton), Harif Rashed (Wendell), Tse-Mach Washington (Joseph), Christopher Knowings (Nate), José Zúñiga (Tommy La La), Isaiah Washington (Vic), Ivelka Reyes (Jessica), **Spike Lee** (Snuffy), Joie Lee (Aunt Maxine),

Vondie Burtis-Hall (Uncle Brown), Bokeem Woodbine (Richard), Peewee
Love (Possom/Greg), RuPaul (Bodega Woman)
35mm, color
110 minutes

1995
LUMIÈRE ET COMPAGNIE *(Lumiere and Company)* (Cinétévé [fr], Igeldo
Komunikazioa [es], La Sept-Arte [fr], Le Studio Canal + [fr], Søren Stærmose AB)
[40 international directors were asked to make a short film using the original
Cinematographe invented by the Lumière Brothers, working under condi-
tions similar to those of 1895. There were three rules: (1) The film could be no
longer than 52 seconds; (2) no synchronized sound was permitted; (3) no
more than three takes.]
Producers: Ángel Amigo (co-producer), Anne Andreu (executive producer),
Neal Edelstein (producer), Fabienne Servan-Schreiber (producer), Søren
Stærmose (co-producer)
Directors: Merzak Allouache, Theo Angelopoulos, Vicente Aranda, Gabriel
Axel, J. J. Bigas Luna, John Boorman, Youssef Chahine, Alain Corneau, Costa-
Gavras, Raymond Depardon, Jaco van Dormael, Francis Girod, Peter Greena-
way, Lasse Hallström, Michael Haneke, Hugh Hudson, James Ivory, Gaston
Kaboré, Abbas Kiarostami, Cédric Klapisch, Andrei Konchalovsky, **Spike Lee**,
Claude Lelouch, David Lynch, Ismail Merchant, Claude Miller, Sarah Moon,
Idrissa Ouedraogo, Arthur Penn, Lucian Pintilie, Jacques Rivette, Helma
Sanders-Brahms, Jerry Schatzberg, Nadine Trintignant, Fernando Trueba, Liv
Ullmann, Régis Wargnier, Wim Wenders, Yoshishige Yoshida, Yimou Zhang
Screenplay: **Spike Lee**
Cinematography: Didier Ferry (Lumière cinematographe), Frédéric LeClair
(Hi-8 video), Sarah Moon (Hi-8 video), Philippe Poulet (Lumière cinemato-
graphe)
Editing: Roger Ikhlef, Timothy Miller
Music: Jean-Jacques Lemètre, Richard Robbins
Cast (in **Spike Lee**'s segment): Satchel Lee, **Spike Lee**
35mm, Hi-8 Video, color
88 minutes

1995
CLOCKERS (40 Acres & a Mule Filmworks/Universal Pictures)
Producers: Jon Kilik (producer), **Spike Lee** (producer), Richard Price (co-

producer), Monty Ross (executive producer), Martin Scorsese (producer),
Rosalie Swedlin (executive producer)
Director: **Spike Lee**
Screenplay: Richard Price (book), Richard Price (screenplay) and **Spike Lee**
(screenplay)
Cinematography: Malik Hassan Sayeed
Production Design: Andrew McAlpine
Editing: Sam Pollard
Music: Terence Blanchard, Bruce Hornsby (song: "Love Me Still")
Cast: Mekhi Phifer (Strike), Harvey Keitel (Detective Rocco Klein), John Turturro (Detective Larry Mazilli), Delroy Lindo (Rodney Little), Isaiah Washington (Victor Dunham), Keith David (Andre the Giant, Housing Police), Peewee Love (Tyrone Jeeter), Regina Taylor (Iris Jeeter), Thomas Jefferson Byrd (Errol Barnes), Sticky Fingaz (Scientific), Fredro Starr (Go), Paul Calderon (Jesus at Hambones), Michael Imperioli (Detective Jo-Jo), **Spike Lee** (Chucky), Harry J. Lennix (Bill Walker), Michael Badalucco (Cop #1)
35mm, Technicolor
128 minutes

1996
GIRL 6 (40 Acres & a Mule Filmworks/Fox Searchlight Pictures)
Producers: Jon Kilik (executive producer), **Spike Lee** (producer), Cirri Nottage (associate producer)
Director: **Spike Lee**
Screenplay: Suzan-Lori Parks
Cinematography: Malik Hassan Sayeed
Production Design: Ina Mayhew
Editing: Sam Pollard
Music: Prince
Cast: Theresa Randle (Girl 6/Judy), Isaiah Washington (Shoplifter), **Spike Lee** (Jimmy), Jenifer Lewis (Lil), Debi Mazar (Girl #39), Peter Berg (Bob), Michael Imperioli (Scary Caller), Naomi Campbell (Girl #75), Gretchen Mol (Girl #12), Richard Belzer (Caller #4, at the Beach), Thomas Jefferson Byrd (Caller #18), Madonna (Boss #3), John Turturro (Murray the Agent), Quentin Tarantino (QT), Ron Silver (Director 2, in LA), Joie Lee (Switchboard Operator), Carol Jenkins (Newscaster Carol), Halle Berry (herself), Rolanda Watts (Reporter Nita), Jim Jenson (Newscaster Jim), John Cameron Mitchell (Rob)

35mm, Technicolor
107 minutes

1996
GET ON THE BUS (15 Black Men/40 Acres & a Mule Filmworks)
Producers: Bill Borden (producer), Reuben Cannon (producer), **Spike Lee** (executive producer), Barry Rosenbush (producer)
Director: **Spike Lee**
Screenplay: Reggie Rock Bythewood
Cinematography: Elliot Davis
Production Design: Ina Mayhew
Editing: Leander T. Sales
Music: Terence Blanchard, Kenneth "Babyface" Edmonds (song: "Put Your Heart on the Line")
Cast: Richard Belzer (Rick), De'aundre Bonds (Junior, a.k.a. "Smooth"), Andre Braugher (Flip), Thomas Jefferson Byrd (Evan Thomas Sr.), Gabriel Casseus (Jamal), Albert Hall (Craig), Hill Harper (Xavier), Harry J. Lennix (Randall), Bernie Mac (Jay), Wendell Pierce (Wendell), Roger Guenveur Smith (Gary), Isaiah Washington (Kyle), Steve White (Mike), Ossie Davis (Jeremiah), Charles S. Dutton (George), Joie Lee (Jindal), Kristin Wilson (Shelly)
16mm, 35mm, color
122 minutes

1997
4 LITTLE GIRLS (40 Acres & a Mule Filmworks/Home Box Office)
Producers: Michele Forman (associate producer), Jacqueline Glover (supervising producer), **Spike Lee** (producer), Daphne McWilliams (line producer), Sheila Nevins (executive producer), Samuel D. Pollard (producer)
Director: **Spike Lee**
Cinematography: Ellen Kuras
Editing: Samuel D. Pollard
Music: Terence Blanchard
Cast: as themselves: Maxine McNair, Chris McNair, Helen Pegues, Queen Nunn, Arthur Hanes Jr., Howell Raines, Harold McNair, Wamo Reed Robertson, Dianne Braddock, Alpha Robertson, Wyatt Tee Walker, Fred Shuttlesworth, Shirley Wesley King, David J. Vann, Andrew Young, Taylor Branch,

Janie Gaines, Ossie Davis, Bill Cosby, Jesse Jackson, Reggie White, **Spike Lee** (interviewer's voice)
16mm, 35mm, B&W and color
102 minutes

1998
HE GOT GAME (40 Acres & a Mule Filmworks/Touchstone Pictures)
Producers: Sonya Burres (supervising producer), Jon Kilik (producer), **Spike Lee** (producer)
Director: **Spike Lee**
Screenplay: **Spike Lee**
Cinematography: Malik Hassan Sayeed
Production Design: Wynn Thomas
Editing: Barry Alexander Brown
Music: Aaron Copland (non-original), Chuck D. (songs, with Public Enemy), Flavor Flav (songs, with Public Enemy), Professor Griff (songs, with Public Enemy), Eric Sadler (songs, with The Bomb Squad), Hank Shocklee (songs, with The Bomb Squad), Keith Shocklee (songs, with The Bomb Squad), Terminator X (songs, with Public Enemy)
Cast: Denzel Washington (Jake Shuttlesworth), Ray Allen (Jay Shuttlesworth), Milla Jovovich (Dakota Burns), Rosario Dawson (Lala Bonilla), Hill Harper (Coleman "Booger" Sykes), Zelda Harris (Mary Shuttlesworth), Ned Beatty (Warden Wyatt), Jim Brown (Spivey), Joseph Lyle Taylor (Crudup), Bill Nunn (Uncle Bubba), Michele Shay (Aunt Sally), Thomas Jefferson Byrd (Sweetness), Roger Guenveur Smith (Big Time Willie), John Turturro (Coach Billy Sunday), Lonette McKee (Martha Shuttlesworth), John Thompson (as himself), Roy Williams (as himself), Dick Vitale (as himself), Bill Walton (as himself), Shaquille O'Neal (as himself), Reggie Miller (as himself), Charles Barkley (as himself), Scottie Pippen (as himself), Michael Jordan (as himself)
35mm, Technicolor
134 minutes

1998
FREAK (Home Box Office)
Producers: Denis Biggs (producer), David Bar Katz (producer), John Leguizamo (producer), Heather Maidat (associate producer), Robert Morton (producer), Krysia Plonka (coordinating producer)

Director: **Spike Lee**
Screenplay: David Bar Katz and John Leguizamo
Cinematography: Malik Hassan Sayeed
Production Design: Wendell K. Harrington
Editing: Barry Alexander Brown
Cast: John Leguizamo
35 mm, color

1999
SUMMER OF SAM (40 Acres & a Mule Filmworks/Touchstone Pictures)
Producers: Jeri Carroll-Colicchio (executive producer), Michael Imperioli
(executive producer), Jon Kilik (producer), **Spike Lee** (producer)
Director: **Spike Lee**
Screenplay: Victor Colicchio, Michael Imperioli, and **Spike Lee**
Cinematography: Ellen Kuras
Production Design: Thérèse DePrez
Editing: Barry Alexander Brown
Music: Terence Blanchard, Pete Townsend
Cast: John Leguizamo (Vinny), Mira Sorvino (Dionna), Jennifer Esposito
(Ruby), Adrien Brody (Ritchie), Michael Rispoli (Joe T), Bebe Neuwirth (Glo-
ria), Saverio Guerra (Woodstock), Patti LuPone (Helen), **Spike Lee** (Reporter
John Jeffries), Anthony LaPaglia (Detective Lou Petrocelli), Roger Guenveur
Smith (Detective Curt Atwater), Ben Gazzara (Luigi), John Savage (Simon),
Jimmy Breslin (as himself), Michael Badalucco (David Berkowitz/Son of
Sam), Michael Imperioli (Midnight)
35mm, Technicolor
142 minutes

2000
THE ORIGINAL KINGS OF COMEDY (40 Acres & a Mule Filmworks/Latham
Entertainment/MTV Films)
Producers: Rylyn DeMaris (associate producer), David Gale (producer), Wal-
ter Latham (producer), **Spike Lee** (producer), Angelia Price (associate pro-
ducer), Butch Robinson (co-producer), Van Toffler (executive producer)
Director: **Spike Lee**
Cinematography: Malik Hassan Sayeed
Production Design: Wynn Thomas

Editing: Barry Alexander Brown
Music: Nelly (song)
Cast: as themselves: Steve Harvey, D. L. Hughley, Cedric the Entertainer, Bernie Mac
35mm, shot on digital video, color

2000

BAMBOOZLED (40 Acres & a Mule Filmworks)
Producers: Kisha Imani Cameron (associate producer), Jon Kilik (producer), **Spike Lee** (producer)
Director: **Spike Lee**
Screenplay: **Spike Lee**
Cinematography: Ellen Kuras
Production Design: Victor Kempster
Editing: Samuel D. Pollard
Music: Terence Blanchard, Erykah Badu (song, "Hollywood"), Chuck D. (song, "Burned Hollywood Burned"), Bruce Hornsby (song, "Shadowland"), Gerald Levert (song, "Dream with No Love"), Prince (song, "2045 Radical Man"), Stevie Wonder (song, "Misrepresented People")
Cast: Damon Wayans (Pierre De La Croix), Savion Glover (Manray/Mantan), Jada Pinkett Smith (Sloan Hopkins), Tommy Davidson (Womach/Sleep 'n' Eat), Mos Def/Dante Beze (Big Black Africa), Michael Rapaport (Dunwitty), Thomas Jefferson Byrd (Honeycutt), Paul Mooney (Junebug), Gillian Iliana Waters (Verna), Ahmir '?uestlove' Thompson (drummer), M. C. Serch (1/16th Black), Gano Grills (Double Black), Canibus (Mo Black), DJ Scratch (Jo Black), Charli Baltimore (Smooth Black), muMs da Schemer (Hard Black), Dina Perlman (Myrna Goldfarb), Danny Hoch (Timmi Hilnigger), Johnnie Cochran (himself), Al Sharpton (himself)
35mm, shot on 16mm and digital video, color
135 minutes

A HUEY P. NEWTON STORY (40 Acres & a Mule Filmworks, 2001)
Producers: Steven Adams (producer), **Spike Lee** (producer), Bob L. Johnson (producer), Marc Henry Johnson (producer)
Director: **Spike Lee**
Screenplay: Roger Guenveur Smith, based on his play
Cinematography: Ellen Kuras

Production Design: Wynn Thomas
Editing: Barry Alexander Brown
Music: Mark Anthony Thompson
Cast: Roger Guenveur Smith
35mm, color
94 minutes

As Producer of Other Directors' Films

1994
DROP SQUAD (40 Acres & a Mule Filmworks)
Producers: Michael Bennett (line producer), **Spike Lee** (executive producer),
Eric Payne (associate producer), Butch Robinson (producer), Kervin Simms
(associate producer), Shelby Stone (producer)
Director: David C. Johnson
Screenplay: David Taylor (story), David C. Johnson and Butch Robinson
(screen story)
Cinematography: Ken Kelsch
Production Design: Ina Mayhew
Editing: Kevin Lee
Music: Michael Bearden
Cast: Eriq La Salle (Bruford Jamison Jr.), Vondie Curtis-Hall (Rocky Seavers),
Ving Rhames (Garvey), Kasi Lemmons (June Vanderpool), Leonard L.
Thomas (XB), Nicole Powell (Lenora Jamison), Eric Payne (Stokely), Crystal
R. Fox (Zora), Vanessa Williams (Mali), Tico Wells (Fat Money), **Spike Lee**
(himself)
35mm, color
86 minutes

1995
NEW JERSEY DRIVE (40 Acres & a Mule Filmworks)
Producers: Bob Gosse (producer), **Spike Lee** (executive producer), Larry Meis-
trich (producer), Rudd Simmons (co-producer)
Director: Nick Gomez
Screenplay: Nick Gomez (also story), Michel Marriott (story)
Cinematography: Adam Kimmel
Production Design: Lester Cohen

Editing: Jane Pia Abramowitz (associate), Tracy Granger
Music: Wendy Blackman, Redman (song)
Cast: Sharron Corley (Jason Petty), Gabriel Casseus (Midget), Saul Stein (Roscoe), Samantha Brown (Jackie Petty), Christine Baranski (Prosecutor), Devin Eggleston (Jamal), Donald Adeosun Faison (Tiny Dime), Heavy D (Bo-Kane), Conrad Meertins Jr. (P-Nut)
35mm, color
98 minutes

1995
TALES FROM THE HOOD (40 Acres & a Mule Filmworks/Savoy Pictures)
Producers: Elaine Dysinger (line producer), **Spike Lee** (executive producer), Darin Scott (producer)
Director: Rusty Cundieff
Screenplay: Rusty Cundieff and Darin Scott
Cinematography: Anthony B. Richmond
Production Design: Stuart Blatt
Editing: Charles Bornstein
Music: Christopher Young
Cast: Clarence Williams III (Mr. Simms), Joe Torry (Stack), De'aundre Bonds (Ball), Samuel Monroe Jr. (Bulldog), Wings Hauser (Strom), Tom Wright (Martin Moorehouse), David Alan Grier (Carl), Brandon Hammond (Walter), Rusty Cundieff (Richard), Paula Jai Parker (Sissy), Corbin Bernsen (Duke Metger), Roger Guenveur Smith (Rhodie), Art Evans (Eli), Rosalind Cash (Dr. Cushing), Lamont Bentley (Crazy K)
35 mm, color
98 minutes

1999
A GUT FEELING
Producers: Shan Browning (producer), Lee Davis (producer), John Murchison (producer), Chuck Wilson (co-producer), **Spike Lee** (executive producer), Sam Kitt (executive producer), Andre Hereford (associate producer), Ross Martin (associate producer)
Director: Lee Davis
Screenplay: Lee Davis
Cinematography: John Bentham

Production Design: Yvette Stapleton
Editing: J. A. Kirby
Music: Ricky Gordon
Cast: Saul Williams (Goines), Ruben Santiago Hudson (Himenez), Arthur French (Silas), Ena Hanna (Mabel), Lauren Greaves (Spirit Girl), Thomas Byrd (Skinny Boy), George Odom (Detective)
35mm, color
11.38 minutes

1999
THE BEST MAN (40 Acres & a Mule Filmworks)
Producers: Bill Carraro (producer), Sam Kitt (producer), **Spike Lee** (producer)
Director: Malcolm D. Lee
Screenplay: Malcolm D. Lee
Cinematography: Frank Prinzi
Production Design: Kalina Ivanov
Editing: Cara Silverman
Music: Stanley Clarke and Lauryn Hill (song)
Cast: Taye Diggs (Harper Stewart), Nia Long (Jordan Armstrong), Morris Chestnut (Lance Sullivan), Harold Perrineau Jr. (Julian Murch), Terrence Howard (Quentin), Sanaa Lathan (Robin), Monica Calhoun (Mia Morgan), Melissa De Sousa (Shelby), Victoria Dillard (Anita), Regina Hall (Candy), Lady Madonna (stripper), Malcolm D. Lee (emcee)
35 mm, DeLuxe color
120 minutes

2000
LOVE & BASKETBALL (40 Acres & a Mule Filmworks)
Producers: Andrew Z. Davis (executive producer), Cynthia Guidry (executive producer), Sam Kitt (producer), **Spike Lee** (producer), Jay Stern (executive producer)
Director: Gina Prince-Blythewood
Screenplay: Gina Prince-Blythewood
Cinematography: Reynaldo Villalobos
Production Design: Jeffrey Howard
Editing: Terilyn A. Shropshire
Music: Terence Blanchard and Ralph E. Tresvant (song, with New Edition)

Cast: Sanaa Lathan (Monica), Omar Epps (Quincy), Alfre Woodard (Camille Wright), Dannis Haysbert (Zeke McCall), Harry J. Lennix (Nathan Wright), Debbi Morgan (Nona McCall), Genndon Chatman (young Quincy), Kyla Pratt (young Monica), Regina Hall (Lena Wright), Gabrielle Union (Shawnee), Monica Calhoun (Kerry), Tyra Banks (Kyra Kessler)
35mm, DeLuxe color
124 minutes

2001

3 A.M. (40 Acres & a Mule Filmworks)
Producers: Danny Glover (executive producer), Callum Greene (co-producer), Anthony G. Katagas (co-producer), Sam Kitt (co-executive producer and producer), Paul Kurta (co-executive producer), **Spike Lee** (co-executive producer and producer)
Director: Lee Davis
Screenplay: Lee Davis
Cinematography: Enrique Chediak
Production Design: Ted Glass
Editing: Susan E. Morse
Music: Branford Marsalis
Cast: Danny Glover (Hershey), Pam Grier (George), Michelle Rodriguez (Salgado), Sergej Trifunovic (Rasha), Sarita Choudhury (Box), Isaach De Bankolé (Angus), Mike Starr (Theo), Paul Calderon (Ralph), Bobby Cannavale (Jose)
35mm, color
88 minutes

As Actor Only

1991
LONELY IN AMERICA (Apple Productions)
Producers: Phil Katzman (producer), Tirlok Malik (producer)
Director: Barry Alexander Brown
Screenplay: Barry Alexander Brown
Cinematography: Phil Katzman
Production Design: Eduardo Capilla
Editing: Tula Goenka
Music: Nikolai Rimsky-Korsakov (from "Scheherazade")

Cast: Tirlok Malik (Max), Adelaide Miller (Faye), Robert Kessler (Jim), David Toney (Duncan), Melissa Christopher (Becky), Frankie Hughes (Carlos), **Spike Lee** (himself)
35mm, color
96 minutes

2001

LISA PICARD IS FAMOUS (GreeneStreet Films Inc./Longfellow Pictures/Sidney Kimmel Entertainment/Stella Maris Films)
Producers: Dolly Hall (producer), Andrew S. Karsch (executive producer), Sidney Kimmel (executive producer), John Penotti (executive producer), Celeste Peterka (co-producer), Mira Sorvino (producer), Fisher Stevens (executive producer), Bradley Yonover (executive producer)
Director: Griffin Dunne
Screenplay: Nat DeWolf, Laura Kirk
Cinematography: William Rexer II
Production Design: Mark Ricker
Editing: Nancy Baker
Music: Evan Lurie
Cast: Laura Kirk (Lisa Picard), Nat DeWolf (Tate Kelley), Daniel London (Boyfriend), Griffin Dunne (Andrew), Linda Blair (herself), L. M. Kit Carson (David Holzman), Carrie Fisher (herself), **Spike Lee** (himself), Penelope Ann Miller (herself), Charlie Sheen (himself), Mira Sorvino (herself)
35mm, shot on digital video, color
90 minutes

SPIKE LEE

INTERVIEWS

Lee Way

MARLAINE GLICKSMAN/1986

'' Y OU SO FINE, I drink a tub of your bathwater." "You need a man like me . . . What's your number?" "I love you. . . ." "Please baby, please baby, please." "You know the minute you get fat, I'm leaving you."

So cajole, plead, woo, and threaten the men—the decent ones and the dogs—in twenty-nine-year-old filmmaker Spike Lee's first feature film, *She's Gotta Have It.* The focus of their attention is Nola Darling. Nola possesses what we have come to know as a man's desire, but is cursed (in society's eyes) with a woman's body. "Some people would call me a freak," she explains at the film's beginning, meaning she's a woman who likes to get down. The story unfolds through Nola's eyes and through the multiple perspectives of those men and women who long to see into and possess them. It is a comedic commentary on the frazzled rules of cat-and-mouse, with Nola as the mouse who scores.

Set entirely in Brooklyn, the film is like the borough's namesake bridge, laced with the tangles and crossed wires of love and its accompanying emotions, as well as a warm and generous sense of humor. Black and white and in the confession style of Akira Kurosawa's *Rashoman, She's Gotta Have It,* was shot in twelve days with a New York State Council of Arts grant of $18,000. Lee worked closely with Ernest Dickerson ("my ace cameraman") as well as a cast and crew with whom he has worked on past films, some of whom he

Published in *Film Comment* 22 (September/October 1986): 46–49. Copyright © 1986 by the Film Society of Lincoln Center. All rights reserved. Reprinted by permission.

has known since undergraduate days at Morehouse College, where he first began "dibbling and dabbling" in film.

Lee also involved almost his whole family in the production. ("If you have a talented family," he says, "you should be shot if you don't use them.") This is the third film that his well-known jazz musician father, Bill Lee, has scored. His sister, Joie, plays Clorinda Bradford, Nola's ex-roommate. And his brother, David, acted as still photographer on the shoot. His straightforward, grainy stills are interspersed throughout the film, contrasting their sense of vanishing time and place with the film's sassy tone, as well as setting the scene for the story. Spike himself plays one of Nola's three main men, the aptly named Mars Blackmon, the four-eyed, hiphopper B-boy who hilariously woos Nola and wars with her other suitors: Jamie Overstreet as Nola's serious and stable suitor, who sees himself as Nola's soulmate; Greer Childs as her self-possessed, Buppie beau; and finally the seductive Opal Gilatrap as Nola's lesbian admirer.

All of the characters in the film are black. Unlike Steven Spielberg's *The Color Purple, She's Gotta Have It* neither needs white context nor white audiences to which blacks have been invited. This time, black women talk to black men, and whites are invited—to learn something about blacks, and also about themselves.

Nola shares her birthday with Malcolm X and paints a commemorative mural, pasted with headlines such as "Honor Student Shot by Cop." Mars wears hi-top sneakers (even when making love to Nola), sports an extra-large eighteen-karat gold nameplate around his neck, and street-talks and jives, repeating himself incessantly. Greer is a *GQ* model who plays scrabble with a dictionary. Jamie is, well, always decent and stable, very predictable. When Nola invites all three to Thanksgiving dinner, the feathers fly. "Chain snatcher," Greer sniffs at Mars. "Pseudo black man," Mars retorts. When Jamie attempts to quiet the ruckus, Greer cuts, "What are you? Henry Kissinger?" In another scene, Nola and Mars share a nice moment after lovemaking and she greases his hair. The film's final credits include the statement "This film contains no *jerri curls* and no *drugs.*" These characters are well-grounded in a largely black neighborhood and, unlike black characters in most other films, speak black dialect *intelligently.* The blacks in Lee's film are real people. And as real people, they speak to us all.

Each lover offers a lover's reason why he isn't Nola Darling's number one man. "To Nola," says Jamie, "we're all interchangeable." Accuses Greer, "I think you are sick. I'm not saying you're a nympho, slut, or whore, but I do think you are a sex addict." When bike-conjoined Mars encounters Jamie on a park bench he opines, "Nola is about as dependable as a ripped diaphragm." But soon the discussion veers off into sports—stopped dead by a female passerby—before the two return to their thoughts about Nola, providing yet another universal observation on the ways men and women navigate and collide. It is Mars who finally figures it out, that all three men comprise an integrated whole for Nola, that it was the men who were really at fault. "We let her create a three-headed, six-armed, six-legged, three-penis monster." In the end, Nola ditches them all and, content to be alone in her bed, reveals the decisive verdict, "It's about control. My body. My mind. Who's gonna own it, them or me?"

She's Gotta Have It uniquely tackles an age-old controversial topic, the discrepancies that exist not only between the sexes but also in the judgments rendered by society. Ironically, the film's willingness to investigate the hot spot where love meets sex landed it in hot water. The MPAA thrice gave the film an X rating. Since the film features a woman and her three lovers, naturally there are sex scenes. But there is no more to be seen than the breasts and butts that grace the lovemaking of white mainstream R-rated films. Spike had to recut his film three times, plus cut in half an overhead shot of Greer and Nola in bed to get down to the R rating dictated by his Island Pictures contract for its domestic release. "It'll be shown the real way in Europe and on tape," Spike said.

Spike is no stranger to trouble. Outspoken, he was almost not asked back after his probational first year at NYU graduate film school when he submitted *The Answer*. The twenty-minute short portrayed a young black screenwriter hired to do a rewrite on a $50 million remake of *Birth of a Nation*. Lee eventually graduated with a Student Academy Award for *Joe's Bed-Stuy Barbershop: We Cut Heads,* about a numbers-running barbershop in the Bedford-Stuyvesant section of Brooklyn. This film also earned him a screening in the New Directors/New Films festival at the Museum of Modern Art in 1983.

It is no surprise, then, that *She's Gotta Have It* this year achieved a spot in the director's fortnight at Cannes, as well as the Prix de Jeunesse. ("We got robbed of the Camera d'Or," Lee says, "but I'm not complaining.") Still, it is often the comments on the long line to the ladies room which serve final judgment on the success of a film, and in the case of this film, perhaps one of the most appropos places to listen. "I want three men, too," said one linestander. "Yeah but I want 'em all at the same time," said another. Perhaps Mars was wrong; perhaps it is Spike Lee who has created the monster.

M G : *The MPAA originally gave* She's Gotta Have It *an X-rating.*
S L : The MPAA said it was filled with gratuitous sex, that it was—and this is an actual quote—"saturated with sex." I edited the film three times and each time they said it was better. But it was still given an X rating. The film will be released unrated in New York, but I have to cut an R-rated film for me to get money, because that's in my contract.

I don't think it's out-and-out racist, but the film portrays blacks outside stereotypical roles and they don't know what to do with blacks in films. They never have any love interest. Nick Nolte is the one who has a relationship in *48 Hours*. And when it comes to black sexuality, they especially don't know how to deal with it. They feel uncomfortable. There are films with more gratuitous sex and even violence. *9½ Weeks* got an R. And look at *Body Double*.

M G : *Why did you set and film* She's Gotta Have It *in Brooklyn—because you're from there?*
S L : I was born in Atlanta, Georgia, but I've lived in Brooklyn all my life. When you are doing independent filmmaking, you don't have the means to go anywhere else. *She's Gotta Have It* was really shot in a one-mile radius, the whole film, in the neighborhood where I lived. That's the only way we could shoot a film in twelve days, only if locations are within a block from each other.

M G : *How did the film come about?*
S L : In the summer of 1984, I attempted to do a film called *Messenger*. We were in pre-production for eight weeks, but I had to pull the plug because it just never really came together with all the money and stuff. So out of that devastation and disaster, we came up with the idea, out of desperation, to do *She's Gotta Have It*. I was determined to do another film the next summer, for as little money as possible. Small cast, small crew. I had a grant from NYSCA (the N.Y. State Council on the Arts) for $18,000 for *Messenger*. NYSCA was kind enough to let me move that money to *She's Gotta Have It*. I also got a grant from American Film Institute for $20,000, but those motherfuckers took the money back. They wouldn't let me move the money. Print that too.

M G :   *You had no private funding?*

S L :   When we started out, there wasn't. But the whole game plan was to raise the money stage by stage. The next stage was to get the film out of the lab. I had the confidence that if we could get it shot, cut, and show it to people, I would be able to raise enough money.

M G :   *Was the $18,000 to shoot enough?*

S L :   No. Monty Ross, the lead actor in *Joe's Bed-Stuy Barber Shop,* who I went to school with at Morehouse, was production supervisor on this film. After we would shoot, everyday, Monty would come home, get on the phone, and call and write everybody we knew in the world asking them to please, please, please help us out, to please, please, please send money, their hundreds, fifties, whatever. So we raised the money at the same time we were shooting. I remember a number of times while Monty, during the shoot, would leave the set and I would fill out the deposit slip and he would run to the bank and deposit the checks. So that's the kind of duress we made the film under. But I'm not complaining. That's the only way that this film could be done.

M G :   *It's wonderful that you had the confidence to go ahead and do the film.*

S L :   Well, I've never lacked confidence. (Laughs.) It's just money. And I've been fortunate enough that I've had people around me like Ernest Dickerson and Pam Jackson, who went to school with Monty and me. She was associate producer of this film.

M G :   *You shot the film on a very small ratio.*

S L :   It's just my style. There's really no need to take eight million takes of everything. We were well-rehearsed. And we try to just get it within the first or second take, move it on to the next shot.

M G :   *Why did you decide to shoot the film in black and white?*

S L :   Well, the images came to me in black and white. This had nothing to do with the budget. I just felt that the subject was a black and white movie.

M G :   *You used color for the birthday scene.*

S L :   Well, we wanted to make that scene, which is a present that Jamie is giving to Nola, a very imaginable scene, to make it different. A little homage to *The Wizard of Oz.* Jamie says to her, "Close your eyes and repeat after me:

There's no place like home, there's no place like home," and you cut to the close-up of her clicking her heels.

M G :   *What is it like to act in your own film?*
S L :   I never acted before. Well, halfway through writing this film, I decided, hey, I should play this role. It was hard. The first day, it was horrible because I was trying to direct and act, and Michael Hunter, who was the gaffer, says to me, "When you're in front of the camera, let Ernest be the director," because I was still saying, "Everybody ready, roll sound, action," all that, and then I'd try to go and act. You can't do that. So when I was in front of the camera, Ernest assumed the reins of the director as far as getting the crew ready, the action, cut, that stuff.

M G :   *Did you ever take acting lessons?*
S L :   I'm really not an opponent of those acting schools. My sister has never acted before either and I think that she's very natural. That stuff—Mars repeating everything—that wasn't scripted.

M G :   *Why do you feel a particular affinity toward the character of Mars?*
S L :   There are a lot of them out there, especially in Brooklyn, a lot of young black youths, and they don't have such a good reputation. Look at the Bernhard Goetz situation. That's why I had stuff like Greer calling him a "chain snatcher." I knew I couldn't attempt to clear their reputation, but I could portray them more positively.

M G :   *Was it more difficult for you to shoot and direct the sex scenes?*
S L :   That's why I used Tracy as an actress. I could have had a known actress, but it was important that I use somebody who was comfortable with love scenes, someone at ease, because her ease would make the audience more at ease.

M G :   *The script was written remarkably from a woman's point of view.*
S L :   I'm a good listener. And I think I really try to be honest. And if you really try to go about the truth and honesty in your work, then you can hurdle my not being a woman. But you have to understand, I have not attempted to make a feminist film. For me, it is about a woman who has three lovers. My friends are always boasting and bragging about how many

women they have. But when word gets back to them that one of the women in their stable is even thinking about seeing someone else, they go berserk. That's insane, that double standard. So I decided, let's make a film about a woman who is actually living her life as a man.

MG: *How did "black" figure into it?*

SL: Another reason I did this film was because there are hardly any films about black people. When you do see films about black people, they're either musicals or comedies. You know, ha-ha, chi-chi, and dancing Eddie Murphy and Richard Pryor, don't even kiss or have any romantic interests in their films.

They don't have a home, no wife, no lovers. And I knew that black people would kill to go into the movie theater and see black people hugging and kissing and, you know, loving each other.

There is so much catching up to do. I know I'm not going to have any problems, for the next three or four years, just dealing with stuff within a black genre. This film has shown a lot of people, especially at Cannes, that black people are just as diversified as any other race. People have been shocked by just how universal this film is, by how they had never seen black people portrayed like this before. I guess all their experiences have been with Hollywood films.

MG: *Is it harder for blacks to work in the industry?*

SL: It is harder for blacks in the industry. But we have to create our own jobs and make our own films. That is why it is important to find close working associates that have the same goals and aspirations that you do.

MG: *Is this film about blacks or men and women?*

SL: I think my love of women is reflected in the work. But I think this film should be the antidote to how the black male is perceived in *The Color Purple*. See, nobody is saying that black men haven't done some terrible things, and what Jamie does to Nola at the end of the film is a horrible act. But Jamie is a full-bodied character, unlike Mister in *The Color Purple* and the rest of the film's black men, who are just one-dimensional animals. I'm not going to blame it all entirely on Steven Spielberg, because if you read Alice Walker's work, that's the way she feels about black men. She really has problems with them. I think people should really analyze why *The Color Purple* was made.

MG: *Why?*

SL: Within recent years, the quickest way for a black playwright, novelist, or poet to get published has been to say that black men are shit. If you say that, then you are definitely going to get your media, your book published, your play done—Ntozake Shange, Alice Walker.

MG: *Do you feel the same way about black male playwrights?*

SL: To me, Toni Morrison could write motherfuckin' rings around Alice Walker. If you look at Toni Morrison's body of work—*Sula, The Bluest Eye, Tar Baby, Song of Solomon*—*Song of Solomon,* I mean, I would like to do that one day. That's going to make a great movie. But still, till today, not one of Toni Morrison's works has been made into film. Why hasn't she won a Pulitzer prize? That's why they put Alice Walker out there. That's why she won the Pulitzer prize. That's why Hollywood leaped the pond to seize this book and had it made. To me, it's justifying everything they say about black people and black men in general: that we ain't shit, that we're animals. That's why this film was made. Of all the black novels, it's not just coincidence that this was the one that they chose. And then they turn around and get some Dutch guy to write the script and get Spielberg to direct it. He knows nothing about black people.

And Whoopi Goldberg—you've got to print this—I've seen her on *Phil Donahue* and she was getting all defensive about the flak the she's getting about *Color Purple,* telling black men that if they can't take a joke, fuck it, and shit like that, and then she's going to try to defend *The Color Purple* by saying, what about *Purple Rain?* What about when Prince had women thrown in garbage cans? Hey, I didn't like that shit either, but that doesn't have a goddamn thing to do with *Color Purple.* And Whoopi Goldberg says that Steven Spielberg is the only director in the world who could have directed this film. Does she realize what she is saying? Is she saying that a white person is the only person who can define our existence? And now, even something more stupid, she's running around with goddamn blue contact lenses in her eyes, telling everybody that she has blue eyes. And that's sick . . . to me. And I hope people realize, that the media realizes, that she's not a spokesperson for black people, especially when you're running around with motherfucking blue contact lenses telling everybody that your eyes are blue. Tell her to read Toni Morrison's *The Bluest Eye.*

M G : *It was a wonderful idea to have "the dogs" speak.*

S L : I'm just amazed at the things men tell women. And when you think about it, the only reason why they say that stuff is that it must work some of the time, because if it never worked, they wouldn't keep on saying that dumb stuff.

M G : *And what do women say to men?*

S L : I don't think they're as. . . . I don't know about that. It might work. But it never happened with me! (Laughs.)

M G : *Whose work are you influenced by? You quote Zora Neale Hurston in the beginning of your film.*

S L : I think it's a very good book *(Their Eyes Were Watching God),* and she's a person that all black female novelists quote. Alice Walker, Toni Morrison, all talk about the influence Zora Neale Hurston had on them. But for film, I like the work of Scorsese, Kurosawa, Coppola. I also like musicals, too, and my next film is going to be a musical.

M G : She's Gotta Have It *was shot in the style of* Rashoman. *Was that scripted?*

S L : Yeah. I called it confessions with people facing the camera. It was also very economical. It doesn't take a whole lot of time to light. And you just shoot. That really helped us to shoot in twelve days.

M G : *Were you influenced by your dad? Does his music influence your work?*

S L : Yeah, his music, jazz. . . . We were raised in a very artistic family. So he was taking me to see him play at the Village Gate, at The Bitter End, at the Blue Note, when I was four, five years old. See him play with Odetta, Judy Collins, Leon Bibb, Peter, Paul, and Mary. I really strive to make music play an important part in all my films. This is the third film that my father has done the music for. And this is the first where the soundtrack is going to be released. (Island Records is releasing.)

M G : *What's it like working with him?*

S L : It's hard. (Laughs.) Because, he's a perfectionist and a nonconformist, and I love him because he's my father, but he's not the easiest person to work with.

M G : *At what stage do you start working with him? In the script?*

S L : Yes. I knew I wanted a theme for Nola played throughout the whole film and I had a lot that had to be recorded before we shot for playback, for the choreography, for the dance scene, and some other stuff. Then I went and shot it, cut it, and when I had a rough cut, that's when we sat down and decided when we wanted music, the type of music, the color of the instrumentation, the length of it. Then he went away and came back and played an idea on the piano. Then we decided what piece was appropriate for each particular scene.

M G : *What is the balance of power working with your father?*

S L : Well, I don't want to sound like a dictator, but film is a director's medium. I try to listen to everybody's suggestions, but the final outcome ultimately is going to be my decision.

M G : *Do you feel like jazz has influenced your writing or editing?*

S L : That's a hard question. Well, I guess it has in the sense that I never try to restrict myself. I just let my imagination go very free. And I like to improvise. So you could say maybe like that.

M G : *Are you a perfectionist?*

S L : No. I haven't been in a situation where I could afford to be a perfectionist.

M G : *What is your next project?*

S L : The next film is a musical called *School Daze* for Island Pictures. I hope to begin shooting in March on a $3 million budget, which feels good. It is set at a black college in the South, during homecoming, on the Spelman/Morehouse campuses. I intend to include a whole spectrum of black music, from funk to jazz.

You know, what we're doing now, people are saying "Spike, this is great, this is great, aren't you excited? You look so blasé." And I say, "Everything we're doing now Monty, Pam, and I talked about when we were in school eight or nine years ago." So this is what we're supposed to be doing. It's no shock.

Spike Lee's Bed-Stuy BBQ

MARLAINE GLICKSMAN/1989

IT'S THE HOTTEST DAY of summer in Bed-Stuy, Brooklyn, where the only thing hotter are people's tempers and a ghetto blaster not only rocks the house but burns it down. While Spike Lee's previous films looked at the under- and crosscurrents of male/female and light/dark-skinned black interactions, in his third feature, *Do the Right Thing,* Lee takes a magnifying glass-under-a-hot-sun look at black/white relations and the result—no surprise—is fire.

Do the Right Thing stars Ossie Davis, Ruby Dee, Danny Aiello, John Turturro, Richard Edson, and Lee veterans Joie Lee, Bill Nunn, Sam Jackson and Giancarlo Esposito, along with newcomer Rosie Perez. It was shot in Bed-Stuy using an almost all-black crew (a rarity in the film industry) during a recordbreaking heatwave.

To pave way for the production, Lee rejected the usual police surveillance from the Mayor's Office of Motion Pictures and instead installed members of the Fruit of Islam. With them, he also cleared the block of three crack houses. Sets were reconstructed from gutted buildings; behind the film's Korean fruit stand stood an empty shell. A pizza parlor was erected, murals painted, the street cleaned up, a block party thrown and the shoot was under way. The Antioch Baptist Church served as canteen, where lunch on some days consisted of ribs and assorted Louisiana hot sauces.

For his role as Mookie, the meandering young black man who is the film's

Published in *Film Comment* 25 (July/August 1989): 12–16. Copyright © 1989 by the Film Society of London Center. All rights reserved. Reprinted by permission.

pivotal character, and who cares less about his girlfriend and young son than getting paid, Lee donned a fade-out flat top and a gold tooth. Cinematographer Ernest Dickerson once again stood loyally behind the lens while the director's brother, David Lee, shot more of the enigmatic stills we saw in Lee's *She's Gotta Have It.*

Lee's film comes at a time when New York City is a racial tinderbox. The alleged black gang rape of a white Wall Street woman this April in Central Park angers whites, smears blacks and triggers Donald Trump to take out a full-page ad in the *New York Times* calling for reinstatement of the death penalty (yet there was no such outcry when Michael Stewart and Eleanor Bumpurs—blacks to whom Lee dedicates his film—*died* at the hands of NYC police in separate controversial incidents). The *Amsterdam News,* favored by a black readership, likened the handling of the Central Park rape to the Scottsboro boys, who were falsely convicted and nearly executed for the rape of a white woman in Alabama fifty years ago. One month later, after a twenty-five-year-old black man died in police custody, one black woman told the *New York Times,* "This is crazy. There's going to be a riot. Somebody is going to get killed and it'll probably be us."

Do the Right Thing takes up the message. Nobody wins when oppressive heat and Raheem's radio causes a meltdown in Sal's Famous Pizzeria. What bubbles up is not mozzarella but the bad feelings hidden beneath. The film, which explores the black underclass, ends with two quotes, the first by Dr. Martin Luther King in favor of non-violence, stating, "The old law of an eye for an eye leaves everybody blind," countered by Malcolm X's "I am not against violence in self-defense. I don't even call it violence when it's self-defense, I call it intelligence." It is on this quote that the film closes.

Lee is no stranger to controversy. The MPAA rated *She's Gotta Have It* with an X—later reduced to R after it was recut—because Lee included a lovemaking scene with nude black bodies. In *School Daze,* Lee broke the conspiracy of silence about prejudice between light- and dark-skinned blacks in his depiction of an all-black college campus during homecoming. *School Daze* also probes blacks' attitudes toward apartheid—income from South Africa helps keep the school running. And in one poignant scene Lee clashes Africa-identifying co-eds with their Jerri-Curled, shower-capped, local "brothers," who spout animosity like ketchup: "We're not your brothers. How come you college mother-fuckers think you run everything? You come into our town year after year and take over. We were born here, been here, will be here all of our lives, and can't find work 'cause of you."

School Daze was criticized by fellow blacks who did not want long-hidden dirty laundry on view for white eyes. But as always, Lee's films are topical. A case before the Atlanta Federal Court highlights the heretofore unmentionable: a woman is suing her former employer, alleging discrimination based on skin color. Both the woman and her employer are black; the plaintiff, however, is light-skinned.

Do the Right Thing, like Lee's other films, is a black insider's perspective on the contradictions and celebrations of African-American life. But Lee's talent lies in creating characters that transcend race and economic status and speak to us all. His Bed-Stuy comes alive with neighborhood people we know: Mother Sister (Dee), matron of the block; Da Mayor (Davis), block philosopher; Sweet Dick Willy (Robin Harris), Coconut Sid (Frankie Faison) and M.L. (Paul Benjamin), the Greek-chorus triumvirate who seek shelter from the sun in beer and beneath a beach umbrella; and even the Puerto Rican helado "icee" man carting his big block of ice and syrup bottles. It is a block where English intermingles with Spanish, where salsa meets Raheem's rap and the air is radio-active with Señor Love Daddy's We-Love show, as he does "the nasty to ya ears" with "da platters dat matter," with black music ranging from rap and juju to reggae and soul—a block where music is a main character.

Nor does this film shy from hot topics within the community. The triumvirate express anger and jealousy over the Koreans' ability to establish a successful business in their neighborhood: "Either them Korean motherfuckers are geniuses or you black asses are just plain dumb!" M.L. declares. It is also where, in a hilarious but biting scene, "You dago, wop, garlic-breath pizza-slinging Vic Damone" is countered by "You gold-teeth, gold chain-wearing, fried-chicken-and-biscuit-eatin' monkey"; where "You slanty-eyed, me-no-speak-American, Korean kick-boxing, son-of-a-bitch," is met by "You Goya bean-eating, fifteen in a car, thirty in an apartment, meda-meda, Puerto Rican cocksucker" and "It's cheap, I gotta good price for you, B'nai Brith, Jew asshole!" It is where the battery-powered message carrier Radio Raheem (Nunn) blasts the word: "Fight the Power," and rules—almost to the end.

Lee's films differ not only in their black perspective—in an industry where few blacks have a voice—but also in their ability to look at both sides of the coin at once. As in real life, his characters are neither all good nor all bad.

And therein lies their—and Lee's—power: the minute he establishes our identification with a character, Lee turns him inside out to reveal the dark side in us all.

Lee's films are unmistakably Spike: direct, outspoken, no-holds-barred, tell it like it is, pointed and hard-hitting. He approaches his subject matter without hesitation, earning him a reputation as both audacious and arrogant. *Do the Right Thing* is not only an assertion of black life but, importantly, of filmmaking. It strikes you with the speed, color and style of graffiti: an urban, in-your-face declaration.

Lee's production company, 40 Acres and a Mule Filmworks, is young and black and located in the heart of Brooklyn, amidst Jamaican patty and spice parlors and other black-owned businesses. Nearby, Lee runs film workshops for minimal fees for those who can't afford the tuition and bureaucracy of film schools but still have a dream.

M G : *How did* Do the Right Thing *come about?*

S L : It started because of the whole Howard Beach incident. I wanted to do something to address that and racism. It's been reported several places that this film is the retelling of Howard Beach. This is a completely *fictional* thing. We took four things from it: the baseball bat, a black man gets killed, the pizzeria, and the conflict between blacks and Italian-Americans.

M G : *How did the ideas develop for the film, and how were they influenced by logistics? It's hot material.*

S L : I wanted it to be one twenty-four-hour period, the hottest day of the summer. I wanted the film to take place on one block in Bedford-Stuyvesant. So that's all the stuff I needed to work with, to start with. From there I could just go ahead and do what I had to do.

The script doesn't come to life till you shoot it. The finished film's always going to be different. I'm always true to what I'm saying, but the most important thing is to do what's right. If I write something, and it comes out in rehearsals that something else is better, we change it.

Every time I do a film, people ask me, 'Did you have full artistic control?' I mean, *She's Gotta Have It, School Daze* and *Do the Right Thing*—we made the films we wanted to make.

M G : *How did the character of Smiley, the Dostoyevskian "village idiot," develop?*

S L : He's not in the script at all. It came about because Roger Smith, the actor, kept hounding me. So we went for something that wouldn't seem like it was just an afterthought.

M G : *Roger Smith, who plays Smiley, doesn't have cerebral palsy in real life?*
S L : No, that was an act. We just wanted him to be a different character.

M G : *Is Smiley a symbol of the black man as handicapped . . .*
S L : I wasn't thinking about that.

M G : *Who is Mookie, the character you play? His relationship with Tina, the mother of his child, is unresolved. We don't really know what his hopes and his dreams are, except wanting to get paid.*
S L : That's all it is. Just live to the next day. He can't see beyond the next day. Mookie is an irresponsible young black youth. He gave Tina a baby. He changes, but up to that point he doesn't really care about his son or her.

M G : *The end of the film is very powerful, and yet, somewhat ambiguous. How do you reconcile the two quotes, one from Dr. King and the other from Malcolm X?*
S L : Well, I don't think it's ambiguous. I think you really have to concentrate on what the final coda of the film is: the Malcolm X quote, not the Martin Luther King quote.

M G : *Malcolm X said, "I am not against using violence in self-defense. I don't even call it violence . . . I call it intelligence." Is the riot then, doing the right thing?*
S L : In that specific case it is, because Mookie and the people around him just get tired of blacks being killed by cops, just murdered by cops. And when the cops are brought to trial, they know nothing's going to happen. There's complete frustration and hopelessness.

They've seen it so many times: Howard Beach, Michael Stewart, Tawana Brawley, Eleanor Bumpurs. Nothing happens. The eight cops that murdered Michael Stewart—that's where we got that Radio Raheem stuff. That is the Michael Stewart chokehold. Except we didn't have his eyeballs pop out of his head like Michael Stewart's did—[the police and medical examiner] greased his eyeballs and tried to stick them back in the sockets. There's a complete loss of faith in the judicial system. And so when you're frustrated and there's no other outlet, it'll make you want to hurl the garbage can through a window.

M G : *If you read about an incident like the one in Central Park in the* Amsterdam News *and then compare it with* The New York Times *coverage there are two different perspectives . . .*

S L : A couple days later a black woman was found raped and murdered in a park. No mention of it—you didn't see nothing—no headlines in the *Post, Newsday, Time, New York Times,* or *New York Daily News.* That's a devaluation of a black life. It's like black life doesn't mean anything, doesn't count for anything.

As long as they see, well, it's niggers killing niggers, they're animals anyway, it's no news. But if a young woman—a young *white* woman, on top of that, from Wall Street—is raped in Central Park, you might as well spit in the face of Jesus or something, because, you know, a great atrocity has happened.

This [black] woman was raped four or five days after the incident in Central Park. *Raped and murdered!* Nobody said nothing. Didn't see no outcry. I didn't see Donald Trump taking any fucking ads out behind that shit.

M G : *The fight in your film was between the most sympathetic white, Sal, and the two least sympathetic blacks. For instance, Buggin' Out, the activist, couldn't get any people on his side except Radio Raheem. John Turturro's openly racist Pino would have been his most likely counterpart.*

S L : See, that's what Hollywood would have had. But that's too easy. Pino didn't pick up that stuff out of the air. Some of it had to have been taught him by his father, Sal.

What's really troubling to some white critics is when Mookie throws the garbage can through the window. Because Mookie's one of those "nice black people." I've heard a lot of white friends tell me, "You're a nice black person, you're not like the rest." They really followed Mookie, they liked Mookie. He was a likable character. [Laughs.] They feel betrayed when he throws the garbage can through the window. Can't trust them. The Moulan yan. Telling him to get a spear. [Screams. Laughs.]

M G : *"Moulan yan" means eggplant.*
S L : Haven't you seen any Martin Scorsese movies?

M G : *Were the events leading to the riot a way to say that even the "nice" whites are willing to hide behind the colonial power structure?*

S L : Sal says, "These people love my pizza." I mean, any time you hear some-one say "youse people," you know what that is.

M G : *Although he seemed proud that everyone grew up on his pizza . . .*
S L : Yeah, but look, as soon as the shit started to happen, all of a sudden he starts saying, "I'll break your fuckin' nigger ass." That didn't come out of thin air. It was there. It just had to be provoked. But it's still there, though.

M G : *Why provoke the fight in a seemingly safe civil arena, a gathering place, rather than on the street?*
S L : Well, that's where a fight like that would start. In the public eye. Buggin' Out's character is a direct reference to a couple days after the Howard Beach incident. Some black leaders got together and wanted all the black people in New York City to boycott pizza for a day. It was one of the most ridiculous things I ever heard in my life. It was stupid.

I mean, Buggin' Out has the right idea. But what's going to be the value of having one black photo up on Sal's wall of fame? Is that going to do any-body any good? But on the other hand, he also has a point, because let's turn it around and say, 'Look, Sal, you make all your money off black people, why don't you have enough sensitivity to have at least one photo up on the wall?' So that's the way the film is to me. Everybody has a point.

M G : *And are you advocating the riot at the end?*
S L : I'm not advocating anything. These are just characters, and this is how they act. This is how *they* acted. And if we turn that around again, I think Sal has a point, too: When you black people get together and have your own businesses, you can do what you want to do.

I don't think that blacks are going to see this film and just go out in the streets and start rioting. I mean, black people don't need this movie to riot. They've been doing it already. Just look at what happened in Miami the week before the Super Bowl, when those cops killed people. Now some people be killed in New York City in summer by the cops, and this movie's not going to help. But it's going to be tense here in New York anyway, with this whole mayoral election coming up. And it's going to be hot, you know. That was the whole premise of the film, that in 95 degrees people lose it anyway.

M G : *Do you think that the "wilding" incident in Central Park will affect the film's reception?*

SL: I never even heard of the term "wilding" before this movie came out. It's like they got this thing, they made it up, you know. I'm very sorry that the young woman got raped. It's a terrible act no matter who it happens to. But I think the whole thing was blown way out of proportion. The media just whipped white New York into a frenzy, and Donald Trump wasn't helping, taking out them ads: bring back the death penalty—they're code words. Anytime you hear Ed Koch talk about "savages" and "animals," you know he's talking about young black males. It was the whole Bernhard Goetz thing right away. And definitely this is being tied into the mayoral race. It'll come up again: a vote for [black candidate] David Dinkins is a vote for wilding. I can see a campaign like that for sure.

MG: *White people fear that you are advocating violence.*
SL: Look, all they have to do is read the last quote of the movie. I'm not advocating violence. Self-defense is not violence. We call it intelligence. People are full of shit. Israel could go out and bomb anybody, nobody says nothing. But when black people go out and protect themselves, then we're militants, or we're advocating violence.

MG: *It seems you almost glossed over the death of Radio Raheem. When Mookie goes to see Sal at the end, he just says, "Radio Raheem is dead."*
SL: Yeah, but that's Mookie's character. What happened that night was tragic, but Mookie's whole character is not going to change overnight. And the reason why he's there that morning is because he wants to get paid. He's been saying that the whole movie, you know, get paid, get paid.

No, I don't think I glossed over it. What's the last thing that Love Daddy says? "The next record goes out for Radio Raheem. We love you, brother."

MG: *When Mookie breaks the window, it's his decision to get off the sidelines, take a stand and really explode the situation. . . . Is that you?*
SL: We've always tried to take a stand no matter what. All creative filming does. I don't think that we're going to change anything. This is just a more explosive, volatile subject matter.

MG: *Is Mookie symbolic of art taking a stand?*
SL: Of art? No. I leave that up to you journalists.

MG: *After the riot, the only people who lose out at the end of the film are the people who live in the neighborhood.*

S L : That always happens. Look at the riots in '67, '68. Anytime there's a riot, the National Guard, police—whatever—they always make sure they contain that riot to the ghetto. And so the buildings they burn down will never be built back. When there were riots in New York City, they were never on Fifth Avenue. There's never been looting in Lord & Taylor's or Saks. It was on 125th Street. So, in a way, we do lose out. But people don't *feel* they lose out, because they feel they lost already. People have nothing to lose.

M G : *Before the riot they had the pizzeria, whatever that meant. But now, the street's the same except it's filled with debris and they don't have a pizzeria anymore.*

S L : They felt better about it, though. They felt that for once in their lives, they'd taken a stand. And they felt that they had some kind of say. They felt powerful.

M G : *It's brought up several times in the film that "it's a free country." Your character brings it up at one point; Clifton, the yuppie who moves into Bed-Stuy, brings it up. It's a very ironic statement.*

S L : Well, yeah. *That* was no accident.

M G : *The street in the film—that was the cleanest street I've ever seen in New York.*

S L : I made that choice because any time you hear people say Bed-Stuy, right away they think of the rapes, murders, drugs. There's no need to show garbage piled up high and all that other stuff, because not every single block in Bed-Stuy is like that.

It would be a fallacy to say that lower-income people always live in burned-out buildings. These are hard-working people, and they take pride in their stuff just like everybody else. So there's no need for the set to look like Charlotte Street in the South Bronx.

Another thing people ask: "Where are the drugs?" Drugs is such a massive subject, it just can't be dealt with effectively as a subplot. You have to do an entire film on drugs. This film was not about that. This film was about *racism.*

M G : *The people in the film are very intelligent. The most ignorant person is Pino. Is there a difference between violence in the hands of the ignorant and violence in the hands of the intelligent?*

SL: Intelligent people will use violence to their advantage and ignorant people just use violence for violence's sake.

MG: *But if you had really ignorant people fighting back the riot would have carried a different weight.*
SL: No. I think that it is good these people were intelligent. Because then it shows this is not just a case of *random* violence. People knew *exactly* what they were doing.

MG: *And if they had jobs? Mookie says several times, "Get a job."*
SL: He gets that really from working for Sal. "Get a job"—that's really a statement on your manhood. Because every man should be able to hold his own weight. And what's the first thing Pino says to the guys who are heckling him, when he's beating up Smiley? "Get a job!" Because a lot of these guys don't have jobs. Therefore, in Pino's eyes it means that they're not men. "All the Moulan yans are on welfare anyway."

MG: *Your screenwriting and filmmaking aren't strictly narrative. They bear a strong resemblance to a musical score. Each character is a note that you play and then bring all together for a crescendo at the end.*
SL: We just don't like to have narratives that show. They're there, but we just don't want to be out in front, because when narratives are out in front, the audience will be able to guess from watching the first ten minutes of the movie exactly where you're going to go. We like to keep them guessing, just let there be work. I think that for the most part, not enough respect is given to audiences' intelligence. They're just spoon-fed everything.

MG: *When* School Daze *was released, it was lumped together with . . .*
SL: *Shoot to Kill* and *Action Jackson.* They all came out on the same day. They just think that the black audience is just one monolithic audience and has no diversity at all—which I think is very disrespectful. There's no way *Shoot to Kill* is a *black* film. Very few black people went to see that film. Sidney Poitier was the only black person in that movie.

MG: *In your book,* Do the Right Thing, *you say that blacks can't be held responsible for racism, that they're victims. It seems that one's self-perception as a victim reduces one's power—as seen in the conversation between M.L., Sweet Dick Willy, and Coconut Sid about the Korean fruit stand.*

S L :   No. How is that going to be "my perception" if black people were taken from Africa as slaves? I'm not imagining that. You must acknowledge that, but not use that as a excuse.

When I was becoming a filmmaker I knew it would be harder for me to be a black filmmaker—to be a filmmaker because I was black. But I realized that you just have to be two or three—four—times better. The same thing as any black athlete. They got to be better than the white boy to make the team. You don't sit there and brood about it. This is something you just know, growing up black. It's a given. The problem starts when people say that's a given and then use that as the excuse.

M G :   *I was reading an article in* Premiere *about blacks in the film industry. And one person was quoted as saying Hollywood films are based on the premise that a black man or woman can't lead you anywhere. Which is to say that whites' moral/ psychological identification can't be with a black person.*

S L :   I truly believe a lot of people—a lot of *executives*—believe that. There's an age-old axiom in Hollywood that black is death at the box office. Except for very few exceptions—Eddie Murphy being one. Look at *Time* the week they had *Mississippi Burning* on the cover. Alan Parker said the realities of Hollywood today demand that this film have two white leads. And I'm not going to hang Alan Parker about that statement. I think that he's just echoing what a whole lot of executives feel, the people who get pictures made.

No matter what you do—you can be as big as Michael Jackson—they still look at him as black first. So, you really can't get around it. But it doesn't bother me.

At Cannes, the jury, led by Wim Wenders, gave no award to *Do the Right Thing*. Says Spike:

"We were robbed.

"Ten films received awards and we didn't get one. I feel we entered the best of the festival.

"Most people on the jury, minus Sally Field—the biggest, most important filmmakers at the world's most important film festival—I don't think they're ready for a young black filmmaker to get the Palme d'Or. I think that it's just reality. When it comes down to between me and somebody else, they're going to give it to the white boy.

"At the party afterward, there's praise for [Soderbergh's] *sex, lies, and videotape:* 'Now we have the future of cinema.' So I guess I'm not in the future—their future at least.

"Jim Jarmusch is a really good friend of mine. I love his work. But you know that Wenders gave him that award because that's his protégé.

"I heard that Wenders said that Mookie wasn't enough of a hero. I think that they saw Spike Lee throwing that trash can through the window.

"One day Wenders is going to get off at the wrong stop on the A-train. He's supposed to get off at 59th Street and he's going to miss the stop—it's going to be express—and get off on 125th Street. And I'll be waiting for his ass. [Laughs.]

"He's going to need wings of desire. And you could say what you want, because I don't plan to be in Germany anytime soon."

He's Gotta Have It: An Interview with Spike Lee

JANICE MOSIER RICHOLSON / 1991

SPIKE LEE IS A FILMMAKER with a vision and an agenda. He makes no bones about it: his purpose is to hold his cinematic mirror up to reflect African-American reality as experienced by his generation. These are the young blacks who grew up after the Civil Rights movement and the assassinations of Martin Luther King, Jr. and Malcolm X. They have seen the dream of a Great Society and Affirmative Action crumble into crackhouses and quota-babble.

Not yet thirty-five, Lee has directed five feature films since 1986—*She's Gotta Have It* (1986), *School Daze* (1988), *Do the Right Thing* (1989), *Mo' Better Blues* (1990), and *Jungle Fever* (1991)—which have earned him a controversial reputation for interpreting contemporary black America to itself and to society at large. He's a man with a commitment and credentials, working in the right medium for the times.

Born in Atlanta into an educated, culturally stimulating family environment—his father is an accomplished jazz musician—Lee moved as a child with his family to New York City, where he lived in middle class Brooklyn neighborhoods. He returned to Atlanta to become a third generation graduate of Morehouse College. After a summer internship at Columbia Pictures, Lee enrolled at New York University's film school where he and friends from Morehouse formed a creative team that has stayed together.

Cultural advantages, solid education, old school ties . . . sounds like upscale America. But it's the middle class family and the college campus that

Published in *Cineaste* 18, no. 4 (1991): 12–14. Reprinted by permission of *Cineaste*.

often incubate American liberal reformers. A shrewd businessman, adept at marketing and public relations, Lee talks freely and concisely about the controversial subjects portrayed in his films. He knows how to work the press, how to take control of an interview and make it serve his own ends. At the same time, he maintains a pose of professional detachment, projecting the high seriousness of an artist and social critic. He directs his gaze slightly away from the questioner, but drops his mask when irritated or amused, replying sharply or bursting into hearty laughter, and sometimes revealing adolescent-like petulance or impish charm. It's hard to tell the public persona from the man and best to take Lee at face value on his own terms. He continues to live and work in Brooklyn as an independent filmmaker at his own company, 40 Acres and a Mule Filmworks, and is currently at work on a feature film on Malcolm X.

The following interview, which took place at the 1991 Cannes Film Festival after the screening of *Jungle Fever,* also incorporates Lee's responses to questions posed at a general press conference and at a panel discussion of American directors.

CINEASTE: *What is the primary purpose of your films?*
SPIKE LEE: I try to show African-American culture on screen. Every group, every culture and ethnic group needs to see itself on screen. What black filmmakers can do is show our culture on screen the same way Fellini's done for Italians and Kurosawa's done for the Japanese.

CINEASTE: *You describe your films as "litmus tests" that measure the pulse of public opinion on issues of social concern. Do you believe that the cinema has significant social power to help eliminate racism and prejudice?*
LEE: I don't think my films are going to get rid of racism or prejudice. I think the best thing my films can do is provoke discussion. In my films, I try to show that there's a very serious problem. Racism is such a broad subject. I think conditions are the same as they've always been. There is still prejudice in the United States and Europe. To me prejudice is based on ignorance. A lot of times, racism is tied directly to exploitation and money. I think the biggest lie that's ever been perpetrated on the American people is 'If you're American, it doesn't matter what race, nationality, religion, or creed you are—you're American, and that's all that matters.' That's a lie and it's always been a lie. The United States is built on the Constitution of the United States.

In that Constitution, it says that black people are three-fifths of a human being and could be sold as property . . . as cattle. Black people have been trained and taught to hate themselves. We've been taught that everything black is negative or derogatory. We've been taught that Africa, our homeland, which is a cradle of civilization, is a place where cannibals run around naked, swinging on trees.

CINEASTE: *You've made two films about confrontation between African-Americans and Italian-Americans. Why did you pick these ethnic groups?*
LEE: New York City is made up of many different ethnic groups. That is not to say that the only conflicts between ethnic groups there are those between blacks and Italians, but these are the most violent ones in my mind. I don't know what it is, but when blacks and Italian-Americans get together, a lot of times you have a conflict. Take the murder of Yusuf Hawkins as an example. One day he wanted to check out a used car and ventured into a neighborhood which happened to be a predominantly Italian-American neighborhood and he was shot.

CINEASTE: *You dedicated* Jungle Fever *to Hawkins. Does that mean there is revenge in the air?*
LEE: No. I don't think there is any revenge in the air. What happened in 1989 happened then. It's two years later. I'm a kinder, gentler person.

CINEASTE: *In your film, you use the term "jungle fever" for the sexual attraction some whites and blacks feel for each other. Have you ever felt jungle fever?*
LEE: No. I've never had a relationship with a white woman.

CINEASTE: *What kind of research did you do? Was the film based on personal experience or invention?*
LEE: Both. A lot of my films are based on personal experience. My mother died in 1977 when I was twenty. My father remarried a white woman. That probably had something to do with it.

CINEASTE: *Did the marriage work?*
LEE: Yes, they're in love. They had a child. I have a little brother.

CINEASTE: *Do you like the woman?*

LEE: We don't get along, but it's not because she's white. I was my mother's first child, so my stepmother's never going to be my mother.

CINEASTE: *What do your father and stepmother think of the film?*
LEE: They haven't seen it yet. It might be hard for him to look at. She ain't gonna like it.

CINEASTE: *Do you think she'll take the issues of the film as a personal slight?*
LEE: What's she gonna do—beat me? I'm a grown man.

CINEASTE: *What are you trying to show in the film?*
LEE: I think what we're trying to do with this film is to show sexual myths. What's important about this film is that the characters Flipper and Angie, played by Wesley Snipes and Annabella Sciorra, are not drawn to each other by love but by sexual myths. When you're a black person in this country, you're constantly bombarded with the myth of the white woman as the epitome of beauty—again and again and again—in TV, movies, magazines. It's blond hair, fair skin, blue eyes, thin nose. If you're black, you never see yourself portrayed in that way—you don't fit that image, you're not beautiful. So we cut away our noses to get a thinner nose . . . we'll cut away our lips . . . wear blue and green contact lenses. Why do we do that? Because that's what's pounded into us constantly. Annabella Sciorra's character bought into the myth that the black male is a stud, a sexual superman with a penis that's two feet long. So those are the two sexual myths that bring these two people together.

CINEASTE: *Are you saying that they wanted to explore the sexual myths—that they were curious about each other's flesh?*
LEE: That was the basis of their relationship. One thing a lot of people aren't picking up on is that the film is not just about interracial marriages and relationships. It's about identity. There are people in the film who are *products* of mixed marriages. My character's wife in the film has a black father and a white mother. The same is true for Flipper's wife. The people in the film are constantly talking about their identity, where they belong. They make a distinction between mulattoes, quadroons, and octoroons. And not just the blacks. In the candy store, the Italian-Americans have the same concern. There are a lot of dark Italians. Sicily is very close to Africa. The charac-

ter Frankie says, "I'm not black. My mother's a dark Italian. I'm as white as anybody here."

CINEASTE: *In one scene, the black women characters speak frankly and openly about sexuality and color. Was it scripted?*
LEE: It was completely improvisational. We did between twenty and twenty-five takes. I find the more you talk the more honest you get.

CINEASTE: *How do you feel about interracial relationships?*
LEE: Interracial relationships and marriages have been going on since we were brought over here as slaves. We're not trying to condemn interracial relationships. People have to realize that this film does not represent every single interracial couple in the world. We're not saying that a black man with a white woman won't work. I think if two people love each other, that's great. There's another interracial couple in the film. The John Turturro character named Paulie and the character Orin. I think they have a chance of having a better relationship because they have a real foundation of friendship, whereas Flipper and Angie's was based on myth. They didn't really love each other. I think if they had, love would have enabled them to withstand the onslaught of abuse they were getting from their family and friends and the two neighborhoods they live in—Harlem and Bensonhurst. In the end, Angie comes to love Flipper, but he still loves his wife.

CINEASTE: *When Angie's Italian-American father finds out that she's been with a black man, did he have to beat her up so badly?*
LEE: He feels he does.

CINEASTE: *Would he have done the same if she'd gotten involved with any other man who wasn't Italian-American?*
LEE: No. If Angie had gotten involved with an Irish or Jewish man, her father might have been upset, but the fact that he's black—that's the ass-whipper.

CINEASTE: *She seems to get the worst of it. Her family's reaction seems much more violent than the one Flipper gets.*
LEE: It's been my experience—I'm not going to say both communities welcome interracial relationships—but it's very rare that black people disown a

relative if they marry somebody white. They might not talk to you for a week or so, but they're not going to lock their door. I know several cases where white people with black partners were thrown out of the family and the family hasn't spoken to them since. They're cut out of the will and all types of stuff. That's the difference.

CINEASTE: *When Flipper's wife discovers that her husband is unfaithful to her, she seemed more upset that her husband was with a white woman than with the fact that he was unfaithful.*
LEE: I think that regardless of whether the other woman was white or black, Flipper's wife would be throwing his stuff out of the window. The fact that he was having an affair with a white woman made it that much worse of an offense.

CINEASTE: *Flipper is a very well-heeled, upwardly mobile professional African-American. Is there a point being made there?*
LEE: Yes. We're saying that one should not lose himself—who they are—while striving to be successful. There are other things more important than success.

CINEASTE: *Why did you wait so long to tackle the issue of the drug problem?*
LEE: I felt that drugs should be a big part of *this* film. It was right for *Jungle Fever.* I had to be the one to determine when drugs would be in my films. I wanted to show the drug problem as a main theme in a film, not just stick it in because the drug topic is trendy, chic, or faddish. In *Do the Right Thing,* drugs would have been a bogus subplot. The main thrust of that film was racism. In *Mo' Better Blues,* I did not want to make another typical story of a jazz musician who's an alcoholic or who's hooked on heroin.

CINEASTE: *Religion is a big theme in this film. In your portrayals of the characters Gator and the Good Reverend Doctor—Ossie Davis's character—you seem to imply a relationship between religion and drugs.*
LEE: That implication's not there for me. Gator's on crack for a lot of reasons. One is the relationship with his father, who's a reverend. The Good Reverend Doctor is out of touch. He goes overboard, and I think religion really had a bad effect on Gator in the film. But I don't think religion is what

turned Gator into a crackhead. His brother Flipper isn't on drugs. I really think people are responsible for their own actions. Gator likes getting high.

C I N E A S T E: *Where did you get the idea for the characters of Gator and the Good Reverend Doctor?*
L E E: The whole idea of the Good Reverend Doctor killing his son is based on Marvin Gaye Sr. shooting Marvin Gaye Jr., who was a cokehead at the time.

C I N E A S T E: *You definitely say 'no' to drugs in the film. You show Flipper wandering through a crackhouse looking for Gator, then crying 'no' as he holds a young addict close to him. Is that your 'no' or the 'no' of the character.*
L E E: Me and him. Flipper's going crazy. He just spent the last two hours in hell.

C I N E A S T E: *Is your portrayal of a crackhouse realistic?*
L E E: Crackhouses aren't that big. It was artistic license. I wanted to show how crack is totally wiping out generations of African-Americans.

C I N E A S T E: *Do you think of yourself as a role model for black filmmakers?*
L E E: No, I don't think of myself like that. I think from the beginning, I never, ever wanted to think of myself as "king of the hill" of African-Americans who make films.

C I N E A S T E: *How did you get started as a filmmaker?*
L E E: When I went to film school, I knew I did not want to have my films shown only during Black History Month in February or at libraries. I wanted them to have a wide distribution. And I did not want to spend four or five years trying to piecemeal together the money for my films. I did my first film, *She's Gotta Have It,* independently for $175,000. We had a grant from the New York State Council on the Arts and were raising money the whole time we were shooting. We shot the film in twelve days. The next stage was to get it out of the lab. Then, the most critical part was when I had to hole up in my little studio apartment to get it cut. I took about two months to do that. I had no money coming in, so I had to hold off the debtors because I knew if I had enough time to at least get it in good enough shape to show, we could have some investor screenings, and that's what happened. We got

it blown up to 35mm for a film festival. What you have to do is to try to get a distributor. You enter as many film festivals as you can. *She's Gotta Have It* was picked up for $475,000 after a lot of distributors saw it at a festival.

C I N E A S T E :   *Your name is often mentioned today as a milestone in black film-making. How do you feel about that?*
L E E :   It's very encouraging. But even though I might be the one who's getting the publicity, there were a lot of people before me who made it happen. If Melvin Van Peebles didn't do *Sweet Sweetback's Baadasssss Song,* none of this would have been possible. And there's Gordon Parks, Ossie Davis—all these people and others put up with a whole lot of stuff. So the people following them twenty or thirty years later are able to do what we're doing now. Because of my success, it's going to make it easier for the next generation that comes up behind us.

C I N E A S T E :   *Do you think you've opened the door for black filmmakers?*
L E E :   I try to make the best films I can, good films that make money to enable things to open up. I'm not saying the door's wide open . . . it's not wide open. But the fact is that blacks are making films instead of the door being shut. I think there were nineteen films by black filmmakers released last year, and that's more than the whole previous decade combined. I think what's important is that we not get too high and start doing cartwheels and say that happy days are here, that Hollywood's in love with black people. That's not the case. We're not getting the same treatment as general market films, which means films for white moviegoers. And this is something we continue to fight. We want to raise the ceiling of how much Hollywood will spend to make and promote our films.

C I N E A S T E :   *As your films get bigger, as you get more success, do you find that you're getting intervention from the moneymen? Do they try to persuade you to do the film their way?*
L E E :   They're always going to tell you what they think. If their suggestions are good, I use them. If they're not, I don't. I think I have the best of both worlds because I'm an independent filmmaker with complete creative control of my films. I hire who I want. I have final cut. But at the same time, I go directly to Hollywood for financing and distribution. I find it's best for me to work within the Hollywood system. It's an individual choice, and you

have to make up your mind. I have a classmate from NYU who hates Hollywood. He's found his financing with Japanese money.

CINEASTE: *Music is an important component in your films. How much of that is your input?*

LEE: I start thinking about the music for my films at the same moment I'm writing the script. It's part of my creative process. I pay as much attention to the music as I do to the cinematography, casting, and production design. I'm the son of a great jazz musician, Bill Lee. He's done the scores for all of my films before *Jungle Fever*. I was raised with jazz. It was played in the house all the time.

CINEASTE: *Stevie Wonder did the music for* Jungle Fever. *You also used some Frank Sinatra songs. Why was that?*

LEE: For juxtaposition. We had three songs by Frank Sinatra at the candy store in Bensonhurst, representing the Italian-American community. We also had four songs by Mahalia Jackson for the scenes with the Good Reverend Doctor and his wife.

CINEASTE: *You often use music and dialog at the same time.*

LEE: A lot of people say you shouldn't do that. I don't agree. If it's the right music, you can play it behind dialog. We had a great ten week mix to make sure we had the right balance, that the music never overrides the dialog.

CINEASTE: *What's your next project?*

LEE: I hope to make a film on an epic scale about Malcolm X. I want it to be on a David Lean scale. The Malcolm X project has been trying to get made for twenty years. There were several directors . . . scripts were written. I thought the first script—James Baldwin's—was the best.

CINEASTE: *When it comes to race relations, would you say that you're an optimist or a pessimist?*

LEE: I think I'm a realist. In my films, I'm not saying, "Throw up your hands, there's no hope," or that black and white people will never get together. Even though some people say my films have a bleak outlook, I think my films are optimistic. I still think there's hope.

CINEASTE: *Do you think the problems of racism and prejudice can change in your lifetime?*

LEE: I don't think racism can be eliminated in my lifetime . . . or my children's or grandchildren's. But I think it's something we have to strive for. I'm going to keep working toward that day coming.

Spike Lee: The *Playboy* Interview

ELVIS MITCHELL / 1991

THERE ARE MANY logical places you might find a famous director, writer, producer or actor—in a bungalow office on the studio back lot, poolside in Bel Air or maybe at a prominent table at Le Dome. But if you're looking for the most successful hyphenate in movies—a man who is the writer, producer, director *and* star of a series of commercially and critically successful films—forget Hollywood and head for a renovated three-story firehouse in the Fort Greene section of Brooklyn.

The fact that Spike Lee has chosen to oversee his burgeoning show-business empire from Fort Greene, his childhood home, is simply one example of his fierce independence. He demands complete control over his often controversial movies, such as *Do the Right Thing, School Daze, She's Gotta Have It, Mo' Better Blues* and the upcoming *Jungle Fever*. He directs and stars in a string of Nike commercials with Michael Jordan. He directs music videos. He oversees books and documentaries about himself and his films. He's starting a record company. He owns a store—Spike's Joint—that merchandises every conceivable type of paraphernalia based on his movies.

"Spike is first and foremost a damn good businessman," says actor-director Ossie Davis, who played Da Mayor in *Do the Right Thing* and Coach Odom in *School Daze*. But Lee is much more than that. With his movies, he has clearly raised the consciousness of Hollywood toward black filmmakers and, more importantly, he has shown that black-themed films can be both commercially and critically viable. But Lee is not satisfied with putting blacks *on* the screen; he is a vocal advocate for getting blacks jobs behind the scenes as well. He stipulates in his contracts—whether for movies or commercials—that blacks be hired, often in capacities that have not been available to them previously. He insists, for instance, that black artists do the posters for his movies and he has built a loyal repertory company of actors and crew, some of whom have been with him since his days as a student filmmaker.

Probably no movie director since Hitchcock has become so immediately identifiable to the public. Part of that fame stems from Lee's acting, both in his films and in commercials. But Lee, thirty-four, has also positioned himself as a spokesman on a variety of racial issues. *Vogue* dubbed him a "provocauteur," and he seems dedicated to living up to that image.

Shelton Jackson Lee—who was nicknamed Spike by his mother—is the eldest child of a middle-class Brooklyn family. His mother, who died in 1977, was a teacher who demanded educational excellence from all five Lee children; his father is a musician who has written the scores for most of his son's films. Lee was the third generation of his family to attend Morehouse College, the so-called black Harvard, and later went to New York University when he decided to pursue filmmaking. His *Joe's Bed-Stuy Barbershop: We Cut Heads* won a student Academy Award and became the first student film ever shown at Lincoln Center's "New Directors, New Films" series.

Despite that success, he was unable to land serious filmwork. Since Hollywood wasn't helping him, Lee decided to help himself. Armed with spit, prayers and a budget of $175,000, he made *She's Gotta Have It,* a dizzying, up-to-the-minute look at a relationship through the eyes of an independent and charismatic young black woman and her three suitors. Lee himself played one of those suitors—Mars Blackmon, the fly-mouthed messenger who does everything, including make love, in a pair of Air Jordans that seem to be as large as he is. (Mars lives on in Lee's Nike commercials.) The movie made $8,000,000 and turned Lee into an overnight sensation.

Had Spike's first film been a fluke? Was it a lucky break or was he really a filmmaker?

Lee answered that with *School Daze,* an ambitious, multilayered tale about life at a black college. Not only did he attempt to examine such sensitive issues as the stratification of light- and dark-skinned blacks and the cliquish assimilation into the middle class that takes place at black colleges, he did it as a musical comedy. *School Daze* was one of Columbia Pictures' biggest-grossing films of 1988.

It was in 1989 that Lee tackled his most heated subject: race relations on the hottest day of the year on a tense Bedford-Stuyvesant block in *Do the Right Thing*. From the flamboyant opening to the tragic climax that ends in one character's death at the hands of the police to the double-barreled closing quotes from Martin Luther King, Jr., and Malcolm X, *Do the Right Thing* was proudly combative. When it failed to earn a chance at an Oscar for Best Picture, Lee was publicly outraged, claiming the snub was racially motivated.

Lee changed pace with *Mo' Better Blues,* a movie about a single-minded jazz musician, but he continued to be a controversy magnet—he was branded as anti-Semitic because of the movie's portrayal of two avaricious, small-minded Jewish club owners. Since his newest movie, *Jungle Fever,* a story about interracial love, promises to be one of his most controversial, we decided the time was right to send Elvis Mitchell, a free-lancer and National Public Radio's *Weekend Edition* entertainment critic, to check in with Lee. Mitchell reports:

"Lee has made my life miserable for the past couple of months. The line 'Elvis was a hero to most, but he never meant shit to me' comes from 'Fight the Power,' the bracing and hard-charging theme of *Do the Right Thing,* and invariably, in phone-tag intramurals preceding our meetings, every message Lee left on my answering machine began with those deathless words, followed by his trademark cackle.

"I first met with him in his office in Fort Greene, where he was putting together an assemblage of *Jungle Fever* to show the studio before leaping into his next picture, an epic on the life and times of Malcolm X. The place is cluttered with boxes and people and Lee was extremely busy. We did manage to talk briefly and schedule our first session, which was to take place on a flight from New York to Los Angeles. He was good-humored and prickly; he loves to catch people off guard and make incendiary comments. For instance, he demanded the right to approve this interview before it was published, but when I told him no, he simply cackled.

"Our first lengthy session, squeezed in between drops during a bumpy flight and a showing of *Dick Tracy,* demonstrated that Lee was a man of many moods. He preferred judging questions to answering them and seemed more combative than comfortable. But our second session, which took place at this New York apartment a few blocks from his office, was far more relaxed

and productive. He responded to the questions with candor and enthusiasm
and even posed some of his own. He asserted his shyness and spoke about
his difficulty with interviews, even as he talked at length.

"We started with the obvious question."

PLAYBOY: *You like to cause trouble, don't you?*
LEE: Sure. I was an instigator as a kid. I just like to make people think, stir
'em up. What's wrong with that?

PLAYBOY: Jungle Fever *certainly seems likely to stir things up.*
LEE: [*Laughs*] You think that one's gonna cause some trouble?

PLAYBOY: *When you write lines such as "You never see black men with fine
white women"? What was the word in the script—mugly? Wasn't that the way
you described the white women black men go out with?*
LEE: [*Laughs*] But that's true. I've never seen black men with fine white
women. They be ugly. Mugly, dogs. And you always see white men with
good-looking black women. But, hey, every time you see an interracial couple somewhere, people stare at 'em.

PLAYBOY: *Come on, Spike. That's a big generalization. We've seen good-looking
interracial couples.*
LEE: I said what I meant to. Never see it.

PLAYBOY: *We know you've said in the past that you won't get involved with
white women.*
LEE: I don't need the trouble. Like I don't go for that, don't like that shit. I
just don't find white women attractive, that's all. And it's way too many fine
black women out there.

PLAYBOY: *Isn't there an interracial marriage in your family?*
LEE: Yes. My father. My father remarried. He married a white woman.

PLAYBOY: *Did that have any effect on your making* Jungle Fever?
LEE: Why? Why would it? I didn't talk to my father about it. I talk to my
father only when it comes to scoring my movies. This isn't about him.

PLAYBOY: *There's another potential controversy in* Jungle Fever. *In the opening, you address the audience directly, not as a character, and tell them that if they think you're a racist, they can kiss your "black ass." You say it twice. Why?*
LEE: I felt it was justified. I wanted to hit all that, about race, before anybody else.

PLAYBOY: *How did test audiences respond to it?*
LEE: The test audiences liked it. I don't think Universal is crazy about that shit.

PLAYBOY: *Will it stay in the movie?*
LEE: I guess it will. I do have final cut.

PLAYBOY: *Why does so much of* Jungle Fever *emphasize racial anger?*
LEE: Why shouldn't it? It's out there.

PLAYBOY: *You've said that black people are incapable of racism. Do you really believe that?*
LEE: Yeah, I do. Let me clear that up, 'cause people are always taking stuff out of context. Black people can't be racist. Racism is an institution. Black people don't have the power to keep hundreds of people from getting jobs or the vote. Black people didn't bring nobody else over in boats. They had to add shit to the Constitution so we could get the vote. Affirmative action is about finished in this country now. It's through. And black people had nothing to do with that, those kinds of decisions. So how can black people be racist when that's the standard? Now, black people can be prejudiced. Shit, everybody's prejudiced about something. I don't think there will ever be an end to prejudice. But racism, that's a different thing entirely.

PLAYBOY: *You've been quoted as saying that no white man could properly do the Malcolm X story, which you're preparing to direct.*
LEE: That's right.

PLAYBOY: *You don't think Norman Jewison, who was originally scheduled to direct, could pull it off?*
LEE: No, I don't. Why do people pull that shit with black people? Don't you think Francis Coppola brought something special to *The Godfather*

because he was an Italian? Don't you think that Martin Scorsese brought something special to *GoodFellas* because he was an Italian?

PLAYBOY: *Marlon Brando's not Italian and he was in* The Godfather. *Isn't the point that there simply aren't enough minorities to be considered?*
LEE: Yeah. Now, when that shit changes, then we can talk. Until there are enough black directors, minorities working in movies so it's not an issue, we have to address it different.

PLAYBOY: *But what about one director having skills another director doesn't?*
LEE: I like Norman Jewison's movies. I respect what he does. I saw *In the Heat of the Night, A Soldier's Story.* I respect his work. But I think a black man is more qualified, especially in this case. Now, I do think black people are qualified to direct movies about white people.

PLAYBOY: *How does that work?*
LEE: Because we grow up with white images all the time, in TV, in movies, in books. It's everywhere; you can't get around it. The white world surrounds us. What do white people see of black people? Look at the shit they have us do in movies: "Right on, jive turkey!" [*Laughs*]

PLAYBOY: *There's a line in* Jungle Fever *that says a black man won't rise past a certain level in white corporate America.*
LEE: It's true. How many black men do you see running Xerox? How many black men you see running IBM? Shit, we need to be black entrepreneurs, run our own shit. That's what it's about.

PLAYBOY: *Is that what's behind your store, Spike's Joint?*
LEE: It started off as this mom-and-pop operation. We sold T-shirts for the movies and stuff, but we just had too much stuff going on. So, yeah, I wanted to get it going the way I wanted. I want to control the business, and it's easier to do it from the store. Black people just have to understand we need to become owners. Ownership is important. I don't mean to get down on Eddie Murphy, but he only owns fifty percent of Eddie Murphy Productions. His two white managers each own twenty-five percent of Eddie Murphy Productions. He don't even own a hundred percent of himself.

PLAYBOY: *You have some other complaints about Murphy, don't you?*

LEE: My problem with Eddie has to do with the hiring of black people. He will maintain he can't do nothin' about getting black people hired at Paramount. That's bullshit. A man who makes them a billion dollars can't do nothing about getting black people hired at Paramount? I can't believe that. In my contract, I demand a black man does the design and artwork for my poster. Eddie built Paramount. He built their house, he can bring some people in there if he wants to.

PLAYBOY: *Overall, you seem to have become less critical about other black performers. Have you mellowed?*

LEE: Look, I was never that critical. When I said that shit about Whoopi Goldberg, I was talking about the contact lenses, she was wearing blue contact lenses. She don't wear them blue contact lenses no more, do she?

PLAYBOY: *What's the deal between you and Arsenio Hall?*

LEE: [*Smiles*] Deal? What deal? I been on his show twice. You have to be specific.

PLAYBOY: *Wasn't there a quarrel between the two of you?*

LEE: I criticized him once. I never criticized him as a talk-show host.

PLAYBOY: *Our understanding is that you appeared on his show last summer and were supposed to go back about a month later and were disinvited.*

LEE: Yeah. They canceled on me at the last minute. Didn't even hear from him. Some assistant said they didn't want me on the show. It's in the past. Nothing to say about it. It's all been worked out. I was on his show for *Mo' Better.*

PLAYBOY: Jungle Fever *and* Do the Right Thing *both deal with the relationships between blacks and Italians in the outer boroughs of New York. Why did you choose to deal with that twice?*

LEE: Well, history has proven that in New York City, those are the two most violent, volatile combinations of ethnic groups. Black people and Jewish people have static, but it rarely ever elevates to a physical thing. Little Italy, Bensonhurst, Bay Ridge, Canarsie—black people know that these are neighborhoods that you don't fuck around in.

PLAYBOY: *What do you remember as a kid about that kind of thing—that feeling of fear you talk about?*

LEE: Well, I grew up in sort of an Italian neighborhood. I lived in Cobble Hill before I moved here to Fort Greene. A lot of Italian people there. And we were really the first black family to move into Cobble Hill. For the first couple of days, we got called "nigger," but we were basically left alone. We weren't perceived as a threat, because there was only one of us. In fact, some of my best friends who lived down the block were the Tuccis. Louis Tucci, Joe Tucci. Annabella's [Sciorra] family [in *Jungle Fever*], they're the Tuccis.

PLAYBOY: *While growing up in that kind of neighborhood, what was your feeling about Italians?*

LEE: I think Cobble Hill is a lot different than Bensonhurst. You had a lot of Jewish people in Cobble Hill, too, so it just seemed to be more—I don't want to use the word intelligent, but—

PLAYBOY: *Tolerant?*

LEE: Yeah, that would be a good word.

PLAYBOY: *It just seems odd that the kind of neighborhood you depict in your pictures is so different from the kind you grew up in. Did you ever have an encounter in one of those places like Bensonhurst?*

LEE: No. See, I went to John Dewey High School on Coney Island. But some of my friends went to other high schools, like F.D.R., Fort Hamilton, schools like that. They used to chase the black kids from the school to the subway station. A lot of my friends got chased.

PLAYBOY: *Do you ever go to Bensonhurst just to see what it's like over there?*

LEE: A couple of days after Yusuf Hawkins got murdered, this reporter from *Newsday* invited me to walk around Bensonhurst with him. Other than that, I never went to it until we shot *Jungle Fever* over there.

PLAYBOY: *What was that walk like?*

LEE: Well, I was a celebrity, so it was "Spike, sign an autograph." "Spike, you bringing Michael Jordan around here?" "Spike, you bringing Flavor Flav?" It was exactly like the scene in *Do the Right Thing* between me and Pino over the cigarette machine, with an allowance. Pino says Magic Johnson, Eddie Murphy and Prince aren't black, they're more than black. That's the way I thought I was being viewed. I was "Spike Lee," I wasn't a black person, so they asked me for my autograph. If I was anybody else, I could have gotten a bat over the head.

PLAYBOY: *How does it make you feel to be a celebrity in the neighborhood where you more or less grew up?*
LEE: Well, I think that people don't necessarily look at me as a celebrity, because they know I grew up here. It's no big thing; they see me every day, buying the paper or walking to work and stuff like that. People say hello, but it's not like [*a throaty scream*] "Spike Lee!" It's not no Beatles shit or anything like that.

PLAYBOY: *What do people on the street say? Do they tell you what they like or dislike about your movies?*
LEE: They come up and tell me how much they like Mars Blackmon, or they tell me what they think I should do for my next movie. I'm always getting these comments from people who know exactly what my next movie should be. It's funny—I guess everybody's a director. Or a critic.

PLAYBOY: *When you were a kid, did you know you wanted to make movies?*
LEE: I didn't grow up thinking I wanted to make movies, be a director. Everybody in my neighborhood saw a lot of movies. There was nothing special about going to the movies. I didn't know what I wanted to do. At Morehouse College, I had a combined major, communications: radio-television, journalism, film—not film right away.

PLAYBOY: *Do you remember the first film you saw that made you want to make movies?*
LEE: Wait a minute. I never had a moment like that. It was never, "I saw *Lawrence of Arabia* when I was two and suddenly I was hit by the magic power of film." That's bullshit. Like I told you, I just went to the movies. Nobody thought about being a director, not me or anybody else. I read that all the time—"After I saw that picture, I knew there was nothing else for me to do"—that's a lie. It's just bullshit when people say that.

PLAYBOY: *Maybe it's a lie sometimes, but certainly, some directors see movies as kids and want to make films.*

LEE: I think it's bullshit. It's just something almost every director says. I have never believed it. I tell you this: It wasn't that way for me. "That's what makes movies seem like this magical thing" or somethin'. That's just Hollywood bullshit, people saying that shit because it makes makin' movies special, and the people who make movies special. The first time I went on a movie set, it didn't look like nothin' magical to me. [Laughs] It was the exact same thing I was doing on my student movies, only it was bigger and they were spendin' more money. That's what keeps black people out of movies— the idea that makin' movies is some special thing, some calling or something. That's what I'm about—demystifying movies. I want to do away with that bullshit.

PLAYBOY: *Do you remember the first Sidney Poitier film you saw?*
LEE: It had to be *Lilies of the Field*. I hated that movie. I must have been six, seven years old, but even at that age, I felt like putting a rock through the screen. Later with these nuns! You better get outta here before one of 'em says that you raped 'em! But we owe a lot to Sidney Poitier, because in order for us to get to where we are today, those films had to be made. And Sidney had to do what he had to do. He was the perfect Negro.

PLAYBOY: *What did you think when you saw* Guess Who's Coming to Dinner—*especially now that you're doing a movie about interracial romance?*
LEE: It was white liberal b.s. You have to look at it in the context of when this film came out. This film came out in the sixties, during the whole civil rights movement. At that time, it was a great advance for black people in the cinema.

PLAYBOY: *That aside, what were you thinking as you were sitting there watching it? Were you bored? Angry?*
LEE: I wasn't angry. It was just that the only way they would accept this guy was because he was a perfect human being: a doctor, from Harvard or whatever it was. Making a long-distance call and leaving the money out. That's the only way the audience would accept him, because he was such a fine, upstanding citizen.

Sidney had a great burden. He was carrying the whole weight of the hopes and aspirations of the African Americans on his shoulders. I think that had a lot to do with the roles that he chose. I think he felt he could not do a "negative" character. That's something I have tried to do, not get into that whole positive-negative image thing.

PLAYBOY: *You must hear that sometimes.*
LEE: *Sometimes?* All the time. Black folks tell me all the time that my image is not a positive portrayal of black people.

PLAYBOY: *Did that start with* She's Gotta Have It*?*
LEE: *She's Gotta Have It* has Nola Darling. She's a negative portrayal of black women and just reinforces what white people think about black women being loose, anyway. And *School Daze*—again, it was negative images of black people, showing fighting all the time. I was airing dirty laundry with our differences, which I feel are petty and superficial.

Do the Right Thing, I've got more negative images. None of the black people in *Do the Right Thing* have a job. It shows we're all lazy or whatever. It shows Sweet Dick Willie pissing against the wall, and that's a negative image of black people.

PLAYBOY: *But obviously, you understand the complaints.*
LEE: I understand what that means, positive black role models, because of the movies and on TV. But it's unrealistic to make every character I come up with a doctor or a lawyer or something that's just a flat character. Like, in *Jungle Fever*, I bring in drugs because it's time. One of the characters is a basehead, because it's appropriate.

PLAYBOY: *What about a movie such as* School Daze, *in which you're showing the environment at a black college? Did that get a negative reaction?*
LEE: Yeah. The schools themselves were saying it would be a negative portrayal of black higher education. That's one of the reasons why, three weeks into shooting, we got kicked off Morehouse's campus. Spelman refused to let us shoot there at all.

PLAYBOY: *In* School Daze, *you showed a part of the black culture—the black middle class—that's not usually shown. Didn't they want that to be shown?*
LEE: Yeah, but a lot of the administration and faculty in these schools, these are *old* schools. To me, they're very backward.

PLAYBOY: *Did many of your fellow students rebel at middle-class traditions at Morehouse?*

LEE: Yeah. We never got a really big thing, but there were students who were not going along with the program. They didn't want to be that "More-house Man."

PLAYBOY: *How many films did you shoot when you were in school?*

LEE: At Morehouse? I might have done one or two. It was there that I had my appetite whet. That's where I became interested in film and that's where I decided I wanted to become a filmmaker. That's why I went to NYU. At NYU, I started making films.

PLAYBOY: *It took you three years to get any work after you graduated from NYU. Did that bother you?*

LEE: I have no bitterness. The way it happens is the way it should happen. We had to struggle for three years, but I was a better filmmaker. I don't think I could have made *She's Gotta Have It* straight out of film school.

PLAYBOY: *What did it take for you to be ready to make it?*

LEE: More maturity. And to be hungrier.

PLAYBOY: *Where did the money come from?*

LEE: Everywhere. Even though the budget for the film was a hundred and seventy-five thousand dollars, we never had that money all at one time. When we began the shoot that July, we only had thirteen thousand in the bank.

Man, that movie was so hard to make. We were cashin' in bottles for change, because we had so little money. I remember, we were shootin' in Nola's loft in the middle of the summer—it musta been a hundred and four degrees up there. When it's so hot, people drink a lot and I remember sayin', "Don't throw away the bottles." That's the one of my movies I can't watch again, *She's Gotta Have It.*

PLAYBOY: *Was it so painful to make?*

LEE: Yeah, it was hard. We only shot for twelve days, but every night, after we finished the day's work, I had to think about tryin' to go out and raise money for the very next day. Things have changed so much now, you know.

We have money for contingencies, reshoots or whatever. Each picture is a little easier. But also, with *She's Gotta Have It,* the acting was bad.

PLAYBOY: *You don't like the performances?*
LEE: No, not at all. They just weren't very good. I didn't really know how to direct. I wasn't good with the actors, in telling 'em hat I wanted from 'em. I was just out of film school, and that was my only experience. In film school, you don't really get to work with actors, you never really have much contact with the actors, and so you're kinda intimidated by 'em. You don't deal with 'em much at all.

PLAYBOY: *What was your personal life like at the time?*
LEE: Everything was wrapped up in getting this film made. We invited the American independent distributors to come to the San Francisco Film Festival, because that's where the world premiere was going to happen. In the middle of the film, there was a blackout in San Francisco. Not the whole city but that particular neighborhood. So for half an hour—the theater was packed, too—people just sat there. I was sitting there in a chair in the dark, on the stage. There was a question-and-answer period while we waited for the lights to come back on. So I answered questions in the dark, and nobody left.

PLAYBOY: *Did you start laughing at that point? You'd been through so much.*
LEE: No. I said it was an act of God. What is happening? At the beginning of the movie, a blackout. But that's where the bidding war started. We sold it to Island Pictures for four hundred and seventy-five thousand dollars and went on to make eight million.

PLAYBOY: *How long before you made your next picture?*
LEE: That has been the biggest gap of all my films, between *She's Gotta Have It* and *School Daze.* I had to stay with that film a long time. Promote it, get it out there. It came out in '86, and *School Daze* didn't come out until '88. But since then, we've made a film every year.

PLAYBOY: School Daze *sounds like it was overly ambitious, going from a four-character piece essentially in one room to a big musical with lots of production numbers and lots of characters.*

LEE: I didn't think that was overly ambitious. I know that has been reflected in some people's reviews of the film. What I wanted to do in *School Daze* was, in that two-hour movie, was compress my four years of Morehouse.

PLAYBOY: *Were you surprised by the response that your next film,* Do the Right Thing, *got at the Cannes Film Festival?*
LEE: That was a big response. You don't know. Sometimes, what might play in the States might not go in Europe, and vice versa. But I knew they would like *She's Gotta Have It.* It had a very European feel to it, the way it was cut and shot and that kind of stuff.

PLAYBOY: *What about what German director Wim Wenders said?*
LEE: Oh, yeah, he said that *Do the Right Thing* was "not heroic"? Yeah, very. I was disappointed. I hold no grudges against Wim Wenders now. I never had anything against Steven Soderbergh [*who won the Golden Palm that year*], because it was not his doing. He made a very good film with *sex, lies, and videotape.* It was not his fault that he got the award. I know he's happy he got it, but I had no ill feelings toward Steven, and we're still friends today. [*sex, lies, and videotape*] was *very, very* heroic. Especially this James Spader character this guy jerking off all the time to the TV. Taping sexual confessions of women. *Very* heroic.

PLAYBOY: *You said that* Mo' Better Blues, *your fourth film, was consciously non-controversial. Not only are you dealing with interracial romance in* Jungle Fever, *but you're also dealing with drugs. Why add two controversial elements?*
LEE: I don't know. I might have given it the interracial thing, but how is drugs controversial?

PLAYBOY: *Because you purposefully avoided, you said, drugs as a subplot previously in* Do the Right Thing.
LEE: Yeah, but I don't think the word is controversy. I'm not gonna let any critic determine my agenda. I find it preposterous that critics would attack me for not having drugs in *Do the Right Thing,* as if drugs were the complete domain of black people. How could you do a film set in Bed-Stuy without any drugs? Easy. We black people aren't the only people on drugs. The reason you've got drugs on the so-called agenda is because you've got young white kids in middle-class America and white suburbia who are doing crack and

whatever. *Then* it becomes a national problem. As long as it was contained within the black ghettos, you would never see that problem being dealt with on the covers of *Time* or *Newsweek*. And if that is the case, which it is, then why have I never read of any white filmmakers being chastised for not having drugs in their films?

PLAYBOY: *Obviously, the critics thought the criticism was valid because of that particular neighborhood.*
LEE: Hey, there's as much drugs in Bed-Stuy as there is on Wall Street or the Upper East Side.

PLAYBOY: *How do you get hooked up with the Fruit of Islam? Some people criticize that group's militancy and its association with Louis Farrakhan.*
LEE: When we did location scouting for *Do the Right Thing*, we needed a block in Bed-Stuy that had two empty lots on the corner that faced each other. We had to build a pizzeria, and build a Korean fruit and vegetable stand. It turned out there were two or three crack houses on the block, or in the vicinity, so knowing the Fruit—they don't play that—we brought them in. They closed down the crack houses and they stayed on for security for the rest of the film.

PLAYBOY: *It seems ironic that the movie doesn't deal with drugs and you had to run the crack dealers off the block.*
LEE: I don't find it ironic. Drugs is a part of our society, but I felt they should not be a part of this story. This film was really about twenty-four hours in the life of this block on the hottest day of the summer. It was really about race relations. I didn't want to put drugs in this.

PLAYBOY: *You seem very sure of yourself, and yet you've consistently portrayed the characters you play in your films as powerless and ineffectual.*
LEE: Yeah, well, I don't see the need to make myself the hero in my movies. What's the point in that?

PLAYBOY: *Why do you keep playing the same kind of character?*
LEE: I'm not that impressed with myself as an actor. I don't think much of myself that way. I don't have a whole lot of range as far as acting. Mars

Blackmon, that was all right. I didn't expect people to like him, the way they did.

PLAYBOY: *What makes you continue to act in your pictures?*
LEE: It really has to do with box office, with having somewhat of a little appeal with the audience. People will be more apt to come to one of my films if I'm in it.

PLAYBOY: *Will you be in* Malcolm X?
LEE: Probably. [*Laughs*] I still need to be in my films.

PLAYBOY: Mo' Better Blues *was criticized for its portrayal of Jews. There's even a story about your father having gone down to apologize to the owner of a Village jazz club because of your portrayal of Jews in that film.*
LEE: Huh? I can't respond to that, because I never heard it before. Look, Siskel and Ebert—I shouldn't say this, 'cause they're fans of mine. Soon as *Mo' Better Blues* comes out, they [start talking about] stereotypes. Then came [*New York Times* critic] Caryn James with her stupid-ass article. Nobody was supposed to take those guys as representin' all Jews. Besides, where was everybody when that what's-his-name movie with Steven Seagal came out?

PLAYBOY: Marked for Death?
LEE: What about that racist piece of shit? That's a number-one hit for a couple of weeks, and where was everybody when that came out? They had nothin' to say about it.

PLAYBOY: *What did you think when you saw it?*
LEE: I didn't see it.

PLAYBOY: *One of the best things in your films tends to be their improvisational quality, the way you handle the interplay between people.*
LEE: Yeah, it helps to have actors who know how to improvise. Not everybody's good at it.

PLAYBOY: *Like who?*
LEE: I don't wanna say.

PLAYBOY: *Wait a second. You're worried about hurting somebody's feelings? When the Oscars came around in 1990, you didn't seem so worried about hurting people's feelings.*

LEE: That didn't have nothin' to do with hurting people's feelings. It was that Fred Schelp——Sheep—— What's that guy's name? That Australian guy?

PLAYBOY: *Fred Schepisi? What about him?*
LEE: You know, the one who did *Driving Miss Daisy*?

PLAYBOY: *You mean Bruce Beresford.*
LEE: Him. Yeah, him. Bruce Beresford. When he was complaining about not getting a nomination for Best Director, nobody made anything of that. Or when [Richard] Zanuck, he started complaining, you know, about *Driving Miss Daisy,* how could it get a Best Picture nomination and not get a Best Director nomination? It was as soon as *I* started sayin' we got robbed on *Do the Right Thing,* suddenly, I'm the one. I'm the problem.

PLAYBOY: *People think you're an artist, and they have higher expectations of you. When you complain about being shut out, people are let down by it.*
LEE: I don't buy that. I don't believe that. I was complaining about the Oscars because we should've got a Best Picture nomination.

PLAYBOY: *A lot of movies that stand the test of time never get nominated for Oscars or they never win Oscars.*
LEE: Oscars, they can mean money. You know, you get a Best Picture nomination and the studios, they can promote a picture, advertise. They can get more people to come out and see it. People were afraid to come see *Do the Right Thing* as it was, afraid there would be riots and shit.

PLAYBOY: *Some people claim that you use racism as a tool to strike out at others, such as in your attack of* New York Times *critic Janet Maslin's review of* School Daze, *when you said, "I bet she can't even dance. Does she have rhythm?"*
LEE: She didn't get the point of *School Daze,* and the way she dissed it, talking about "my little musical." Race is an issue, and I don't always use it. You'd think I don't like critics. I don't like the *New York Times.* Well, I read Vincent Canby.

PLAYBOY: *You've always had a dicey relationship with the press. Stanley Crouch, in his essay "Do the Race Thing," discusses how you tried to have it both ways with* Do the Right Thing," *discusses how you tried to have it both ways with* Do the Right Thing, *by quoting Martin Luther King and* Malcolm X.

LEE: That ignorant motherfucker. He has no idea what he's talking about. Shit, what about all those motherfuckers like Joe Klein at *New York* sayin' *Do the Right Thing* would cause a riot, because it was released during the summer? Or David Denby callin' it irresponsible? That's irresponsible. And it's lazy. When the riots didn't happen, when Dinkins got elected, neither one of them, none of the people who said that shit, said they were wrong in print or apologized.

PLAYBOY: *What about the Nike Air Jordan controversy?* New York Post *columnist Phil Mushnick wrote that you and Michael Jordan glamourize expensive shoes and sometimes kids are killed in robberies over them.*

LEE: Shit. What about it? It's my fault, it's Michael Jordan's fault, that kids are buying those shoes? That's just the trigger. There's more to it than that. Something is wrong where these young black kids have to put so much weight, where their whole life is tied up—their life is so hopeless—that their life is defined by a pair of sneakers. Or a sheepskin coat. The problem is not the coat or the sneakers. I mean, we tried to explore that with *Do the Right Thing* with the radio. These young black kids who are lost. Radio Raheem [*the character who's killed by the police*]—his life was that radio. That really defined his existence. I mean, without that radio, he's invisible; people don't notice him. But with that radio blasting Public Enemy and "Fight the Power," you had to deal with him. It made people notice him. It gave him self-worth. And when Sal killed his mother or his father, or himself. That's why he tried to choke the shit out of Sal.

PLAYBOY: *What about that* Sports Illustrated *article where Jordan was almost reduced to tears? He's publicity remorseful, disturbed by what his endorsement may have caused.*

LEE: What the fuck? You think I'm happy black men are dying over shoes? Hell, no! Hell, no! I'm upset about it, too. Is every black man who wears those shoes a drug dealer? Hell, no! You know how that is. Look at you. You're wearing Pumps. Are you a drug dealer? Hell, no! They're oversimplifying the issue.

PLAYBOY: *OK, let's ask an easy question: What is Michael Jordan really like?*

LEE: Mike's a down brother. Mike just had a lot of confidence in me. He was a young brother. He liked *She's Gotta Have It*. He felt like I did, that it was important that we hook up. Mike pulled me to the side and said, "Look, there's been some grumbling where Nike is trying to ease you out. But as long as I'm around, you're around." I said, "I hear you, Mike. Thank you for getting me back." That's why I did those commercials. I thought it was important that me and Mike do something together. Young black people in different fields, hooking up.

PLAYBOY: *Did your parents encourage you to go into the arts?*
LEE: Not really. Whatever you wanted to do was fine with them. They encouraged us, but they never pushed me in any direction. I will say that we had great exposure to the arts at a young age. We had to. My mother taught art; she liked the theater and liked music. My father is a jazz musician—he played with folk singers, too, like Theodore Bikel and Josh White—so music was always being played in the house. I remember my mother dragging me to *The King and I* with Yul Brynner when I was little. I started crying; I was scared to death. She had to take me home.

PLAYBOY: *What was the first thing you remember sitting through and really enjoying as a kid, even if it didn't make you want to be a filmmaker?*
LEE: When I was real little, I saw *Hatari*. Remember that? John Wayne in a safari film, with the rhinoceros. And *Bye Bye Birdie*. My mother would take me to see James Bond films, *Goldfinger* and *Dr. No*. I remember her taking me to see *A Hard Day's Night*.

PLAYBOY: *Did you like that?*
LEE: Yeah. I liked the Beatles when I was little. My father would turn down the radio when he came in the house.

PLAYBOY: *He didn't like the Beatles?*
LEE: He didn't like *no* music besides jazz. [*Shouts*] "Turn that bad music off!"

PLAYBOY: *Did you always know you were going to college?*
LEE: Yeah. I mean, what else was I gonna do? My father and my grand-father, they went to college, so it was there for me, too. What else would I

do, work at a McDonald's? Go work for somebody else? I never thought about rebellin', not goin' to college. It was what I was gonna do.

PLAYBOY: *You sound like you were a practical kid, not a troublemaker.*
LEE: I grew up as the oldest, so I had to be practical. The oldest child has to take care of the younger kids. They're always the most practical.

PLAYBOY: *What was your relationship with the kids in the neighborhood?*
LEE: I was always a leader. I was the one organizing stuff.

PLAYBOY: *Did you like school as a kid?*
LEE: Not really.

PLAYBOY: *Did you do well?*
LEE: Just good enough to get by.

PLAYBOY: *Which must not have made your mother too happy, since she was a teacher.*
LEE: She was always on me. I'd get an eighty and I'd be happy, but she'd be like, "Well, you shouldn't be content with an eighty. Them Jewish kids are getting ninety-five." [*Laughs*] But she was right.

PLAYBOY: *Do you wonder what it would be like if you were growing up now?*
LEE: It would be frightening, with the violence and the access to weapons and guns, and the drugs. Before, we used to be terrified if we even saw somebody taking a puff on a joint. But now, if you're a parent, you pray to God that's all your child is doing is smoking marijuana.

PLAYBOY: *Do you think there's a lack of emphasis on education now?*
LEE: Right. Half of the young black males here in New York City don't even finish high school. But this is not to say that I'm blaming them. I'm not trying to point a finger at the victim. I think that the educational system has failed. At the same time, I've never been one just to blame white people for everything, for all of our ills. We have to take some responsibility. If stuff's going to be corrected, it's up to us. It's up to the parents. What are these kids doing outside late at night? Eight years old and hanging out later than I am.

Running in the streets at two, three, four in the morning. Where are their parents?

When we were growing up, people looked out after each other. Other parents could tell you something. If somebody else's mother saw you doing something wrong, that mother would treat you as if you were her child.

PLAYBOY: *But you also got straightened out in school, right?*
LEE: Yeah. I think that discipline, that's what's really lacking. I'm not saying let's go back to the Dark Ages when they were hitting kids in school with rulers, but discipline is really lacking.

PLAYBOY: *Does it make you leery of having a family?*
LEE: No, not really at all. When I do have a family, I don't want to send them to private school, because I feel that's too sheltered.

PLAYBOY: *Even given the problems with the educational system?*
LEE: I will be able to get my kids in the best public schools here. I mean, there are good public schools here, but there aren't that many. I went to public school, my brother Chris went to public school. But David, Joie and Cinqué went to private school. I always could tell a difference in them because they went to private school. Their negritude got honed or harnessed going into these predominantly white private schools. That's where my mother was teaching.

PLAYBOY: *Do you talk about this?*
LEE: They know it. Most of their friends were white. Not that I have anything against that, it's just that there is definitely an argument for being around your own people.

PLAYBOY: *A lot of the parents who send their kids to private schools today went to public schools themselves. They fear their children won't get a good education or be safe at a public school.*
LEE: They're justified in thinking that. People are getting shot and stabbed in school. That's not supposed to happen in a school.

PLAYBOY: *Did your mother try to keep you away from the bad kids in the neighborhood?*

LEE: No. There were never any gangs. I don't remember ever seeing any. There were people who would steal your lunch money, but that wasn't no gang thing. I mean, now they'll shoot you. When I was growing up, they might take a quarter from you. You give it up.

PLAYBOY: *Or fight.*
LEE: Yeah, but it's not like "Give us your leather coat or I'll shoot you."

PLAYBOY: *Since the educational system is so bad, why should kids be unemployed college grads when they could sell crack and make a lot of money?*
LEE: That is something that is going to have to be dealt with, the economics. Forget about the moral issue, even though it should play into it. It's not going to weigh when these kids are faced with the fact of making minimum wage at McDonald's or making three and four thousand a week selling crack. Not everybody, but a lot of them are going to sell that crack and make that money. You're not thinking about how you might end up dead, eventually, or end up in jail. That's not the point. Now you can buy that BMW or whatever. Gold chains and gold teeth. Kangols [*hats*] and Kazals [*glasses*].

PLAYBOY: *Where do you think that materialism comes from?*
LEE: Well, when people don't have anything, they have to try and show they do have something. And you show that by what you wear or the car you drive. "I'm not like all the rest of these poor niggers. I got something."

PLAYBOY: *Don't some black kids view education itself as white?*
LEE: There's something very sick where if you speak well and you speak articulately, that's looked at as being negative and speaking white. I remember when I was growing up, people used to tell me, "You sound white." I've been reading of various cases where kids flunk on purpose so they'll be considered "down" with the home boys and stuff. That's crazy when intelligence is thought of as being white and all the other stuff is being black and being down. I think that one has to be able to navigate both worlds. You ought to be able to speak with your brothers on the street but at the same time be able to go to a job interview, fill out the application and speak proper English. You've got to have both. I don't think it makes you any less black by being articulate.

PLAYBOY: *Where do you think that attitude comes from?*

LEE: I think all this stuff you could really trace to our hatred of ourselves. Everything we do, eventually, if you keep going back far enough, you'll see that we've been taught to hate ourselves. And until we stop that, all this other shit we're doing is just going to continue to happen.

PLAYBOY: *Comedian Franklyn Ajaye said that one of the things he didn't like about* In Living Color *when he was a writer there was that everybody talked like they were down. He didn't see any kind of reflection of articulate black life in the show, and that bothered him.*

LEE: Me and Keenen [Ivory Wayans] talked about it. He was on the cover of *New York* magazine, and in the article, they said they had thirteen writers and only three or four were black. The rest were all these Jewish kids that went to Harvard. So I just asked Keenen what's up. He explained to me all he's done for black people, as far as the show is concerned. I'm not going to dispute that. I'm not saying it's because they did the skit on me, but if you have some white kid from Harvard joking about Malcolm X-Lax—I don't think that shit is funny. I don't think they'd allow a black person to make a joke about Golda Meir.

PLAYBOY: *Do you think being educated means that you're not black?*

LEE: In a perverse kind of way. Everything has been kind of turned upside down. I think we've just got a lot of things turned around.

PLAYBOY: *When did that happen?*

LEE: A lot of things happened after the civil rights movement, where we thought we were making strides and progress. Somewhere from the end of the sixties up to now, we got off the path. Or we were led off the path. I think that we really haven't advanced a lot. For me, the biggest problem is that people get tricked. Because of the visibility of a couple of African Americans who are able to split through, mostly in entertainment or the sports industry, it gives off the perception that black people have made great strides and that everything is all right. But the reality is, we're not all right. You look at all the black people who are dying of cancer, hypertension, AIDS. The permanently unemployed. The black underclass now is larger than it's ever been. But people are tricked into not really taking that stuff into account. I'm not blaming these people. They're tricked because they see Oprah Winfrey, they see Bill Cosby, they see Spike Lee, they see Eddie Murphy, they see Michael Jordan, they see Bo Jackson, Paula Abdul, M. C. Hammer, Janet Jackson, Arsenio Hall. But we're the exception, not the rule. We were able to slide through that microscopic crack that was open for a second.

PLAYBOY: *Is it because you think there are so many visible black people that—*
LEE: Wait. If you look at the context of all the shows that are on TV and all the movies that are made, and then look at the percent, it's not that many. It's just the *perception* that there's a lot of us.

PLAYBOY: *Based on that perception and the fact that you can say there may be more successful, visible black people than ever, the perception is that—*
LEE: We've arrived. And that's not the case at all. I mean, there's not one person outside of Eddie Murphy, really, not *one* African American in Hollywood who can green-light a picture. Who can say, "I want this picture made," and that's it.

PLAYBOY: *You can't get that done?*
LEE: No matter what? For me to get a film made, I have to present a script, and they either do it or they don't. But every studio has people who are the guardians of the gate. They're the ones who say this picture gets made and this picture doesn't. and there are no black people in that position in Hollywood. I mean, we're getting ready to have a big fight with the Teamsters here in New York because they don't have *no* black people. We used the Teamsters on *Do the Right Thing, Mo' Better* and *Jungle Fever,* and the amount that we paid for the Teamsters for all three films is like three quarters of a million dollars. And there are only three or four black Teamsters in the whole union, here in New York. I refuse to give money to organizations that are openly into hiring practices that may exclude blacks. So we're about to go toe to toe with them on *Malcolm X.*

PLAYBOY: *You're not going to use them?*
LEE: If they don't get some more black people in it, they can kiss our ass. We told them that. They even refused to sit down with us and meet. They said, "We will let no one dictate to us who to hire."

PLAYBOY: *So they deny any discriminatory practices?*

LEE: The Teamsters, man, it's predominantly Irish. This particular branch I'm talking about here in New York. The Teamsters who work on movies.

PLAYBOY: *How long have you been talking to them about this? Since you started to use them?*
LEE: Yeah. They've been appeasing us. They might give us one or two, but we told them we wanted a black Teamster captain and we wanted five black people to get their books. They trick you sometimes. Let me now use the word trick, but they might put black people on your film, but they don't have their books. Meaning they're not full-fledged members of the union and don't receive the full benefits of the union. If you're a Teamster here in New York, they have the best benefits of any union in the country. Any of their children, they can go to college—free. Whatever college you choose. The union will pay for it.

PLAYBOY: *And there are just a handful of black people in the union?*
LEE: A handful. I mean, they just admitted one who got his book recently. But the last time one got admitted before that was *1962*. There's too much money being made. I refuse to give money to an organization like that that's just so overtly racist in their hiring practices.

PLAYBOY: *There is obviously now a big trend toward trying to increase the African-American inclusion in the movie mainstream. We've heard that people are already expecting a backlash. Remember when* The Wiz *and* Ragtime *failed—*
LEE: That was it. They said, "Black people don't support these films. Let's stop making black films." The blame was never put on Sidney Lumet, or the score, or the casting of Diana Ross. That is not to disrespect any of them, but the blame was put solely on "black people who failed to support this film." Whereas, if a white film doesn't work, it would be the director or whoever.

PLAYBOY: *In some ways, there seems to be a renaissance of black participation in popular culture. There's you and Robert Townsend,* In Living Color *and the enormous effect of rap.*
LEE: Yeah, that's true. They've finally realized black people contribute, and black audiences are a power in the entertainment market. Studios know there's just too much money to be made now from black audiences. And that people wanna see us, too.

PLAYBOY: *Do you worry that history will repeat itself?*

LEE: I think that this is a very crucial time. Every film studio, if you're black and even look like you're a director, they're signing you. And it's very important that all these people who are getting opportunities really be serious. I'm not trying to speak like I'm the grandfather of black cinema. But I think there are a lot of people who are getting deals now—and more power to them—but I don't know if they're going to last. They just think that you can just walk off the street and direct a movie—and it's not true. This ain't just no bullshit; "Well, I'm just directing a film. I don't need to know nothing about film grammar or film history," or any other thing that one needs to know to become a film director.

PLAYBOY: *You talked about being attacked for the Nola Darling character in* She's Gotta Have It. *Do you think you're becoming more enlightened about your portrayals of women?*

LEE: This is something I've known all along. Every filmmaker has a weakness, just like athletes.

PLAYBOY: *But we're not talking about every filmmaker.*

LEE: No, I'm saying every filmmaker, every athlete has weaknesses. If you come into the league hitting fifty percent at the free-throw line, you've got to do something about your foul shooting if you want to be a complete ballplayer. My female characters were something I needed to work on. It was lacking. It's something I've tried to concentrate on.

PLAYBOY: *We always thought one of the interesting things about Nola was that she lived her life the way she wanted to.*

LEE: Yeah, but that wasn't the only film where they talked about the female characters. *School Daze*—they weren't as multidimensional as the male characters. There weren't enough of them in *Do the Right Thing*. And in *Mo' Better,* all they wanted was the man; they didn't have a life of their own—which I don't agree with for that particular film.

PLAYBOY: *How does this affect your personal relationships? Do women have preconceived notions about you?*

LEE: I don't really think you can break that question down to a sex thing, as far as male-female. I think that's just in general. Any time you're out in the public eye, people, when they meet you in person, they expect you to live up to that expectation of what that person is. A lot of people expect me to be more animated, and they're kind of disappointed. "I didn't know you were quiet." So that really has nothing to do with male-female.

PLAYBOY: *What about your relationships with white people? It's clear that a lot of white people are afraid of you.*
LEE: I guess you fear stuff you don't understand. I don't think any white folks have anything to fear from me.

PLAYBOY: *Still, almost all of the movie industry is white. All they ever see are other white people.*
LEE: With a small smattering of Jewish people. [*Laughs*] I don't know why some Jewish people get upset when you say that there are a lot of Jewish people in the movie industry. That's the truth. That's like saying there are blacks in the NBA. That's not making a judgment, that's just a fact.

PLAYBOY: *Do they really get sensitive when you say there are lots of Jews in the industry?*
LEE: Yeah. The *New York Times*, there was this whole black-Jewish Hollywood thing. It was sparked by the convention the NAACP had in Hollywood where they said that Hollywood is racist and so on, and that it was run predominantly by Jewish people.

PLAYBOY: *You must get a lot of calls whenever something like that happens.*
LEE: Hooo, from around the world! The phone rings off the hook at our office. I think that this is what happens when the media appoints their so-called spokesperson for black people. This is something I have never wanted to achieve. It's not something I've chased after. And, for the most part, I don't say anything. But there are instances where stuff has to be spoken on. But, for the most part, I only answer about five percent of their questions.

PLAYBOY: *What do you think about the future for African Americans?*
LEE: If you look at the eight years of Reagan and maybe another eight years of Bush, and the way they're dismantling affirmative action and all that stuff we fought for and died for, or the Supreme Court that's being appointed—Bush tried to pull this thing where it's discriminatory for schools to have

scholarships for black students, and then they get this Uncle Tom handkerchief-head Negro to announce it as assistant secretary [of the Education Department]. Nobody even heard of this motherfucker, but the moment that this program has to be implemented and an announcement has to be made, they pull this Negro off the shelf. How are we supposed to go to school? It's a shame that we've still got Uncle Toms like this around. That guy should be beat with a Louisville Slugger in an alley. He got used. That's the only reason why they hired him, for something specific like that that was going to affect black people. So by the Bush Administration having this black person make this announcement, it can't be racist—we got a black person saying it.

PLAYBOY: *Do you wonder if there has been some complacency since the civil rights movement?*
LEE: I think America just really arrived at the point where it said, Look— and I think the mandate was handed down by Reagan—where it said, Look, we are tired of you niggers. You've got about as much as you're gonna get from us, and that's it. Period.

PLAYBOY: *Some black people say they don't want special consideration.*
LEE: Special? I don't think it's special, the fact that we were brought here as slaves and we've been robbed of our heritage and everything else. I mean, I don't consider that special.

PLAYBOY: *So we take it you don't have much truck with black conservatives.*
LEE: They'll sell you out in a minute. They sold us out. I mean, they're trying to make a big deal out of this what's-his-name, Colin Powell.

PLAYBOY: *You don't think that he's a formidable figure? He's the Chairman of the Joint Chiefs of Staff—that shows black progress, doesn't it?*
LEE: So what? So we've got a black general that's going to be head of the Army that kills black people in Panama? Kills black people in Nicaragua? People of color in the Middle East? How come every war now is against people of color in Third World countries? They talk about fighting for democracy: Is South Africa democratic? I know it would be too far-fetched to ask Bush to send troops into South Africa to fight for black people, so let's not talk about that. But how about sanctions? He's trying to lift the motherfucking sanctions! Saddam does not compare to what de Klerk and all them

crooks down there in South Africa are doing and have been doing. But they're white, so it's not perceived as that.

PLAYBOY: *So you think it's another instance of racism?*
LEE: Yes. I'm not going to say that Saddam might not be a maniac, but if you just study the way the press portrays Noriega, Ortega, Hussein, the ayatollah and the way they portray people like Botha, de Klerk, Cecil Rhodes—I mean, it's the difference between night and day. I have to give in, they have a point on Hitler and Mussolini, but since World War Two, there is a difference in the way they portray dictators.

PLAYBOY: *But look at the way the Soviets were portrayed.*
LEE: That was really during the Cold War. They didn't send no troops into Lithuania and shit. They bogarted that country the same way that Hussein bogarted Kuwait. For me, the United States is not on the moral ground to judge anybody, because it's the most hypocritical country in the world. So, to me, they really can't say shit about nobody, because they got a lot of shit with themselves.

PLAYBOY: *Do you think that after the civil rights movement lost its figureheads—Martin Luther King and Malcolm X—it lost momentum?*
LEE: It did, but that's a mistake of putting emphasis on personality and people instead of the movement. As long as we continue to do that and make cults around our leaders, all they have to do to stop it any time we're making ground is just kill us off, kill off that leader.

PLAYBOY: *What have you learned in your research for the Malcolm X movie?*
LEE: That Malcolm was a very complex person. There were three or four different Malcolms. He was constantly evolving, his outlook and his ideology, and always trying to seek the truth. If he found it, he was not scared of being called a hypocrite. If he found a higher truth, he would say, "I was wrong. All that stuff I said before is wrong, and this is what I believe." That's something that very few people do.

PLAYBOY: *Have your feelings about him changed since you started doing the research?*

LEE: I think that I've really grown to love Malcolm more. What he stood for and what he died for.

PLAYBOY: *What did you think when you first read his autobiography?*
LEE: It was just a revelation. I have deep respect for Dr. King, but I've always been drawn more to Malcolm. I just cannot get with Dr. King's complete nonviolence philosophy.

PLAYBOY: *Malcolm was moving in that direction himself, wasn't he?*
LEE: No. Malcolm never moved away from defending oneself, the right to protect the self. He never moved away from that. Malcolm would never say, "Go to a march, get hit upside the head, and hopefully, after you get enough knocked upside the head, the white man will see how evil he is and will stop." He never said that, and he was never moving toward that. He's always been about the right to protect oneself. Malcolm never advocated violence. He said one should reserve the right to protect oneself.

PLAYBOY: *Doesn't it seem interesting that there has finally come a time when a major studio will give you——*
LEE: Yeah, twenty years and more since he's been dead and buried. He no longer seems such a threat. This film would not have been done in 1966, the year after he got assassinated. No way.

PLAYBOY: *But look at what you get a chance to do now.*
LEE: It's a great opportunity.

PLAYBOY: *Are you up for it?*
LEE: Yeah. Everything I've done has really prepared me for this film. It's led me in this direction. I've got no intention of dropping the ball.

Our Film Is Only a Starting Point: An Interview with Spike Lee

GARY CROWDUS AND DAN GEORGAKAS / 1993

IN ADDITION TO OUR Critical Symposium on *Malcolm X*, *Cineaste* felt it was important to talk to Spike Lee and incorporate his comments in our overall perspective on the film. In the following interview, Lee explains his primary desire to introduce Malcolm X to young viewers and his awareness that the time limits of even a nearly three and a half hour movie prevented him from producing anything more than a "primer" on one of America's most charismatic black leaders. His additional comments about the difficulties of attempting to produce an epic political film within the budgetary constraints imposed by Warner Bros. and in light of the many other pragmatic and political considerations involved are important aspects in arriving at a fully informed appraisal of the artistic achievement and political significance of *Malcolm X*. Spike Lee spoke to *Cineaste* Editors Gary Crowdus and Dan Georgakas in mid-December 1992, just three weeks after the film's nationwide premiere.

CINEASTE: *What sort of research did you do for the film? And what was the role of your Historical Consultant, Paul Lee?*
SPIKE LEE: I read everything that I could, including a new book by Zak Kondo about the assassination that was very important in helping us recreate the assassination in the film. Paul Lee was a great help because he's someone who's really devoted his life to Malcolm X. Paul, who lives in Detroit, was in the Nation, I think, when he was twelve years old. As far as

Published in *Cineaste* 19, no. 4 (1993): 20–24. Reprinted by permission of *Cineaste*.

scholars go, I don't think there's anyone who knows more about Malcolm X than Paul Lee.

I also talked to a lot of people, including Benjamin Karim, who's Benjamin 2X in the film, Malcolm's brothers—Wilfred, Omar Azziz, and Robert—his sister Yvonne, Malcolm's widow, Betty Shabazz, and Malcolm Jarvis, who's Shorty in the film. I also went to Chicago and talked to Minister Farrakhan. That's where a lot of the good stuff came from, going around the country and talking to people who knew Malcolm. Not just his relatives, but people who were in the Nation with him, in the OAAU, and so on.

CINEASTE: *Have you had any dealings with the Socialist Workers Party? They got to Malcolm early, gave him podiums numerous times, and published a lot of his speeches.*
LEE: Pathfinder Press? No, I just used their books, because they're fine documents.

CINEASTE: *Of the various screenplay adaptations of* The Autobiography *that had been written, why did you feel that the James Baldwin/Arnold Perl script was the best?*
LEE: I read 'em all—the David Mamet script, Charles Fuller's two drafts, Calder Willingham's script, and David Bradley's script—but the Baldwin/Perl script was the best. James Baldwin was a great writer and he really captured Harlem and that whole period. He was a friend of Malcolm's.

CINEASTE: *What did your rewrite of the Baldwin/Perl script involve?*
LEE: What was lacking, I felt, in the Baldwin/Perl script was the third act—what happens during the split between Malcolm and the Nation, between Malcolm and Elijah Muhammad. A lot of stuff about the assassination had not come out then. William Kunstler was a great help on that. He represented Talmadge Hayer and gave me a copy of Hayer's affidavit where he 'fessed up to the assassination. I mean, if you look at the credits of the movie, we name the five assassins, we *name* those guys—Ben Thomas, William X, Wilbur Kinley, Leon Davis, and Thomas Hayer.

I also wanted to tie the film into today. I did not want this film just to be a historical document. That's why we open the film with the Rodney King footage and the American flag burning, and end the film with the classrooms, from Harlem to Soweto.

The speeches in the Baldwin/Perl script were not really Malcolm's best speeches, they did not really show the growth politically of Malcolm's mind, so we threw them all out. With the help of Paul Lee, who gave us copies of every single speech that Malcolm gave, Denzel and I chose and inserted speeches. Baldwin had stuff out of order. He had Malcolm giving speeches at the beginning of the movie that didn't really come until 1963 or 1964, so we had to get rid of those.

CINEASTE: *So Denzel was involved somewhat in working on the script?*

LEE: Yeah, Denzel was very involved. He has a good story sense. We both knew a lot was riding on this film. We did not want to live in another country the rest of our lives. We could not go anywhere without being reminded by black folks, "Don't fuck up Malcolm, don't mess this one up." We were under tremendous pressure on this film. We can laugh about it now, but it was no joke while we were doing the film.

CINEASTE: *Given the difficulty of portraying about forty years of a man's life in any film, even one nearly three and a half hours long, are there some aspects of Malcolm's life you felt you weren't able to do justice to?*

LEE: No, this is it, this is the movie I wanted to make. Our first cut was about four hours and ten minutes, I forget exactly, and we had more speeches and stuff, but this is the best shape the film can be. Of course, people say, "Why did you leave this out and why did you leave that out?," but you cannot put a man's whole life in a film.

People have told us, "The most important year in Malcolm's life was his final year," and "Why didn't you show his whole pan-Africanism thing?" But it's limited. We've never said that anyone who sees this film doesn't need to know anything else about Malcolm X. I mean, the man had four or five different lives, so the film is really only a primer, a starting point.

CINEASTE: *But don't you think that showing him meeting heads of state in Africa would have added to his dimension at the end, especially for people who don't know?*

LEE: But people don't know who Kwame Nkrumah is anyway. Besides, we didn't have the money. I mean, we just barely got to Egypt. We shot in the U.S. from September 16, 1991 up to the Christmas holiday and after the holidays we did what we had to do in Cairo and then we went to South Africa.

But I don't think we would have gained anything by showing him meeting with Nkrumah or others. Besides, at that point in the film, we're trying to build some momentum.

CINEASTE: *Cassius Clay/Muhammad Ali is sort of dropped from the film, too.*
LEE: What, and get someone to impersonate him? I think it was important to have Muhammad Ali in the movie, but we show him in a newsreel clip in the montage at the end.

CINEASTE: *You don't think it dissipates some of the anti-Vietnam War feeling that was in the Nation?*
LEE: They weren't really anti-Vietnam. Malcolm was, but Elijah Muhammad never said anything about the Vietnam War, he had already been kicked out of the Nation.

CINEASTE: *Do you feel a film of this financial scale has built-in 'crossover' requirements in terms of its audience?*
LEE: We felt so. We felt that everybody would want to see the film and we've received a large white audience to date. This is my first PG film—the previous five have all been rated R—because we wanted to get a young audience. We feel this is an important piece of American history and people, especially young kids, need to see this.

CINEASTE: *Is that why the few sex scenes in the film are considerably milder than those in the published screenplay?*
LEE: Yes, because we made the decision for a PG-13 rating. We did not want to give teachers, schools, or parents an excuse why they could not take their children to see this film. I think when you weigh it, it's much more important for young kids to be exposed to Malcolm X than to see that other shit. We're preparing a classroom study guide on the film that'll be out in January.

It's amazing, I've seen this film with ten, eleven, and twelve-year-olds and they're just riveted in their seats. You know the attention span of young people at that age—they're usually throwing popcorn at the screen—but there's not a sound, they're riveted for three hours and twenty-one minutes. A whole generation of young people are being introduced to Malcolm X and people who've heard of him or had limited views of him are having their views expanded. Above all, we hope that black folks will come out of the theater inspired and moved to do something positive.

CINEASTE: *What sort of message would you like white viewers to come away with from the film?*

LEE: I think that, as with any film I've done, people will take away their own message. For a large part of the white audience, however, I think we're helping to redefine Malcolm X because for the most part their view of Malcolm came from the white media which portrayed him as anti-white, anti-Semitic, and pro-violence. It's funny, when we had the national press junket for this film, many of the white journalists said they felt they'd been robbed, that they'd been cheated, because they'd never been taught about Malcolm X in school or they had only been told that he was anti-white and violent. A great miseducation has gone on about this man.

CINEASTE: *In that regard, we heard that Warner Bros., presumably concerned about defusing any controversy about potential violence at screenings, held advance showings of the film for police departments around the country.*

LEE: That was Barry Reardon's decision. I did not agree with that. I thought it was inappropriate. I mean, if they do that to us, they should do it to *Terminator*. How many cops got killed in those films? Actually, it was the exhibitors. Before the film came out, exhibitors were calling Warner Bros., they were scared shitless, they were requesting extra police protection. One theater in Chicago even installed metal detectors!

CINEASTE: *What was the response at the police screenings?*

LEE: Oh, the cops loved it. In Los Angeles, they showed it to Willie Williams, the new Police Commissioner there. It was the exhibitors and also the press who were waiting for that violence so they could destroy the movie. *Do the Right Thing* was really hurt at the box office when the press—people like David Denby, Joe Klein, and Jack Mathews—predicted that the film was going to create riots. In Westwood, in Los Angeles, for example, nine police were at the theater on the opening weekend, some mounted on horseback.

What's interesting for me now in reading a lot of the reviews of *Malcolm X* is how so many critics had predetermined that the film was going to be inflammatory.

CINEASTE: *To a great extent that's because of their unfamiliarity with Malcolm X other than what they've read in the mainstream press.*

LEE: And with me, with the combination of Malcolm X and Spike Lee. They were expecting a film that for three hours and twenty-one minutes would be saying, "C'mon, black folks, let's get some guns and kill every single white person in America," but in the end the critics were saying, "This film is *mild.*"

CINEASTE: *In the published screenplay, there are two sort of 'dramatic book- ends' scenes. In the first scene, Malcolm brushes off the well-intentioned young white woman outside Harvard who asks how she might be of help in his struggle. The second scene, which occurs later at the Hilton Hotel in New York, involves the same type of encounter but this time Malcolm has a completely different response. The two scenes emphasizes Malcolm's evolution on this question, but only the first scene appears in the film. Why?*

LEE: We shot that other scene, but the acting just didn't work. Anyone who's read the book knows that Malcolm's response to that young woman was one of his biggest regrets. I wanted to give Malcolm a chance to make up for it, so I wrote the scene where he could answer that same question again, but it just didn't work.

CINEASTE: *Are you concerned with how the dramatic weight has now shifted to that first scene? At the two screenings we've attended, that scene always gets a big laugh.*

LEE: Who's laughing? Black viewers or white viewers?

CINEASTE: *They've been mixed audiences.*

LEE: White people don't laugh at that because for the white audience that young white woman is *them*. We shot the second scene, but it just didn't work, so what were we supposed to do? In any case, I think we see Malcolm change when he comes back from Mecca.

CINEASTE: *In terms of* The Autobiography's *portrayal of Malcolm's youthful criminal career and the extent of his drug abuse, Malcolm was much more critical of himself in the book than the film is. Do you think that aspect of the book is exaggerated?*

LEE: I've talked to Malcolm's brothers and they said that he was not that big of a criminal. He was a street hustler and not even a pimp, just a steerer. I think he was a wannabe, a wannabe bigtime gangster, but he wasn't. The description in the book was not so much to build himself up but to lower the depths from which he rises. That's OK, but I don't buy this Bruce Perry bullshit that Malcolm was a homosexual, that he used to crossdress, or that Malcolm's father burned down their house in Omaha or that Malcolm fire-bombed his own house in Queens. That's bullshit! He did a lot of research, and some of the interviews were good, but Bruce Perry's book reads like *The National Enquirer.*

CINEASTE: *Many feminists are critical of the Nation of Islam's sexist attitudes towards women. In fact, one of their well-intentioned slogans refers to women as "property."*
LEE: We didn't make that up. That was an actual banner.

CINEASTE: *No, we understand that was historically accurate, but since you've taken so much heat from feminists in the past . . .*
LEE: Hey, you know who should be taking more heat than me? Oliver Stone!

CINEASTE: *Oh, he has taken a lot of heat.*
LEE: Not as much as me, though, about women.

CINEASTE: *In a historical film like this, the dilemma seems to be whether one can—or should even attempt to—deal with such an issue by presenting an anachronistic, retroactive 'politically correct' perspective on the Nation's attitudes towards women.*
LEE: We just showed it the way it was.

CINEASTE: *We thought you dealt with this issue well in at least one scene where you intercut Elijah Muhammad's various strictures against women with Malcolm's conversation with Betty where he parrots pretty much the same line.*
LEE: Yeah, he's a mouth piece. [*Lee at this point does a pretty good impersonation of Al Freeman as Elijah Muhammad*] "She should be half the man's age plus seven. She must cook, sew, stay out of trouble." [*Laughs*] Sure, I've been

at some screenings where women go, "Ugh!," but, look, those are not my views.

CINEASTE: *You often have scenes where there's no obvious interpretation, you leave it up to the viewer.*
LEE: A lot of my work has been done that way. Some things I'll slant, but a lot of time I let people make up their own minds.

CINEASTE: *We're thinking especially of the scene where Denzel is watching television, and you intercut newsreel footage of police repression of civil rights demonstrations with a slow zoom into his face.*
LEE: Yeah, and with John Coltrane's "Alabama" on the soundtrack.

CINEASTE: *There are a couple of different levels of interpretation there. You can think that he's despising Martin Luther King, Jr. and his nonviolent approach, or you can think that he's regretting that he's not involved in action like that. In this regard, we also wondered about the little smile you see briefly on Malcolm's face just before he's shot.*
LEE: That was Denzel's idea.

CINEASTE: *I guess that's also open to interpretation.*
LEE: Well, Denzel and I felt that he just got tired of being hounded. In actuality, you know, there were several assassination attempts. The CIA tried to poison him in Cairo, and the Nation tried to kill him numerous times. There was a big assassination attempt in Los Angeles, another in Chicago, and one night he had to run into his house because guys with knives were chasing him. So he was hounded for a year, the last year of his life, and Denzel and I thought about it and just felt that, you know, he was happy to go. It was Denzel's idea to smile right before he gets the shotgun blast—like, "You finally got me," and it was over.

Malcolm knew that he was going to die—even in the book he says, "I'll be dead before this comes out"—and that idea is played through that montage where Malcolm, his aides, and the assassins are all driving in separate cars to the Audubon Ballroom—an idea we got from *The Godfather,* by the way ('props' to Francis)—accompanied by the Sam Cooke song, "A Change Is Gonna Come."

CINEASTE: *In terms of FBI and CIA involvement in the assassination, do you think it was more a case of them letting it happen rather than actually doing it?*

L E E : In my opinion they definitely stirred things up between Malcolm and the Nation. The FBI's COINTELPRO operation had infiltrated the Nation and was writing letters back and forth. Then I think they just stood back and let it happen. I don't think the FBI or CIA needed to assassinate Malcolm because, if you read *Muhammad Speaks* at that time, the Nation was going to do it themselves.

C I N E A S T E : *The FBI did the same thing on the West Coast, fomenting a rift between the Black Panthers and Ron Karenga.*
L E E : Oh yeah, they're great at that. A very important book in this regard is *Malcolm X: The FBI File*. Two new books coming out—*The Judas Factor: The Plot to Kill Malcolm X* by Karl Evanzz and *Conspiracys: Unravelling the Assassination of Malcolm X* by Zak Kondo—both say the Nation was responsible. Of course, Amiri Baraka's saying that I'm part of some great government conspiracy and that the reason the studio let me make the film is because I was going to pin the assassination on black people. That's bullshit!

The five assassins were from Temple No. 25 in Newark, New Jersey, and the orders came from Chicago. I don't know if they came from the Honorable Elijah Muhammad, but it was from somewhere up high. That's the truth. I mean, Baraka should talk to Betty Shabazz, he should ask her who killed her husband. She told me the same thing. I'm not part of some conspiracy to turn black folks against the Nation of Islam. That's bullshit!

C I N E A S T E : *Has the Nation had a response to the film yet?*
L E E : The Thursday before the movie opened we had a special screening in Chicago for Minister Farrakhan.

C I N E A S T E : *How did that go?*
L E E : He was there, and I got a note from his secretary saying he was going to respond by letter, but we haven't heard from him since. But Minister Farrakhan has been supportive. While we were shooting the film, he said, "Look, Spike, I support your right as an artist." That's been it.

C I N E A S T E : *Do you think they'll make an official pronouncement, one way or another?*
L E E : I think they'll just let it blow over.

C I N E A S T E : *In making this film, did you arrive at a more sympathetic understanding or appreciation of Islam?*

LEE: Yeah, I mean you had to have respect. Denzel and I were reading the Koran before we began to shoot. We *had* to. If we didn't have a sympathetic attitude toward Islam, why would the Saudi government allow us to bring cameras into Mecca to shoot the holy rite of *hajj*? You have to be a Muslim to enter Mecca, so we had two second units, Islamic crews, who in May 1990 and June 1991 were permitted, for the first time ever in history, to film in Mecca.

I think the Saudi government realized this film could be good publicity for Islam. I mean, Islam and the Arabs in general have been taking a bashing in the West—what with Khomeini and the Gulf War and everything—and in Islam Malcolm is considered a martyr. That's why they let us bring cameras in.

CINEASTE: *Will the Islamic countries be an important overseas market for the film?*
LEE: Yeah, we're going to try. We've got to be careful, though, because the same people who gave us the stamp of approval, the Islamic Court, are the same cats who sentenced Salman Rushdie to die, so we don't want to fuck around.

CINEASTE: *Some felt that the film's Mecca scenes were a little saccharine, somewhat like Christian movies of Jerusalem.*
LEE: If the man says this was a deeply religious experience, you have to be true to that, no matter how you feel personally about religion. I mean, if up until that point the man felt that every single white person was a blue-eyed, grafted devil, and he no longer believed that after his visit to Mecca, something must have happened.

CINEASTE: *A very powerful scene in the film is when the young man, after seeing Malcolm and other members of the Nation confront the police, approaches Malcolm and says he wants to become a Muslim. It showed the power of the Nation to influence people and change their behavior.*
LEE: People can talk about Elijah Muhammad all they want, but there's never been a better program in America for black folks to convert drug addicts, alcoholics, criminals, whatever. Elijah Muhammad straightened those guys out and, once they were clean, that was that.

CINEASTE: *A lot of people felt Malcolm would have left Islam, but we always thought he was as devout a Muslim as King was a Christian.*

LEE: No, he would never have left Islam. He would have moved on to other stuff, but he would have remained a Muslim. He would not have made it a requirement to join his organization because he saw it was too regimented. He wanted to include as many people as possible. People wanted to follow him but they weren't willing to give up pork, or sex, or whatever.

CINEASTE: *There was always this tension between Malcolm and King which some people saw as a contradiction but which we saw as more of a dynamic tension.*

LEE: I agree. At the end of *Do the Right Thing,* when I use the statements from Malcolm and King, I wasn't saying it's either one or the other. I think one can form a synthesis of both. When Malcolm was assassinated, I think they were trying to find a common ground, a plan they could both work on.

Some people felt I took a low blow at King in the film in the scene where John Sayles, as an FBI agent listening in on a phone tap on Malcolm, cracks, "Compared to King, this guy is a monk." I don't think that's a low blow. J. Edgar Hoover had made tapes of King with other women and he confronted King with them, saying, "If you don't commit suicide, I'm going to send these tapes to Coretta," and he did. Afterwards things weren't the same between Coretta and Dr. King, but I'm not taking a low blow at King. The low blow was the FBI doing this to Dr. King. But some black people told me, "Spike, you know, you shouldn't have done that."

CINEASTE: *They have a hard time dealing with King as a sexual being. Baldwin also thought that there was this dynamic, this dialectical tension, between Malcolm and King. Toward the end, Malcolm seemed to be saying, "You'd better deal with King, because, if you don't, you'll have to deal with me." It's the Ballot or the Bullet.*

LEE: He said that all the time. He told King, "I'm good for you."

CINEASTE: *Some people would have liked you to have included the scene where Malcolm went down to Selma and spoke to Coretta King. Did you think of putting that in?*

LEE: [*Covers his head in a defensive manner and laughs uproariously*] We couldn't do everything! We knew going in that, at best, we'd just get the essence of the man, that's the most we'd be able to do. Besides, Henry Hampton of Blackside—you know, the guy who did *Eyes on the Prize*—he's preparing an eight hour series on Malcolm. They'll be able to do a lot more than we did, and I'm glad.

CINEASTE: *We've also heard that there are plans to re-release, at least on video, the 1972 feature documentary on Malcolm.*
LEE: Marvin Worth's film. It's good. I think if more people can learn about Malcolm X, that's cool.

CINEASTE: *We thought you might have done more with Ossie Davis's eulogy.*
LEE: What, you mean see him delivering it? Then we'd have to restage the funeral and I didn't want to see Denzel in a casket. Besides, by that time we show footage of the real Malcolm X. I gotta give my props here to Oliver Stone. Barry Brown [*the editor who cut* School Daze *and* Do the Right Thing] and I saw Oliver Stone's *JFK* the first day it came out, and I said, "Barry, man, look what they're doing. C'mon!" That film gave us great inspiration.

You remember the opening newsreel montage in *JFK*? Well, we tried to do the same thing, or better it, with our montage at the end where Ossie Davis delivers the eulogy. We also had some of the black and white thing going, like newsreel footage.

CINEASTE: *So you were directly influenced by* JFK?
LEE: Yes. There are other similarities between *Malcolm X* and *JFK* but what makes our film stand out is the performance of the lead actor. I think Kevin Costner is an OK actor, and I know that's probably the only way Oliver could have gotten the film made with the amount of money he wanted to, but I love that film *despite* Kevin Costner's performance. In *Malcolm X*, Denzel *is* the film, he's in every single scene. I hope he gets nominated for the Academy Award and I hope he wins.

Another thing we're really proud of with this film is the craft. Far too often with my films the craft is overlooked, but I think everything here—Barry Brown's editing, Ruth Carter's costume design, Terence Blanchard's score, plus the source music we used, and Ernest Dickerson's cinematography—is outstanding.

CINEASTE: *The cameo appearances in your film are another similarity to* JFK.

In some ways they're amusing, and people love them, but, on the other hand, they seem to disrupt the dramatic intensity, because people are saying, "Hey, that's Al Sharpton," or "There's Bill Kunstler," or "Did you see Bobby Seale?"

LEE: Not that many viewers know who these people are, and for me it just added weight to the stuff. I don't think I was making jokes or trying to make it campy or funny. I actually wanted Clint Eastwood to play the cop in the Peter Boyle scene, but he was shooting *Unforgiven.*

CINEASTE: *Has Warner Bros. been supportive in terms of the advertising campaign and the national release?*

LEE: Yes, ever since they saw the rough cut. I mean, for a while there during production we went at it toe to toe, but since they've seen it they've been behind the film. We're on 1600 screens nationwide. I have no complaints.

CINEASTE: *In terms of the highly publicized dispute during production between yourself, Warner Bros., and the Completion Bond Company, to what extent do you feel racism was involved?*

LEE: Racism is part of the fabric of American society, so why should the film industry be exempt? I think it's a racist assumption that white America will not go to see a black film that's not a comedy, or that doesn't have singing and dancing, or that doesn't star Eddie Murphy. I think there are racist tendencies that keep this glass ceiling on the amount of money that is spent on black films, to produce them or to market and promote them. I mean, how is it that Dan Aykroyd, a first-time director, can get $45 million to do *Nothing But Trouble?* $45 million! They're willing to give more money to these white boys right out of film school than they are to accomplished black directors.

In terms of the controversy, films go over budget all the time, so why I am on the front page? I wasn't calling up these newspapers and saying, "I'm over budget and the Completion Bond Company is taking the film over."

CINEASTE: *Wasn't there some sort of misunderstanding about the delivery date of the film?*

LEE: No. Here's what happened. Any time a director and the lead actor are shooting, that is first unit, that is principal photography. The Completion Bond Company tried to say that what we did in Africa was second unit. But Denzel and I were shooting, so that's principal photography. We finished shooting in Soweto in late January 1992, and five weeks later they wanted a first rough cut!

The Bond Company was mad because they were getting stuck by Warner Bros. and were having to deal with a $5,000,000 overage. Usually the studio will help out the bond company, but in this case Warner Bros. said, "Fuck you. We paid you a fee and this is your job." So the Bond Company said to us, "Look, until we work this agreement out with Warner Bros., we're not paying you anything." So they fired all our editors. We had no money coming in to complete the film, so that's when I made the phone calls to these prominent African-Americans—Oprah Winfrey, Bill Cosby, Magic Johnson, Michael Jordan, and others.

CINEASTE: *And their contributions were gifts.*

LEE: These were gifts—not loans, not investments. So for two months we continued to work and neither the Bond Company nor Warner Bros., knew where the money was coming from. That really fucked 'em up. I chose to announce what we had been able to do on May 19th, Malcolm's birthday, at a press conference at the Schomburg Center. *Miraculously,* two days later, the Bond Company and Warner Bros. worked it out. They say it was just a coincidence, that it would have happened anyway. I say bullshit.

But I hope this will be a precedent. Next time, maybe myself or some other filmmaker will bypass Hollywood altogether for financing and go directly to people like Oprah or Bill or Magic or Michael who'll finance the production, and then just go to Hollywood for distribution once the film is done. There are plenty of black people with money, plenty of black entrepreneurs. It can be done.

CINEASTE: *Are there other major black historical figures that you'd like to do films on?*

LEE: Yeah, Walter Yetnikoff and I are working to acquire the rights to Miles Davis's life story. I heard that Robert Townsend may direct and star in a film on Duke Ellington. Right now, Touchstone is getting ready to do the Tina Turner story, with Angela Bassett, who plays Betty Shabazz in *Malcolm X,* as Tina and Larry Fishburne as Ike Turner. What we hope, what we're praying for, is that with the success of *Malcolm X,* you'll be able to eventually see films about Miles Davis, Paul Robeson, Harriet Tubman, Sojourner Truth . . . you can go right on down the line.

Doing the Job

JAMES VERNIERE/1993

JAMES VERNIERE: *How long have you been thinking about making* Malcolm X?
SPIKE LEE: Since I made *Do the Right Thing*. I read *The Autobiography of Malcolm X*—the most important book I'll ever read—when I was in junior high school. I began to look at the world with a new set of eyes. It showed me how we are portrayed in the media, how African-American stars in sport and show business smile and say all the right things, but never speak out, and how it all ties in.

JV: *Malcolm X often comes down very hard on Christianity, especially African-American Christian ministers. Do you share his views?*
SL: He had a thing about Dr. King, but a lot of that might have been jealousy because King was the object of so much adulation.

JV: *At the conclusion of* Do the Right Thing, *you quote both Martin Luther King, who speaks in conciliatory terms, and Malcolm X, whose words have been interpreted as a call to arms. What was your point?*
SL: I think we have to get out of this either/or thing. I think black America has to form a synthesis between the two views and make it work.

JV: *In a story in a recent issue of* New Yorker, *the writer argues that Dr. King*

Published in *Sight and Sound* (February 1993): 10–11. Reprinted by permission of the British Film Institute.

appealed to the middle class, while Malcolm X spoke to the more oppressed, lower classes, the people in the ghettos. Why was Malcolm X's message stronger for you, the product of a middle-class background and education?

S L :   I don't think Malcolm's message excluded the middle class; he was just strongest among the underclass. To me, Malcolm's greatest power was that he could make everything so crystal clear, so simple. He'd say, "A plus B equals C," and you'd smack your head and think, "I never saw it that way before."

J V :   *In the newsclips you use at the end of* Malcolm X, *I noticed several shots of him smiling and looking cheerful. But the only pictures I remember of him on television or in newspapers when I was a boy made him look angry and accusing.*

S L :   Malcolm had his own photographer, and one day he got upset with him because the guy was taking pictures of him looking mean and angry. He said, "I don't need you to do that. I can get the *New York Times* to do that." People have to realize that the media know what they're doing. They know how to shape a person's image and make the American public believe it.

J V :   *I wonder if we'll ever see a movie by Spike Lee released without a host of combative headlines and contentious, often negative stories about you to go with it.*

S L :   I long for that day. It's not that I wake up in the morning and say, "What can I come up with today?" I get misquoted a lot. It must look as though I slip somebody some money so I'll get blasted in the papers and get publicity for the film. But this stuff always just seems to happen.

J V :   *You don't enjoy the attention at all?*

S L :   It gets to be a nuisance after a while because I end up having to explain stuff I never said in the first place.

J V :   *A cover story about you in a recent issue of* Esquire *magazine ran with the headline, "Spike Lee Hates Your Cracker Ass." What did you think of that?*

S L :   You know, I was on a plane and somebody sitting next to me was reading that story and he turned to me and said, "Did you really say that?" No, I did not say that. I don't feel that way. I never have. The writer from *Esquire* (a white woman named Barbara Grizzuti Harrison) turned me off from the first minute of the interview because I guess she felt she had to tell me all about her black boyfriend and how they went to see Billie Holiday and. . . .

Right there I stopped her and said, "C'mon, you're here to do a job, I'm here to do a job. Let's talk about *Malcolm X*. You don't have to convince me you're a bleeding-heart liberal. It's not necessary." Then she asks, "Do you have any white friends, Spike?" What the fuck is that? What white film director would get asked questions like that?

JV: *Do you think the media are racist?*
SL: Yes. Madonna swears by that old saying, "Print anything you like about me as long as you spell my name right." I'd rather be out of the papers than see some false shit about how I'm anti-Semitic or how I hate white people. I'd rather not be in the papers at all, whether or not my name is spelled right.

JV: *Those same accusations were leveled against Malcolm X. What do you think his legacy is?*
SL: I think the resurgence of Malcolm is about a void that young people are trying to fill. Ossie Davis said it best when he delivered the eulogy at Malcolm's funeral: "He was our shining black prince, our manhood." Young black men today need role models, and it's a shame we have to dig up a dead man instead of finding someone who walks among us.

JV: *Don't you fulfill that kind of role for a lot of people? Aren't you a kind of role model, at least to young black filmmakers who've sprung up in the last two or three years?*
SL: If I really considered myself to be a role model, it would be a hindrance. I means you can't have anything negative connected with you—Michael Jordan can't be photographed drinking a beer. I'm an artist. I can't wear that straightjacket.

JV: *But don't you think that the integrity of your work and the discussion it generates make you a role model, someone worthy of the respect and admiration of young people?*
SL: I'm not saying that's not possible. I just try to lead by example. I think that twenty years from now, black athletes will dominate in golf because kids today have seen Michael Jordan with a golf club in his hand. I remember at the first LA premiere of *She's Gotta Have It*, a skinny black kid walked up to me and said, "Hi, my name is John Singleton and I'm in high school now, but I'm going to make movies just like you." For me, that's where the reward

is, though that's not to say I'm the father of black cinema. I'm just going down the same road that Ossie Davis, Oscar Micheaux, and Melvin Van Peebles went down. Their success made it easier for me, and every success I have makes it easier for others. Young black kids need concrete examples of people like them who make films, because until you see someone like you doing something, you can never imagine yourself doing it.

JV: *So how do you feel now about Matty Rich, John Singleton, Reginald and Warrington Hudlin, Carl Franklin . . . the new black filmmakers who have sprung up in your wake?*
SL: I think it's great. I never wanted to be the only one out there. Let them take some of the bricks.

JV: *Do you think this film will appeal to white audiences?*
SL: Yes. I've always had a large white following, but it's been kept quiet because if that gets out, it just empowers me even more. This film is going to crush that old axiom that white audiences will not go to see black people in a movie, unless it's a musical or a comedy or an Eddie Murphy film. When that axiom dies, studios can no longer tell black filmmakers they can't give them a decent budget because their films are too much of a risk.

JV: *Your budget for* Malcolm X *was about $34 million, but you only got $28 million from Warner Bros. How did that work out?*
SL: We raised the extra money because I kicked in half my salary and because we got gifts from people like Michael Jordan, Bill Cosby, and Oprah Winfrey. The important thing is that it looks like there's a $60 million budget when you see it on screen. I told Warner Bros. at our very first meeting that this was going to be an epic on the scale of a David Lean film, and that it was going to cost over $30 million and be over three hours long. And you have to remember that $34 million is not a lot of money for an epic. But whenever I asked Warners for more money, I was told, "But Spike, you made *She's Gotta Have It* for less than $5,000. Why do you need more money now?" I've had my differences with Warner Bros. but never with the people who market and sell the pictures. Barry Reardon, Rob Friedman, John Dartigue, Charlotte G. Kandel—they are behind the film 100 percent, and they are going to sell it.

JV: *At one time,* Malcolm X *was set to be directed by Norman Jewison, but you publicly complained that the film should be directed by a black director, presumably yourself. Why was that?*

S L: It wasn't a personal thing. Norman Jewison is a fine filmmaker, but he wasn't the person for this job. I've never said that only black people can direct black films, and only white people can direct white films. But I think there's no way that someone who wasn't Italian-American could have done what Francis Coppola and Martin Scorcese did in films like *The Godfather* and *GoodFellas*. Somebody else could have done those films, but they wouldn't have had that flavor.

J V : *As usual in your films you've cast yourself in* Malcolm X *in a part designed primarily to provide comic relief.*

S L: In basketball terms, I'm like the sixth man off the bench—I'm a spot player, a utility man, a person with limited abilities who knows what his role is, doesn't try to play outside his game, gets the job done and lets the real actors take over—Denzel Washington, Ossie Davis, Ruby Dee, John Turturro, Anthony Quinn, people like that.

J V : *Your film is being released at a time when racial tensions are peaking in America. What do events such as the Rodney King beating and the riots in Los Angeles say about racism in this country?*

S L: I think the inclusion of the Rodney King video footage in the opening of our film along with the image of the burning American flag and the words of Malcolm X, say that things haven't changed much. Things have opened up to some individuals, but not to the masses. There are more black people in the underclass than ever before; under Reagan and Bush, the country seemed to be moving backwards.

J V : *What can this movie do for the masses?*

S L: What can any work of art do? We want people to come out of the film spiritually uplifted and enlightened.

J V : *In the past, you've been accused of being a provocateur—a columnist for* New York *magazine once accused you of trying to incite riots with* Do the Right Thing. *Do you think that sort of criticism is racist?*

S L: In a lot of ways, yes. How is it that black audiences are going to see a film and then re-enact what they saw on the screen, while the white masses can go in droves to see *Terminator 2* with no problem? How many cops did Arnold Schwarzenegger kill in the first *Terminator* movie? Did we hear any complaints from the police about that? Yet Ice T does a song which is pure fantasy, and the whole world comes down on him.

J V : *Do you think some of your potential white audience might be turned off by the impression that Malcolm X doesn't belong to them?*
S L : One of Malcolm's biggest regrets was that he once told a young white co-ed that there was nothing she could do to help improve the conditions of black people in America. Later, he changed his mind. We wrote that scene and shot it, but we had to cut it out. . . . I think Malcolm belongs to anyone who is ready to hear his message.

J V : *Was there any thought of having Alex Haley, the co-author of the Malcolm X autobiography, appear as a character?*
S L : He was a character in one version of the script, but I felt it was not the right thing to do. The film should not be about Malcolm X telling his story to Alex Haley.

J V : *There was also a David Mamet version of the script.*
S L : Mamet wrote that script for Sidney Lumet when Lumet was attached to the project. The script that I rewrote was by James Baldwin and Arnold Perl. Unfortunately, Baldwin is not mentioned in the credits because his sister, who controls his estate, petitioned the Screenwriters' Guild to remove it. Her objection was that we had rewritten a lot of it, but I think she made a mistake.

J V : *How concerned were you about the reaction of Louis Farrakhan, the leader of the Nation of Islam? Elijah Muhammad is still a revered figure to many Muslims today, and Farrakhan is reportedly concerned about how you portray him in the film.*
S L : I flew to Chicago to discuss the film with Farrakhan, and he let me know that he'd be watching very closely. He wouldn't say anything until he saw the film. But he didn't want us to trash the image of the Honorable Elijah Muhammad. He let me know that he would be very upset if we did.

J V : *And how would his "upset" manifest itself?*

s L: I might find out. He hasn't seen the film yet, and there are things in it I know he's not going to like.

J V: *Despite some striking similarities, your film isn't JFK. You don't speculate about who killed Malcolm X, you present the assassination as a matter of fact.*
s L: I don't think there's any doubt that the Nation of Islam was behind the assassination. The five assassins were from Temple Number 25 in Newark, New Jersey. That's not to say that the Honorable Elijah Muhammad ordered the killing, but somebody in Chicago gave the word. And the FBI and the CIA were also involved—they knew it was about to happen but stood back and did nothing to stop it.

J V: *You have no problem stating that as fact?*
s L: It's common knowledge, and there are recently released FBI files to support it.

J V: *Why do you have such vocal critics within the black press? Such influential New York journalists as Armond White and Stanley Crouch are among your most vehement detractors.*
s L: It would be presumptuous for me to think that all black critics are going to love my work. Black people are among the most disunited people on earth—I mean, Stanley "Crotch" wrote a story about *Jungle Fever* in which he mentioned my height about ten times. What's that got to do with anything?

J V: *Have you had a chance to think about your next movie?*
s L: I'm going to rest, refuel, and crank up again. I don't know what I'll be doing next, but it will be a small film.

J V: *What do you see as the future for you and African-American filmmakers? Is it risky for directors to pigeonhole themselves by making films for a specific market?*
s L: I don't think there's one specific film any black filmmaker should be making, because there's not one monolithic audience out there. Every filmmaker should be allowed to make the film he or she wants to make. But I hope each of us strives to make great cinema, because if not, we'll just be another trend, and we'll soon be over.

Interview with Spike Lee

CHARLIE ROSE/1994

CHARLIE ROSE: *In the eight years since he scraped together $175,000 for his first commercial movie,* She's Gotta Have It, *Spike Lee has become a major player in the filmmaking community. To date he has produced and directed seven films, from* Malcolm X *to the no-sex, no-violence, no-drugs of* Crooklyn. *Filmmaking is just one of the hats he wears. He's also an executive producer; he owns a music label; he has apparel shops in Brooklyn and Los Angeles; he's writing a script for a CBS pilot; he's starting an ad agency; he's teaching at Harvard; and he has started his eighth film. All of that shows remarkable energy, and I'm pleased to have him back. Welcome.*
SPIKE LEE: Glad to be here.

CHARLIE ROSE: *You are a fixture of the Knicks game. Every time I've ever been to the game, you are sitting right there. You get to sit right there on the front row, too.*
SPIKE LEE: Season tickets.

CHARLIE ROSE: *Season tickets. Why do you love the Knicks? I mean, why do you love basketball? What is it about this game?*
SPIKE LEE: Well, the first sport my father introduced me to was baseball, I think. Most fathers, you know . . . it's baseball first, then football, or basketball. But he started taking me to these triple headers they used to have at the

From *The Charlie Rose Show*, New York, New York. 17 June 1994. Published by permission of Rose Communications.

old Garden. Holiday festival. You could see Providence with Jimmy Walker, and [Kareem Abdul] Jabar with UCLA.

CHARLIE ROSE: *And NIT [National Invitation Tournament], probably. You probably went to NIT.*
SPIKE LEE: NIT. You know, we'd to triple headers in the morning, triple headers at night. And so, I grew up a big Walt Frazier fan. At the time of *She's Gotta Have It,* my season tickets were in the blue, you know, Bob Uecker seats, and I have just moved down each film.

CHARLIE ROSE: *There is nowhere else to move.*
SPIKE LEE: Now I'm in better seats.

CHARLIE ROSE: *When I was sitting next to you one night you were talking to [Vernon] Maxwell from the Rockets. You were giving him such a hard time. Does your wife like basketball as well?*
SPIKE LEE: Loves it. I mean, my friends can't get in now.

CHARLIE ROSE: *Your friends can't come to the game anymore.*
SPIKE LEE: Yeah, they're out.

CHARLIE ROSE: *Tell me a couple of things about sports. Mike Tyson.*
SPIKE LEE: I've been to visit Mike six times since he's been in the joint, and he's in great spirits. He's been doing a lot of reading, a lot of reflecting, and I'm looking forward to when he gets out—I think he is going to box again.

CHARLIE ROSE: *Is that what he wants to do? That's the only thing he knows.*
SPIKE LEE: That's what he says. That's what he knows. He regrets the circumstances that put him there, or the stuff, the bad karma he might have compiled. But, he's all right.

CHARLIE ROSE: *You're not making a movie? This is just friendship?*
SPIKE LEE: No, I don't know how the press turned that around. This is just a friend visiting somebody who is in prison. I have no intentions of doing any films about Mike Tyson.

CHARLIE ROSE: *What change have you noted in him? He says he is sorry.*
SPIKE LEE: You know, when you are in prison, it gives you a lot of time to reflect. And you look past on your actions. Some of them might not have been good, and what goes around, comes around. And he's sorry, about stuff that happened.

CHARLIE ROSE: *Do you know the fight game pretty well?*
SPIKE LEE: A little bit.

CHARLIE ROSE: *Teddy Atlas was here the other day, was in the corner with . . .*
SPIKE LEE: The guy who pulled a gun on Mike, right?

CHARLIE ROSE: *Exactly. And we, well, we mentioned that, as a matter of fact. He says he—I think it was Teddy Atlas who told me, in that interview—that he doesn't think Tyson will ever be the champion again because he thought he's lost it: he's lost his step, or he's lost something. Do you have any sense of that?*
SPIKE LEE: Look at the heavyweight champion division now.

CHARLIE ROSE: *Lennox Lewis.*
SPIKE LEE: Mike Tyson will be champ again. He's going to kill them all.

CHARLIE ROSE: *How about Riddick Bowe?*
SPIKE LEE: Kill him.

CHARLIE ROSE: *Kill him? No question in your mind?*
SPIKE LEE: No question.

CHARLIE ROSE: *He hasn't lost it? And he knows, he thinks in his head that he will be the champion again?*
SPIKE LEE: He knows it.

CHARLIE ROSE: *That he can take anybody that he sees out there?*
SPIKE LEE: He's going to have to take a year to get the title shot.

CHARLIE ROSE: *What do you think of the people surrounding him?*
SPIKE LEE: Well, as I said before, he's had a lot of time to do reflection, and there is going to be some housecleaning.

CHARLIE ROSE: *And who, who is going to go?*

SPIKE LEE: Charlie, all I am saying is, I think he is going to clean house.

CHARLIE ROSE: *Could you possibly get involved in his career?*

SPIKE LEE: I am there for support. I just want him to be righteous and to win the heavyweight championship. There is no personal gain on my part at all.

CHARLIE ROSE: *Why him for you? What is it about him that appeals to you?*

SPIKE LEE: He's from Brooklyn. East Brownsville, New York.

CHARLIE ROSE: *And so was Riddick Bowe.*

SPIKE LEE: Yeah, but he moved away. And he's never really claimed Brooklyn.

CHARLIE ROSE: *But is it something more than that though?*

SPIKE LEE: Just, you know, I think Mike has led a tragic life, and my heart always went out for him, even before the Desiree Washington thing.

CHARLIE ROSE: *What do you think about that? Do you think he got an unfair deal, wasn't represented well, all that? Or do you think he should put it behind him? He's served his time, let him come out?*

SPIKE LEE: He's going to hopefully get out early—three years—and just move on. And, hopefully, learn from past mistakes.

CHARLIE ROSE: *You are not a Muslim, are you?*

SPIKE LEE: No.

CHARLIE ROSE: *Is he? Has he converted?*

SPIKE LEE: Yes, he converted.

CHARLIE ROSE: *That's what I thought. In prison.*

SPIKE LEE: Yes, he did.

CHARLIE ROSE: Crooklyn. *Tell me about this movie.*

SPIKE LEE: We're very happy with the response to it.

CHARLIE ROSE: *It's lighter than what you've done before.*

SPIKE LEE: Yes. I think it's light, but I don't think it's the vast departure that some people said. Like all of a sudden, this is a warm and gentler Spike Lee, like I never had those qualities, or those qualities were never in any of my other films. I just felt that as far as my career goes and the types of films that I want to make, that it was important to do something different, and not duplicate what we did with *Malcolm X*, or the other two films dealing with race, *Jungle Fever* and *Do the Right Thing*. And, you know, stuff between black people, *School Daze*. I just felt that it was time for a change of pace, and I think it just really shows the versatility that I have and the types of films I want to make. I don't always want to do a film that deals with the racial climate in this country.

CHARLIE ROSE: *Did you feel like it was necessary for a change of pace after* Malcolm? *Because that was a long-time project.*
SPIKE LEE: Two years.

CHARLIE ROSE: *And you devoted night and day to it.*
SPIKE LEE: Two years, night and day. And I really don't want to box myself into that corner.

CHARLIE ROSE: *I want to stay on* Crooklyn *because we don't have that much time. How do you feel now when you can look back on the* Malcolm *experience? You made the film you wanted to make?*
SPIKE LEE: We made the film that we wanted to make.

CHARLIE ROSE: *And you think the Academy Awards were unfair because they didn't give you the fair shot?*
SPIKE LEE: We don't even worry about that.

CHARLIE ROSE: *All right, you're moving on.*
SPIKE LEE: We made the film that we wanted to make, and I think that history will bear us out and *Scent of a Woman* and all that other stuff, it's not going to hold up to *Malcolm X* twenty, thirty years down the line. I truly feel that.

CHARLIE ROSE: *Did it change you in any way?*
SPIKE LEE: It made me stronger because it was the hardest thing I ever had to do in my life, and there were hurdles in front of us.

CHARLIE ROSE: *In terms of raising the money, in terms of being able to make the film you wanted to make?*

SPIKE LEE: Everything. I mean, they have been trying to make that film twenty-two, twenty-three years before me, so it didn't start with me, you know. That's been like a quarter of a century trying to get this film made.

CHARLIE ROSE: *It says something about you that you ended up making the film, something about your own tenacity and your skill.*

SPIKE LEE: I think that it was just timing. I think it was meant to be made when it was made, and Denzel [Washington] and I were the people that were meant to do it, I think.

CHARLIE ROSE: *He is a great actor, isn't he?*

SPIKE LEE: Great. Big basketball fan, also.

CHARLIE ROSE: *Oh, he likes basketball too? But he doesn't like the Knicks. He's a big Laker fan.*

SPIKE LEE: He likes the Knicks, but he lives in L.A., so he has season tickets for the Lakers.

CHARLIE ROSE: *Well, not a great year there, was it?*

SPIKE LEE: No, no. Down year for them.

CHARLIE ROSE: *Do you think Pat will be here next year? Riley?*

SPIKE LEE: Yeah, he's not going anywhere. The players are going to go before him.

CHARLIE ROSE: *Like who?*

SPIKE LEE: I am saying if anybody is going, it will be players, before he goes.

CHARLIE ROSE: Crooklyn. *The idea, the story came from your . . .*

SPIKE LEE: My sister. Joie. It was her original idea. She wrote the first couple of drafts, with my brother Cinqué. They came to me not to make the film, but to say, "Do you know anybody who could help us get this made?" I read it, and I said, "I will make it." And that's that.

CHARLIE ROSE: *Let me tell you what some of the critics say about this, in case you don't know.* The Washington Post, *listen to this: "For those who can overlook the occasional flat note,* Crooklyn *is a spiritual rendering of African American family life in the early 1970s, modulating from heavy to light, from angry to lyrical, and so on. The movie is an enjoyable emotional symphony." You like that?*
SPIKE LEE: Who wrote that?

CHARLIE ROSE: The Washington Post, *Desson Howe. You like that?*
SPIKE LEE: Mm-hm.

CHARLIE ROSE: *All right, how about this?* "Crooklyn *is so mild that it is the first Spike Lee film with the potential to be turned into a television show. More importantly, it is the first one to display real warmth of heart." Do you like that? I mean tell me if you agree with this. Are you interested in what the critics think?*
SPIKE LEE: I don't think it's a mild picture. I just have to do the films I want to make. I do a film like this, they say it is too mild. I do *Do the Right Thing,* they accuse me of trying to incite thirty-five million Americans to burn down America.

CHARLIE ROSE: *Well, are you guilty on both counts or neither count?*
SPIKE LEE: Not guilty.

CHARLIE ROSE: *All right, not guilty, he says. Now listen to this. This is from* The New Yorker. *You read that magazine don't you? "Spike Lee's* Crooklyn *is slight in everything but length. The picture runs well over two hours, and you feel every moment of it because Lee can't seem to find . . . a theme or style to shape this."*
SPIKE LEE: No, the movie is under two hours, so maybe he felt like it ran over to him, but I just have to continue to make the films I want to make. Knock on wood: I will get a chance to continue to do that.

CHARLIE ROSE: *Is there anything you want to do? I mean, do you feel like anything Spike wants to do, with enough dedication, enough hard work, enough energy, he can do it?*
SPIKE LEE: Sure, I've always felt that. I mean I just think that I was inspired by my parents and grandparents. They always gave us confidence to go down swinging, at least.

CHARLIE ROSE: *And that's defined your life?*
SPIKE LEE: Go down swinging, if you've got to go down.

CHARLIE ROSE: *What do you want?*
SPIKE LEE: Well, I am doing what I want to do. I think I am blessed. I'm able to make films. I mean, I think you have to go back a long time to see an African American filmmaker able to go from film to film to film. When we start *Clockers,* from the Richard Price novel, in July, that will be our eighth film in the last ten years.

CHARLIE ROSE: *And did Scorsese buy the rights to that and get you to do it?*
SPIKE LEE: No, Universal bought it for him, and he was going to do it at first, but he is doing *Casino* now, with [Joe] Pesci and [Robert] De Niro, so he is still going to be the executive producer on it.

CHARLIE ROSE: *And have you cast it?*
SPIKE LEE: Yes, Harvey Keitel is going to play Rocco.

CHARLIE ROSE: *Not bad.*
SPIKE LEE: Delroy Lindo is going to play Rodney. John Turturro's going to play Mazilli.

CHARLIE ROSE: *God, these are great actors. Did you get pretty much who you wanted?*
SPIKE LEE: Yes. That's the people we wanted. And we start shooting in July, and it will be out next summer.

CHARLIE ROSE: *Why Harvey Keitel? Just right?*
SPIKE LEE: Well, we liked his frontal nudity in *The Piano* and . . .

CHARLIE ROSE: *Yeah, come on, come on.*
SPIKE LEE: . . . and *Bad Lieutenant.*

CHARLIE ROSE: *Did you like* The Piano *as a movie?*
SPIKE LEE: Yes, I think Jane Campion is a great filmmaker.

CHARLIE ROSE: *Who has influenced you the most?*
SPIKE LEE: As a filmmaker?

CHARLIE ROSE: *Yeah.*
SPIKE LEE: I'd have to say Mr. Scorsese.

CHARLIE ROSE: *Really?*
SPIKE LEE: It's an honor working together with him. And he's always taken an interest in my work, even when I was just a runny-nosed NYU film student going up to him and asking him questions. You know, he took time out. He didn't know who I was. But he did.

CHARLIE ROSE: *Do you talk a lot about making films now?*
SPIKE LEE: With him?

CHARLIE ROSE: *I mean do you see him?*
SPIKE LEE: We see each other infrequently because we're both so busy. But when we get together, it is non-stop, just talking about cinema.

CHARLIE ROSE: *My impression is, and tell me if this is just wrong, is that for young African-American filmmakers, this is a good time. We got you leading the pack. The Hughes brothers [Albert and Allen], [John] Singleton.*
SPIKE LEE: Mario Van Peebles.

CHARLIE ROSE: *Mario Van Peebles, who just made* Posse *and is probably doing something else now.*
SPIKE LEE: Yes, he's doing the Black Panther story now.

CHARLIE ROSE: *Doing one character or another of . . .*
SPIKE LEE: Huey [Newton].

CHARLIE ROSE: *Huey. Okay. I mean, there really seems to be a group of you.*
SPIKE LEE: Ernest Dickerson. Matty Rich. Julie Dash. I would say that there has never been a better time than now. But I want to preface that by saying the door is still not wide open, and the type of films that we are able to make are still limited. Either it's a comedy, or it's a hiphop, gangsta 'hood, rap movie. So we are still not allowed the leeway. But I guess it's going to come.

CHARLIE ROSE: *But are you included? Not you? I mean, you can do whatever you want to. I mean,* Jungle Fever . . .

SPIKE LEE: Budgetary, budgetary . . .

CHARLIE ROSE: *Jungle Fever was a love story, I thought, Yeah?*
SPIKE LEE: You're very . . .

CHARLIE ROSE: *No, no, no, I know, I am kidding you. It was a broad theme, this was not a "street" theme.*
SPIKE LEE: I think I can make any film I want within budgetary constraints. And I'm grateful for that. But it is still not like that across the board.

CHARLIE ROSE: *No, but you are the exception, in a sense, for the most part.*
SPIKE LEE: Well, I've been fortunate.

CHARLIE ROSE: *What did it cost,* Jungle Fever?
SPIKE LEE: I think it cost like fourteen million, same price as *Crooklyn.*

CHARLIE ROSE: *And it made, what,* Jungle Fever?
SPIKE LEE: I think thirty-three.

CHARLIE ROSE: *Now, Wesley Snipes?*
SPIKE LEE: Can't afford him anymore. He's $8 or $9 million a movie.

CHARLIE ROSE: *Does he get more than Denzel?*
SPIKE LEE: Yes.

CHARLIE ROSE: *Is that because his films have been more successful? Is it simply bookkeeping?*
SPIKE LEE: I don't know what it is. I guess they, the people who pay out the money, say that Wesley, you know, he has that action crowd.

CHARLIE ROSE: *The Sylvester Stallone group. And Arnold Schwarzenegger.*
SPIKE LEE: So I guess they pay him more. But I can't afford Wesley anymore. I tell him that all the time.

CHARLIE ROSE: *And what does he say? "You're right, brother."*
SPIKE LEE: He laughs.

CHARLIE ROSE: *But it's true, he won't do it? Suppose you went to him and*

said, "Look, do this for me. This is an important film. You are the right guy. You know, you and Denzel will knock them dead."
SPIKE LEE: He would tell me to go talk to his agent at CAA, and his manager Louis Robbins, who would tell me take a hike.

CHARLIE ROSE: *They would?*
SPIKE LEE: They would.

CHARLIE ROSE: *Now what about Wesley and Denzel together?*
SPIKE LEE: It's going to cost.

CHARLIE ROSE: *Like Redford and Newman? A buddy picture?'*
SPIKE LEE: You would think so. But I don't know if they want to spend that much, you know. If, in Hollywood, they don't think it can cross over. If they don't think that a white movie-going audience is going to see it in Peoria, they're not going to want to make that type of film.

CHARLIE ROSE: *Are they right?*
SPIKE LEE: I don't think they are right. I think that audiences will come out to see a good film if it is marketed correctly.

CHARLIE ROSE: *Tell me what delusions you think there are. The people who are responsible for what movies America sees—do they not trust the audience?*
SPIKE LEE: I think that the people that make movies are very disrespectful to the intelligence of the American movie-going audience. I think that they play down to the lowest common denominator, the lowest level, and they just try to play the audience like they're stupid. And I think that's when you end up making $75 million bombs.

CHARLIE ROSE: *Like* Last Action Hero *or something?*
SPIKE LEE: Why do you want me to name films, people, players? Who is Mike Tyson getting rid of? You know, I can't . . .

CHARLIE ROSE: *You are an out-front, candid guy, that's why.*
SPIKE LEE: Yeah. But this, this is the new, warm, gentler Spike Lee.

CHARLIE ROSE: *Oh, is it? Now, tell me this, has Spike changed at all? I mean you are married now.*

SPIKE LEE: Now I am married.

CHARLIE ROSE: *Has that changed you?*
SPIKE LEE: That's what my friends tell my wife all the time.

CHARLIE ROSE: *I know. That's what I hear. How has it changed you?*
SPIKE LEE: I myself cannot see the change.

CHARLIE ROSE: *Do you feel different? I mean do you feel some sense of mellowing?*
SPIKE LEE: I just think that you have a greater sense of responsibility, married. That it's not just you anymore. And that's the way it should be when you get married.

CHARLIE ROSE: *Had you been looking for a long time?*
SPIKE LEE: No, I wasn't looking; it just happened.

CHARLIE ROSE: *What happened? You met her in an elevator or something, what was it?*
SPIKE LEE: It was at the Congressional Black Caucus in D.C. two years ago, and I was going down the escalator, and she was going up an escalator.

CHARLIE ROSE: *Oh boy, this is a movie, this is a movie.*
SPIKE LEE: And then I went back up the escalator real quick.

CHARLIE ROSE: *And what did you say to her when you got there?*
SPIKE LEE: "You got a minute?"

CHARLIE ROSE: *And she said? "What's up?"*
SPIKE LEE: "Yeah," she said, "I got a minute." And I said, "I got to talk to you." And then we got married. No, it was like a year after that.

CHARLIE ROSE: *So you had a chance to get to know each other.*
SPIKE LEE: Mm-hm.

CHARLIE ROSE: *But it's made you feel better about yourself? You know what I mean.*

SPIKE LEE: Yes.

CHARLIE ROSE: *It sort of gives you a larger perspective, if you've got somebody in your life to live for.*
SPIKE LEE: It makes you whole.

CHARLIE ROSE: *Other than just yourself. Before this it was all for Spike. Now it's for Spike and Tonya.*
SPIKE LEE: I think that when you find the right partner in your life, it makes you whole and complete.

CHARLIE ROSE: *Let me ask you this. You live in Martha's Vineyard.*
SPIKE LEE: No, no, no, I live in Brooklyn, New York.

CHARLIE ROSE: *Yeah, but you have a house in Martha's Vineyard.*
SPIKE LEE: I have a house in Martha's Vineyard. That's different. I have a house in Martha's Vineyard.

CHARLIE ROSE: *No, it's more than a house. How many acres you got up there? Come on, tell me.*
SPIKE LEE: It's two, two and a half.

CHARLIE ROSE: *Two and a half acres! On the water, right there . . .*
SPIKE LEE: It's not on the water. It's on the Sengekontacket Pond.

CHARLIE ROSE: *Why Martha's Vineyard? Although, there has always been an African-American community there.*
SPIKE LEE: Since the early '40s. One of my best friends, John Wilson, his grandmother has had a house there since the '40s. And when we were in college at Morehouse, he used to invite me up to Martha's Vineyard for 4th of July, Labor Day, Memorial Day. I loved it. And I've been fortunate enough to buy a house there.

CHARLIE ROSE: *Great to see you.*
SPIKE LEE: Thank you.

CHARLIE ROSE: *Spike Lee. The mook. The movie is called* Crooklyn, *just out, been out for several weeks. Spike's next film is* Clockers, *which he is directing, with Harvey Keitel and others.*

Between "Rock" and a Hard Place

STEPHEN PIZZELLO/1995

HAVING INFILTRATED America's major cities, crack cocaine (or "rock") has spawned a complex and dysfunctional culture with its own laws, language and legacy. In the jargon of this limbo world, a "clocker" is a low-level runner (so named because the runner is on the street "around the clock") who serves as a conduit between dealers and addicts. Eager to make instant profits on the street, clockers spend their days preparing and distributing a product that exerts a viselike grip on its obsessive users. But the quick cash often exacts a heavy price of its own; in any criminal enterprise, trust and loyalty are strong-armed aside by paranoia. Detailing the downward spiral of a clocker whose time is running out, director Spike Lee's new film provides a stark, unflinching look at crack's deadly impact on a fictional New York neighborhood.

The film's somber tone is established during its startling title sequence, which presents a grisly series of stills that re-create actual autopsy photographs of drug-related murder victims. In preparing the sequence, Lee spent two weeks at the New York crime scene unit headquarters, where the lieutenant in charge allowed him to inspect what the officers refer to, with typical gallows humor, as the "family album." The pictures he selected were later restaged with actors and photographed by his brother, David Lee. Recalls the director, "I saw the most gruesome autopsy photos you could imagine. Of course, it would have been in bad taste to use the actual photos in the film,

Published in *American Cinematographer* 76, no. 9 (September 1995): 36–46. Reprinted courtesy of *American Cinematographer*.

so we duplicated them. We did this for effect; we wanted viewers to know, before they even settled into their seats, that our film was about serious business. This movie is the exact opposite of the big-budget action films you see, which are full of cartoony killings. We weren't going to treat life cheaply in *Clockers*, because when you take a life, it's forever. There are too many kids being killed on the streets of this country, and it's no joke to me."

Given the opportunity to make such a statement to a mass audience, Lee has crafted a harrowing tale that is both visually inventive and remarkably realistic. The director's desire for authenticity was so great that he even recruited actual crack addicts for a montage sequence in which fictional dealers are shown peddling their wares. "We always had a six a.m. call time, and when we got to the location we'd see all of these crackheads scurrying around," Lee recounts. "Not everyone in the projects is a crackhead, but that element is a part of the environment, and I wanted to think of a way to incorporate them into the movie. One day, it was raining. We could have gone to a cover set, but instead I told my A.D., Mike Ellis, to round up some crackheads so we could work them into a scene. I think it was an effective tactic."

Adapted for the screen by screenwriter/novelist Richard Price from his own book, *Clockers* was originally slated to be directed by Martin Scorsese, with Robert De Niro starring. The story certainly presents a Scorsesean milieu, featuring betrayals, double-dealings, and a youthful protagonist in search of redemption. De Niro was to have played Rocco Klein, a veteran homicide detective who believes that a teenaged clocker named Strike is responsible for the shooting death of a convenience-store clerk—despite the fact that Strike's straightlaced older brother, Victor, has confessed to the crime. As the detective pressures Strike to confess to the murder, the clocker's relationship with his dealer sours inexorably, leaving him no place to turn.

Before the film came to fruition, Scorsese and De Niro opted to pursue a different project *(Casino)*, sending Universal Pictures on a search for another director for *Clockers*. Under Scorsese's auspices as executive producer, the studio offered the film to Lee, who felt the project was a perfect fit with his own sensibilities, concerns and aesthetics. "I read the novel and looked at the various scripts that Marty and Richard Price had worked on," says Lee. "But as I did, I started getting ideas about how to add my own vision while still being true to the book. I met with Marty, Richard and De Niro, and they all seemed to be in line with what I wanted to do, so I went ahead and made the movie."

Lee worked out a new draft of the script with Price, casting Harvey Keitel, a veteran of four Scorsese films, in the role of Rocco Klein. The players also include a pair of Lee mainstays: John Turturro *(Do the Right Thing, Jungle Fever, Mo' Better Blues)* as Klein's partner, Larry Mazilli, and Delroy Lindo *(Malcolm X, Crooklyn)* as crack dealer Rodney Little, whose neighborhood grocery store serves as a front for his drug-running operation. The pivotal role of Strike went to new face Mekhi Phifer; Isaiah Washington essayed the role of Strike's upstanding brother, Victor; and another first-time actor, Tom Byrd, portrayed Errol, Rodney's drug-addled henchman.

Phifer and Byrd weren't the only newcomers to benefit from Lee's patronage. In a rare move that bucked Hollywood's traditional system of personnel advancement, which often occurs at a glacial pace, Lee decided to give a former member of his electrical crew, twenty-six-year-old Malik Sayeed, the promotion of a lifetime to director of photography. A 1990 graduate of Howard University, Sayeed earned his degree in film studies and later attended the Maine Photographic Institute, where he benefitted from courses taught by cinematographers Ralf Bode, ASC, Rob Draper and Billy Williams, BSC. "A major part of my education was reading any book I could find on motion picture photography," he says. "Reading was my foundation; it really helped me to understand the actual process during my practical training."

Having worked his way into I.A.T.S.E. as an electrician in college, he was later able to gain a position on the electrical crew for Lee's epic biopic *Malcolm X*. Of his entry into the film business, Sayeed relates, "A friend of mine who was an electrical intern introduced me to the gaffer on *Malcolm X*, Charlie Houston, and I just kept hanging around until one day they finally needed some extra people. That film was shot in New York in the dead of winter, and it was *seriously* cold outside. But I was just thankful for the chance to watch Ernest Dickerson [ASC] work. When I went home at the end of the day, I spent all of my free time reading up on films, watching videotapes and making notes."

Sayeed's studious attitude paid off with a promotion to best boy on Lee's subsequent film, *Crooklyn*. Prior to that assignment, he had gaffed a few smaller projects for *Crooklyn* cinematographer Arthur Jafa (a.k.a. A.J.), whose credits include *Daughters of the Dust*. "I had also bought a pair of cameras, a Bolex and an Arri 2C, and was shooting anything I could," says Sayeed.

"After I worked on a docudrama with A.J. called *Seven Songs for Malcolm X,* we became really tight. He's definitely influenced my style. We both try to express our creative energies through cinematography, in the same way a musician uses his instrument. I get visual ideas while listening to music, but not in a physical sense; it's more an emotional tone. I especially admire Thelonious Monk. With Monk, it's all about timing, and where to place the emphasis. He broke all the rules. Monk took what he learned and built something else; he never said, 'I can't do this.' I applied that attitude to *Clockers.*"

In the days before his big break, Sayeed compiled an impressive reel of work which included his collaborations with top music video director Harold "Hype" Williams. After watching the young cameraman's reel, Lee invited Sayeed to shoot a series of television commercials with him. The director soon decided that Sayeed had what it took to tackle a full-length feature.

Lee recounts, "When *Clockers* came around, I talked to a lot of cinematographers, including Janusz Kaminski, who was already committed to another project. Finally, I said, 'Wait a minute. You've got to cultivate your own.' I knew Malik might not get another chance for a long time, and I didn't want him to be in video hell forever, so I rolled the dice and gave him a shot."

The director does admit that he is still adjusting to life without Dickerson, who served as his right-hand man on five pictures—all visual stunners. "When I was working with Ernest, if I got lax in saying where the camera would go while we were setting up a shot, it never mattered, because he always put the camera exactly where it was supposed to be," says Lee. "Now that Ernest has gone off to be a director, I can't use him as a crutch anymore. Malik is more inexperienced, so he was thinking primarily about the lighting on this film. I had to step up and do what a director is supposed to do—set up the camera and design the shots. I have to say that I was really fortunate to have done a lot of films with Ernest, because I really benefitted from his visual sense."

Asked to assess the talents of his new cameraman, Lee offers, "What I like most about Malik's style is that it's uncontaminated. Some cameramen get bogged down in thinking about what you can and can't do. To those guys, it's just a job. I want to work with people who think like artists, not just technicians. That's not to say that Malik doesn't know his stuff; he's really on top of the technology. He knows about all the new lights and equipment that's out, and he wants to try new and interesting things."

This sense of creative chutzpah is certainly apparent in *Clockers,* which offers a cornucopia of unusual ideas and techniques. The most startling was Sayeed's gambit of shooting a significant portion of the film on Kodak's 5239 film stock, an Ektachrome reversal film that isn't even mass-produced. The stock, which is rated at 160 ASA, was once used in a 16mm incarnation during the days before news reporters shot exclusively on video. Lee concedes that he had "never even heard of the stuff" before Sayeed brought it to his attention. According to the cinematographer, the only reason Kodak still makes the stock is that NASA and the U.S. Air Force continue to use it. "When the *Challenger* space shuttle exploded, NASA had a lot of video cameras on board, along with one film camera, and the only camera that survived was the film camera," he says. "So NASA started putting more and more film cameras on the shuttles. They used this Ektachrome stock because their labs had been set up to handle it for years. When we first started shooting *Clockers,* we discovered that 5239 doesn't even have edge numbers on it; we had to have Kodak make up a special batch with numbers for us. But once we got rolling, everything went smoothly. We processed it in a negative bath, and then printed from there on standard Eastman print stock."

Sayeed had tested a wide variety of stocks during eight weeks of preproduction, searching for one that would reflect his own vision of life in the projects of New York. He even sought the advice of renowned film stock alchemist Robert Richardson, ASC, who had read a treatment of the film while Scorsese was still attached. "He was very, very helpful," Sayeed says with admiration. "Because he had read an earlier version of the story, he had a lot of opinions. He stayed on the phone with me for hours; I was really grateful that he took the time to talk to me."

In discussing the look of the film, Lee and Sayeed referenced a few other films, such as the raw, urban cop dramas *Bullitt* and *The French Connection.* But Sayeed testifies that the visual style of *Clockers* was more influenced by still photography. The production designer, Andrew McAlpine, had introduced the filmmakers to a book called *Juke Joint,* by Birney Imes, which presents photographic essays on rural areas in Mississippi. "Imes shot photos of little clubs that are barely standing," says Sayeed. "The designs on the walls of these places are very interesting. We used that look at Rodney's store and in Strike's apartment. You can find the same visual style in Brooklyn, Senegal and the Caribbean—colors like blue-green against black and yellow, in a variety of different patterns. Some other inspirations for me were Bruce Davidson's book *Subway,* and two books of photos that Leni Riefenstahl shot in Africa. Her politics are a matter of debate, but her aesthetics are incredible."

Both Lee and Sayeed felt that a unique look was needed to convey a true sense of daily life in a New York housing project. Working on location at the Gowanus Housing Project in Brooklyn (rechristened as the Nelson Mandela Projects in the film) they agreed that the gritty look they sought would be difficult to achieve using today's clean, sharp film stocks, and decided that it was worth the risk to shoot scenes in the projects on 5239. Lee points out that while a few sequences in Steven Soderbergh's recent film *The Underneath* were shot with 5239 and cross-processed, *Clockers* represents the most significant use of this technique in recent memory; the director estimates that approximately three-quarters of the movie was shot on the reversal stock. He admits, however, that the decision gave him a few sleepless nights. "At one point, some experts from Kodak showed up on the set and said, 'We don't know if this negative's going to last.' There was some question about the fixer process, and they wanted us to stop shooting with it. We went ahead anyway, but I did a lot of praying."

The potential problem with the fixing process was solved by Joe Violante, Vice President of Producer Services at Technicolor New York. Violante, a twenty-five-year veteran who had done the cross-processing on Soderbergh's film, was eager to help Sayeed and Lee with their project. "Almost five years ago, Technicolor New York began to experiment with cross-processing the reversal films in a negative bath," he says. "When we first started doing this we were just using stills, and we were working mainly with commercial cinematographers. At first, we didn't have such great success, because the process was cooking the reversal. Slowly but surely, we worked up to 400-, 1,000- and 5,000-foot rolls. Through trial and error, I discovered that I could create a stabilized product by re-fixing the negative. When *Clockers* came along, we felt ready to jump right into it, but we were still very careful. Malik and I personally supervised every frame, and we isolated this film from the others Technicolor was handling at the time.

"As far as the results are concerned, I love the way this film looks," Violante concludes. "I think it's very unique."

Kodak Production Account Executive Mike Brown, who handled the *Clockers* account, adds his own note of caution to anyone who might want to try the cross-processing technique. "Anyone attempting to use such a process on a motion picture should perform extensive testing with the lab, and should also consult Kodak," he says. "The special films used on *Clockers* had to be special-ordered well in advance. Kodak still considers cross-processing to be a highly unconventional approach, so it's better to be safe than sorry."

Looking at the experiment from a historical point of view, Sayeed points out, "Filmmakers were trying this kind of thing all the time in the twenties, thirties and forties, because nothing was set in stone yet about how things should be done. Everybody was using different processes. Still, I did run up against a wall when I first suggested this technique. One big lab, whose name I won't mention, told me, 'No way, never, we can't believe you're going to do this.' But Technicolor New York and Joe V. went the extra mile for me. Some people still think I'm crazy for doing it, but I felt it was the best approach for the story. 5239 was the one stock that was best able to convey the atmosphere of the locations we were using. The standard Eastman negative didn't have the emotional weight that this technique gave us. I saw the film process itself as a metaphor for what exists in the ghetto; you have this really messed-up environment, but there's still a beautiful culture within that environment. Likewise, the 5239 has a completely raw grain structure, but it also has intense, vivid colors. It really records red and purple, so we took advantage of that. In one scene near the end of the film, for example, Spike had practically everyone in the frame dressed in red."

Sayeed admits that the stock presented some photographic challenges. With little under- or overexposure latitude, the cinematographer had to perform extensive tests to zero in on the relatively narrow exposure range. "There were a couple of scary moments, but in general we had no problems," he maintains. "The most difficult situations were strong sunlight and shade. Those are tough situations even if you're shooting normally, but our strategy really made it extreme. I was going for a very naturalistic level of fill light, because I don't like to use fill to the point where it looks like fill. It also helped to try to shoot in confined areas; I didn't want to confine the story, but things got tougher when we had really big shots. I did a lot of exposure pulls on this film, and there were a few times when I made little mistakes. For example, there's a scene in which the two detectives go to arrest Rodney at his store. The shot starts outside, where it's really bright, and then goes into the dark interior. We definitely had to do an exposure pull, but I think it was a little extreme. The street was very hot, but I think I came down a bit too much. This stock did lend itself to exposure pulls, though, because the contrast is so extreme that you can go a little further without seeing a notice-able shift; most of them are invisible."

The filmmakers applied a variety of other stocks as well, depending upon the requirements of a scene. In addition to the 39, Sayeed tapped 5298 for night sequences, 5248 for scenes in the police precinct, and 93 for select shots. He also cross-processed 7251, a 16mm Ektachrome reversal film, for a surreal flashback in which Rodney tells Strike about the first time he killed a man.

To further heighten that sequence's queasy tension, Lee filmed several shots with anamorphic lens. Although *Clockers* was shot in 1.85 to exploit New York's vertical skylines, Lee felt that the subtle use of anamorphic would heighten the "shock value" of certain scenes. He had previously employed this strategy for a twenty-minute uncorrected anamorphic sequence in *Crooklyn,* with highly controversial results; the squeezed images prompted Universal to prepare printed disclaimers at theaters exhibiting the film. Still determined to defend his choice, Lee says, "People had problems with the anamorphic sequence in *Crooklyn,* but in that film I was trying to show the difference between life in the city and life in the suburbs. I wanted to present this distorted suburban world through the eyes of the little girl, Troy, who had grown up in a completely different environment. If I had to do it again, I'd still do it the same way.

"On *Clockers,* we just used anamorphic for very specific shots. For the Rod-ney flashback, we used Clairmont's Swing-and-Tilt lenses in combination with anamorphic, which gave us an unusual perspective. I didn't want to do the whole film in anamorphic, because I don't like going through the correc-tion process."

Sayeed's use of moving streaks of light added to the strange quality of this flashback. "I had two of the electrics hold lights and pan them like search-lights across the actors' faces," he reveals. "We were trying to achieve a voy-euristic point of view. We wanted to show real-life consequences in a very graphic way."

The film's other flashback sequences were shot in equally interesting ways. For scenes detailing Victor's past, Sayeed used an Ektachrome still pho-tography reversal film, 5017 (ASA 64), which Kodak spliced into 1000-foot rolls that would run through an Arri 535. "The pitch worked fine in the Arri camera," says Sayeed. "I knew I could get the look I wanted, but it was a matter of whether the lab would be willing to cross-process the film. We used the Swing-and-Tilt lenses on some of the other flashbacks as well, such as one in which Harvey Keitel appears in another character's flashback."

According to Lee, the idea of physically placing Keitel's character in a small boy's memory of a shooting incident was culled from the classic film *The Boston Strangler,* in which a police investigator revisits the past with serial killer Albert De Salvo (Tony Curtis). "Martin Scorsese is one of the greatest film buffs ever, but after he saw that sequence he got all excited and asked me, 'How did you think of that, Spike?!!' " Lee recalls with a guffaw. "I said, 'Marty, c'mon, it's from *The Boston Strangler.* I was kinda surprised that one slipped by him!"

Lee further enhanced this sequence by employing a trick he has used to great effect in previous films: placing the camera and actors on a moving dolly to create a strange, otherworldly feeling of movement. In one particularly eye-catching shot during the boy's flashback montage, Keitel seems to float along in mid-air as the boy rides his bike. Sayeed explains, "To do that shot, and others like it, we used a plywood sled built by the key grip, Bobby Andres. It's a platform setup made out of Speedrail, plywood, twenty-foot lengths of black pipe and some wheels. You run two pieces of pipe, which connect together with a few twists of an Allen wrench. The pipes are on top of wooden planks, and the sled goes on top of the pipes. It's very, very smooth, and you can make it run as far as you want by adding more pipe. You can even put another dolly on top of it; it's big enough to handle two Pee-Wees. And if you want the platform to be bigger, you just add planks. For the bike scene, we mounted the bike and lights on top of it and put the camera on sticks."

Commenting on his frequent use of such dolly shots, which can be also seen in *Mo' Better Blues, Jungle Fever* and *Malcolm X,* Lee states, "It's just a different way of having characters move. I think the best application of this technique prior to *Clockers* occurs in *Malcolm X,* during the scene in which Malcolm is on his way to the Audubon Ballroom. I did research and found out that Malcolm seemed to know he was going to be assassinated that day. The dolly technique really fit in with the mood of that scene; it created a weird sense of disorientation."

Lee and his team used a variety of methods to add movement to other scenes. A Steadicam, operated by John Corso, was used several times to follow Strike's movements, and the film is bookended by dramatic Louma Crane shots—an establishing overview of the convenience store, and a climactic shot of a slain clocker. For an early sequence that tracks the movements of the clockers on their daily routine, the filmmakers covered the action with long lenses, in a shaky style that resembles police surveillance. "We shot that scene with three cameras," notes Sayeed. "We positioned ourselves as outsiders peeping in. To get the look we wanted, we did a lot of rack-focusing, hand-zooming and swish-panning."

The lively camerawork in Lee's films is not without a philosophical basis. Practical concerns always come into play, but the director maintains that modern times call for modern methods. "I want vibrant energy, movement and life in my films," he explains. "Shooting any other way, for me, is too much like television. It costs $7.50 to see a movie today, plus extra for parking, popcorn and soda. If you don't give the audience something interesting to watch, they're going to stay right on that sofa at home, where they have 150 channels to choose from."

The advantages of this forward-thinking stance are evident throughout *Clockers,* even during exchanges of dialogue. Rather than simply ping-ponging between talking heads, Lee often incorporates movement into what would otherwise be standard setups. A good example from *Clockers* is a conversation between Klein and Strike, which takes place on a pancake-shaped concrete platform in a neighborhood park. As Klein tightens the screws on Strike, trying to coerce a confession, the camera revolves around them, capturing the essence of their cat-and-mouse relationship. "As soon as I saw that big pancake, I pulled out the circular dolly tracks," Lee notes with a chuckle.

The director's fondness for dialogue led him to shoot most of the film with two cameras running simultaneously—the Arri 535 and a Moviecam Compact. "It can be a drag shooting two people talking, and a lot of times actors give their best performances when they're reading their lines offscreen," he says. "Actors love it when you use two cameras, because they don't have to wait for the turnaround."

Sayeed agrees that the two-camera setup preserves the spontaneity of performances, but he notes that this technique does come with a price. "The cameras are usually pointed almost directly at each other, so the optimum light placement is always in the other camera's shot," he points out. "It's a major challenge to light both angles effectively."

Although Lee has been faithful to Arri since his student days at New York University, Sayeed was interested in testing out the Moviecam unit. "Spike has used Arris since his earliest film, *Joe's Bed-Stuy Barbershop,* and he's got a

Tracy Camilla Johns and Spike Lee, *She's Gotta Have It*, 1986

Giancarlo Esposito and Spike Lee, *School Daze*, 1988

Spike Lee and Danny Aiello, *Do the Right Thing*, 1989

Denzel Washington and Spike Lee, *Mo' Better Blues*, 1990

Wesley Snipes, Veronica Webb, Spike Lee, and Annabella Sciorra, *Jungle Fever*, 1991

Denzel Washington, *Malcolm X*, 1992

Alfre Woodard and Delroy Lindo, *Crooklyn*, 1994

Harvey Keitel and Mekhi Phifer, *Clockers*, 1995 (Photo: David Lee)

Theresa Randle and Isaiah Washington,
Girl 6, 1996

(Front row, left to right) Andre Braugher, Hill Harper, Hosea Brown III,
DeAundre Bonds, Charles Dutton, Steve White; (back row, left to right)
Gabriel Casseus, Thomas Jefferson Byrd, Ossie Davis, Isaiah Washington,
Roger Guenveur Smith, Harry Lennix, and Bernie Mac, *Get on the Bus*, 1996

Bebe Neuwirth and John Leguizamo, *Summer of Sam*, 1999
(Photo: David Lee)

John Leguizamo and Adrien Brody, *Summer of Sam*, 1999
(Photo: David Lee)

Jada Pinkett Smith and Damon Wayans, *Bamboozled*, 2000 (Photo: David Lee)

good relationship with the company," Sayeed notes. "That was fine with me, because the Arri 535 is an excellent camera. But I also wanted to try the Moviecam, because it's lightweight and very versatile. I knew we were going to be doing some handheld in this movie, and I thought the Moviecam would be easier on the operator, Gary McCloud. It's the camera of choice for Steadicam operators. It's also versatile in terms of where you can put the magazine; you can configure it so it's much smaller than the 535.

"You can also do speed changes with the Moviecam, and we did one for the scene near the end of the film in which Strike is trying to avoid a confrontation with Errol, Rodney's henchman. We shot Mekhi Phifer on our sled setup in slow-motion as he walked along in the park, and we switched to real-time after he spotted Errol and tried to hide by a fence. It was subtle, but it looks pretty good. We also used a speed change for the flashback where Victor is working at a burger joint."

Except for a few brief sequences, Sayeed kept his lenses unfiltered throughout the shoot. "Most of the film was shot with Zeiss Superspeeds, mainly primes. We had an Angenieux 25-250, but we didn't use it very much. We also used 300, 400 and 600mm Nikkor lenses. Our standard lens was a Zeiss 25mm prime. I like being at 35 for normal shots, but Spike prefers to go a little wider at 25. Another lens I like is the 65. For slightly wider close-ups we used the 65 or an 85, and for extreme close-ups we used a 135."

One particularly eye-catching shot was executed with the help of a Zeiss macro lens. As detective Klein grills Strike in an interrogation room at the police precinct, the filmmakers cut to a giant closeup of Keitel's eyeball, which engulfs Strike's reflection. "The thing about the macro lens is that once you get in really tight, it stops down automatically, because there's a macro exposure compensation," Sayeed notes. "You really have to pump in the light, so it was blazing in that small room. The lights were on stands that were placed outside the curvature of the reflection in Harvey's eye, which became almost like a fisheye lens; it took in almost everything in the room."

During the film's other interrogation sequences, Sayeed and Lee paid homage to Robert Richardson by emulating the hot, haloed look he pioneered in the Oliver Stone film *JFK*. To create the "Richardson aura" around the actors, Sayeed loaded up the ceiling of the interrogation room with HMIs, supplementing the look with Kinoflos placed on the floor. He also added a Fogal net to the lens for a touch of filtration. "It was unbelievably hot in there; everyone was sweating," he recalls. "It doesn't look that hot on film, because of all the blue-grey metal in the room, which lent everything a cool feel. But the heat was so intense that Harvey's hair started smoking! I had told the makeup department not to put any grease in his hair but they did, and his head had curls of smoke coming off it. I wasn't trying to burn anybody, but I thought the look was appropriate for those scenes. We were shooting with the 5239, and it really got the feel I was after. We bounced the lights off some boards I placed on the interrogation table. I was getting so much ambient light off the bounce that I didn't need to add anything to the actors' faces."

The interesting qualities of the 5239 stock are especially apparent during one of the interrogation scenes, in which Klein questions a young boy about his role in a shooting, under the watchful eye of Andre, a neighborhood cop intent on keeping the drug trade in check. Sayeed split his lighting in the scene, creating a strange, almost matte-like separation between the foreground characters and the cop in the background. "The 5239 has some really interesting densities," the cinematographer attests. "You can get different tones and contrasts based on your exposure. With the 5239, there are some places underneath the 18 percent mid-range where you can get some unique tones. In the scene involving Andre, the lighting was a little bit different on him—a little bit 'down'—and it produced that odd look of separation."

Elsewhere in the film, Sayeed's approach was dictated by the desire to shoot the locations as naturalistically as possible. Most of the film's night scenes, for example, were shot without the help of any movie lights. "A lot of our setups made use of existing practical lights—even some of the interiors, such as the bar where Strike and Victor meet early on in the film. For street scenes at night, I had the art department and the electrical crew change a lot of the bulbs in the storefronts to high-output fluorescents. That approach felt more appropriate to me than just washing the entire street with Muscos. Kodak's 5298 stock helped a lot in those situations, because it's got incredible latitude. I actually pushed most of the night stuff one stop; I could even push it two stops without it breaking up."

For a scene in which a detective on drug detail confronts Strike in the park at night, Sayeed used a combination of sodium-vapor and mercury-vapor lights to augment the existing fixtures. "The sodium lights are not high-output, but with the 98, it was the most appropriate strategy," he says. "Mercury-vapor lights go green on film; it's even slightly apparent to the naked eye. We played with the fact that the film stock was not going to compensate for the green content in these gaseous-output lights. We put a cool white fluorescent tube in the background and just let it go. We did that in a number of other scenes as well, just to add some visual pop. Robert Richardson did a similar thing for the supermarket sequence in *Natural Born Killers*. He used a more neon green, while we were trying for a blue-green. If you use an 85 [filter] and a cool white light with tungsten-based film—or if you put an 85 on the lights—it will go straight green. But if you take the 85 off and let the cool white go, it will go bluish green.

"We wanted to take a realistic approach to the lighting of the film," he reiterates. "Any expressionistic or interpretive elements were done with camera movement or the use of film stocks."

With *Clockers* at the top of his resumé, Sayeed has shown that he is a young cameraman to watch. He and Lee recently completed principal photography on their second collaboration, *Girl 6*, which was shot partially with Sony digital cameras. Summing up his feelings about the need for experimentation in the cinematic art, Sayeed declares, "The types of things we did on *Clockers*, and which Robert Richardson has been doing in the past few years, are just the tip of the iceberg; there's a world of room in terms of playing with stocks and even digitally manipulating tone, contrast and texture. If the labs are willing to push the envelope, there's no limit to what you can do. It's a very detailed process, but it is possible. I think there are a lot of stories that could be told in these different textures."

Spike Speaks

ALAN FRUTKIN / 1995

MENTION SPIKE LEE, and you're bound to get a heated response. After all, one of Lee's great talents is stirring up controversy. He's traded barbs with gays, women, and Jews over their depictions in various of his eight films. Still, few dispute his artistic gifts. Lee's latest film, *Clockers*—the rough tale of a young Brooklyn drug dealer, or "clocker"—has been hailed as his finest. Among the film's urban nightmares is AIDS—through the HIV-positive, drug-addicted thug featured in the story is not gay.

You'd be hard-pressed to find more than a handful of gay and lesbian characters in Lee's entire oeuvre. What references to gays there are in his films have been insulting—a fact not lost on gay media watchdogs. "It's referring to us as objects of derision without showing who we really are," says Donald Suggs, a spokesman for the Gay and Lesbian Alliance Against Defamation. "When I see a Spike Lee movie, I see a black community I can relate to as an African-American. But I don't see the personal contributions lesbian and gay people make to that community."

But is Spike Lee homophobic? In his first conversatoin with *The Advocate*, the director answers in typically confrontational style.

AF: *In* Clockers *the kids who are working the street, the clockers, call the homicide detectives "homo-cide." Does your use of the words* homo *and* faggot *in your films contribute to homophobia?*

S L: No. What gets me is, have you ever called up Martin Scorsese and asked him how many times he uses the fucking word *nigger?* In *Mean Streets,* in *GoodFellas,* in *Raging Bull?* This is the way these characters speak. Because I use the words *faggot* and *homo,* people try to pin me as fucking homophobic, and that's bullshit. If homosexuals don't think people call them "faggots" and "homos," then they're stupid.

A F: *Well—*
S L: Wait a fucking minute. Has anybody ever gone to Quentin Tarantino and asked him how many times he uses the fucking word *nigger* in *True Romance, Reservoir Dogs,* and *Pulp Fiction?* He uses the word, and nobody says a motherfucking thing about it.

A F: *I understand that—*
S L: You don't understand, because I'm always getting this shit from the homosexual community—that I'm homophobic. Because I have a character in a movie say "faggot," that means that automatically Spike Lee is homo-phobic, and I'm sick of this fucking bullshit. Why are gays always able to make that distinction with Martin Scorsese—and they don't make it with me?

A F: *When the same respect black people have struggled for is not extended to our community, it takes us by surprise. You can see that, right?*
S L: Yeah, I could see that taking you by surprise. I can see that, sure.

A F: *So I think that's one of the reasons why you're singled out and not Scorsese.*
S L: You're saying, Scorsese's white, so he doesn't know better? But, Spike, you're black, so you should know better? I'm not buying that. I know every-body looks after their own, but you just can't talk about being antigay and then dismiss racism.

A F: *Do you think Scorsese's racist?*
S L: No, because I know the man. He grew up in Little Italy, and I grew up in Brooklyn. A lot of my high school classmates were from Bensonhurst, and that's the way those guys speak. You're telling me in order not to offend black people, Scorsese shouldn't have his characters say "nigger"?

AF: *I'm not saying that.*

SL: No, I'm asking you a question. Should he not use those words because it might offend black people?

AF: *I don't think I can speak—*

SL: No, answer the question. Why can't you answer that question?

AF: *I can't speak for the black community. If people in the black community aren't offended by that, that's their business.*

SL: Their offense is not toward Scorsese. Their offense is toward people who think like that. People have to understand that just because you have a character say a word, that is not necessarily the view of the director.

AF: *But we should take offense at your characters who represent homophobic members of the black community?*

SL: Yeah. Sure.

AF: *Would you ever make that point in a film—that it is offensive to gay people?*

SL: I don't do that. I can't tell audiences how to feel.

AF: *But so much of your work is political and does attempt to fight racism. Yet you've never addressed homophobia.*

SL: Well, it hasn't happened yet.

AF: *Is it something you would avoid?*

SL: No, I don't think I'd avoid it.

AF: *Would you be opposed to creating a positive gay character in a movie?*

SL: No, I'm not opposed. If you look at *Clockers,* it's indicative of how I work—where people are good and bad.

AF: *Let's discuss gay images in your films. In* She's Gotta Have It, *Nola Darling is pursued by her lesbian friend, Opal, who's a sort of sexual predator.*

SL: We weren't trying to make Opal be the evil lesbian. We just wanted to show that Nola wore her sexuality on her sleeve and that it was a turn-on to men and to women. Opal was just doing what the men were doing.

A F : *In your second film,* School Daze, *a rival fraternity ridicules the Gamma Phi Gammas by calling them fags.*

S L : That movie is about my four years at Morehouse College. When I went to school, for good or worse, homosexuals were ridiculed. Morehouse has always had a large gay presence, it being a predominantly black-male school. Because of that, I think homophobia is probably bigger there than at a coed school. By showing it I don't think I'm endorsing it. It's a reality. The gay community should know African-Americans are more homophobic than anybody.

A F : *Why do you say that?*

S L : For the most part we're very conservative, and we still have a very strong religious background. Because we still have a strong stense of the black church, homosexuality is frowned upon. That's just my sense.

A F : *With science indicating that homosexuality is not a choice but a result of genetics, will the black community change the way it views the gay community?*

S L : It might change over the years, but in my opinion African-Americans are probably more homophobic than other groups. As time goes on, I think African-Americans will catch up to the rest of white America as far as attitudes on homosexuality.

A F : *Is that something you might address in future films?*

S L : I don't know that I'm capable of doing it because I don't think I have the knowledge. Let some gay filmmaker—an African-American gay filmmaker—step up and do that. They would be more knowledgeable on the subject.

A F : *For the record, what do you think of homosexuality?*

S L : I think people are free to pursue whatever they want to.

Interview with Spike Lee

CHARLIE ROSE/1996

CHARLIE ROSE: *This summer it will be ten years since the release of Spike Lee's feature debut,* She's Gotta Have It. *His latest film,* Girl 6, *is the first time he has returned to a female-centered story. It is a story sure to inspire as much discussion as any of his previous works. The film follows an aspiring actress who is down on her luck and becomes a phone sex operator in order to pay her bills. As she becomes immersed in the fantasy world, she learns more about her acting skills and her self-image than she ever did with any acting job. Joining me now to talk about movies and phone sex and other things is Spike Lee, filmmaker. Welcome.*

SPIKE LEE: How you doing?

CHARLIE ROSE: *I'm doing good. It's good to have you here.*

SPIKE LEE: Glad to be here.

CHARLIE ROSE: *You're on your way to watch the Knicks, and we'll talk about that later. Reggie [Miller]. You like Reggie, don't you?*

SPIKE LEE: Yeah, I like him.

CHARLIE ROSE: *Yeah. Even though . . . a little . . .*

SPIKE LEE: That got blown out of proportion. We like each other.

CHARLIE ROSE: Girl 6.

SPIKE LEE: The new movie, number nine.

From *The Charlie Rose Show*, New York, New York. 20 March 1996. Published by permission of Rose Communications.

CHARLIE ROSE: *Number nine meaning what?*
SPIKE LEE: The ninth film I've done.

CHARLIE ROSE: *Oh, the ninth film.*
SPIKE LEE: No, the Beatles song.

CHARLIE ROSE: *The notion of you returning to a movie in which the central character is a woman: any significance in that?*
SPIKE LEE: We thought it was time. Ten years has been long enough if you don't count *Crooklyn*, where the lead character was a girl, ten years old. So we felt that—this August, it'll be ten years since we did *She's Gotta Have It*—it was time to go back and try to do something else where the lead was a female.

CHARLIE ROSE: *Where did the story come from?*
SPIKE LEE: Well, the story really came from thinking about *She's Gotta Have It,* and how in that film Nola Darling has three lovers at the same time. Man, people thought that was cute and stuff like that, but that was before AIDS, and now ten years later, that kind of conduct or behavior, is dangerous. And ten years ago the phone sex business was not a multi–billion dollar industry, you see. So, [with] these two things, it's really a look at how things have changed in the past ten years.

CHARLIE ROSE: *And why does she get involved in phone sex, your character?*
SPIKE LEE: Why? Quick money. She's a starving actress living in New York, and like most starving actors here in the city, they feel that if they can get to Los Angeles, if they can just get to Hollywood.

CHARLIE ROSE: *Get the break, they'll be a star.*
SPIKE LEE: Get the break, they'll be a star. And she needs this quick cash to finance the trip to Hollywood.

CHARLIE ROSE: *Who's the lead actress?*
SPIKE LEE: Theresa Randle. Theresa's a very fine actress, was in two other of my films, *Jungle Fever* and *Malcolm X*. I'm in the film, also, and I play her neighbor and confidant.

CHARLIE ROSE: *Oh, imagine my surprise!*

SPIKE LEE: I have dreams of my own. I'm a sports memorabilia collector, and so I'm getting out of why she has forsaken her acting career to do this phone bone stuff, as I say.

CHARLIE ROSE: *Why do you put yourself in your films?*

SPIKE LEE: Well, the very simple reason is that the people who do like my films, like to see me in them.

CHARLIE ROSE: *This is an Alfred Hitchcock kind of thing?*

SPIKE LEE: No, because I do more than cameos.

CHARLIE ROSE: *I know you do, but it's the idea that people always looked for him to be in his films even though it was a cameo.*

SPIKE LEE: Yeah. The first film, *She's Gotta Have It,* the only reason I was in that film playing Mars Blackmon was because we couldn't afford to pay anybody else, and Nike liked it enough to pair me and Michael Jordan together, so that's where it started.

CHARLIE ROSE: *You like it?*

SPIKE LEE: No. I don't like acting.

CHARLIE ROSE: *You don't. Why not?*

SPIKE LEE: It's rough. It's very hard to be a good actor, and I think what I do is limited, so I just try to do my little part and get out of the way and let the great actors like Denzel, Wesley, Anthony Quinn, John Turturro, Danny Aiello, people like that, Ossie Davis . . .

CHARLIE ROSE: *Yeah, but this is a principal character in this film.*

SPIKE LEE: Well, not really, Charlie.

CHARLIE ROSE: *No, it is. Come on.*

SPIKE LEE: No, really. This is a star vehicle for Theresa Randle and so Isaiah, Isaiah Washington, who plays her ex-husband . . .

CHARLIE ROSE: *Who's a kleptomaniac.*

SPIKE LEE: Yes. We're supporting players to her star part.

CHARLIE ROSE: *You've got a lot of roles by friends of yours, I assume. Madonna plays a little cameo role.*
SPIKE LEE: Madonna, John Turturro, Ron Silver, Naomi Campbell, Peter Berg, Aiello . . .

CHARLIE ROSE: *And Quentin Tarantino.*
SPIKE LEE: Quentin Tarantino plays the hottest director in Hollywood.

CHARLIE ROSE: *And there's a great scene in which she comes in, and he asks her to . . .*
SPIKE LEE: Yeah, the movie opens with the audition, where he's casting actors for the greatest African-American romance ever filmed to be directed by him, and he asks her to take off her top. She does it, but she leaves in a huff.

CHARLIE ROSE: *Yeah. And then later at the end of the movie . . . Are we giving the movie away if we come all the way back?*
SPIKE LEE: Yes.

CHARLIE ROSE: *Okay, let's stay away from that then.*
SPIKE LEE: One of Girl 6's problems is that a lot of times she has difficulty distinguishing reality from fantasy.

CHARLIE ROSE: *Said another way—I mean, I don't want to prompt the great director, but said another way is that she gets into the role.*
SPIKE LEE: Well . . .

CHARLIE ROSE: *Let me talk about this controversy that was on the cover of* People *magazine. Tell me about that.*
SPIKE LEE: Well, *People* magazine chose a very opportune time to come out with this article about how black people, minorities, are not really represented in the film industry. And the timing was good because the Academy Awards are Monday night, and this year, there were 166 nominees, and only one of those nominees is an African-American. No Latinos, no Native Americans.

CHARLIE ROSE: *Why do you think that is?*

SPIKE LEE: I think that those numbers really reflect the membership of the people who vote, and I think that, to be honest, we're treated as second class citizens.

CHARLIE ROSE: *Who should have been nominated but wasn't?*
SPIKE LEE: Well, I think Don Cheadle for his performance in *Devil in a Blue Dress,* Delroy Lindo for *Clockers.* I think that "Babyface" [Edmonds] should have been nominated for best song by Whitney [Houston] and . . .

CHARLIE ROSE: *"Waiting . . ."?*
SPIKE LEE: Yeah, for "Waiting to Exhale." You know, there's a lot of technical stuff, too, but I guess we're not talented enough to get these nominations.

CHARLIE ROSE: *That's not what you think.*
SPIKE LEE: No. I believe that. We just don't have the talent, Charlie.

CHARLIE ROSE: Jackie Robinson, *a movie that you very much want to make.*
SPIKE LEE: Yes. We've been working on this for the last two years, and we had a development deal with Ted Turner, Turner Pictures, and they put it in turnaround, so they won't be making it, but hopefully, we will be able to find somebody to spend the necessary amount of money to make this film correctly.

CHARLIE ROSE: *Forty million dollars.*
SPIKE LEE: No, no. We do it for thirty-five, and that's the average budget for a Hollywood film today.

CHARLIE ROSE: *Okay, here's what somebody told me. They said Spike said he could make* Malcolm X *for less than he could, and he knew that but he wanted to get the money in order to make the movie.*
SPIKE LEE: First. Who said I could have made it for less?

CHARLIE ROSE: *No, [they] said that you knew it was going to take more than twenty-five million to make it, but you only said twenty-five million because you didn't think you could get that much money to make it.*

SPIKE LEE: No. that's not true, Charlie. Oh, we told Warner Brothers from the very beginning that . . .

CHARLIE ROSE: *Forty million?*
SPIKE LEE: No. We told them it was going to cost thirty-three, what it actually cost. And they said they were only going to give us twenty domestically, and they said you could sell the foreign rights, and we sold the foreign rights to Largo [International, Inc.] for eight. So we were still $5 million short.

CHARLIE ROSE: *Five million dollars short. So you went out and raised it from Oprah and Bill Cosby, and people like that.*
SPIKE LEE: They got some, and then finally Warner Brothers kicked in with the rest of the money. I've always said from the get go that it was going to cost thirty-three.

CHARLIE ROSE: *So you didn't deflate what it was going to cost in order to make sure everybody was on board because this was a movie you wanted to make, and you realized you can't do that the second time?*
SPIKE LEE: Cannot do that. I was surprised—I was telling them it would cost thirty-three, and I was surprised that the bond company and Warner Brothers and Largo signed up on the budget knowing I was saying it was going to cost thirty-three from the beginning.

CHARLIE ROSE: *The reason you can't raise $35 million to make a movie at a very appropriate time about Jackie Robinson would be, what, some anniversary of his?*
SPIKE LEE: Ninety-seven will be the fiftieth anniversary of Jackie breaking the color barrier.

CHARLIE ROSE: *And you can't raise $35 million to make that film.*
SPIKE LEE: Not now.

CHARLIE ROSE: *Turner was going to do it, and then they backed down.*
SPIKE LEE: For whatever reason, they said they just don't feel comfortable.

CHARLIE ROSE: *What did they say?*
SPIKE LEE: They don't want to make the movie.

CHARLIE ROSE: *Okay, fine. Then, you said, "Why?" and they said what?*
SPIKE LEE: No. Because a lot of times . . .

CHARLIE ROSE: *So, pulling stuff out of you is a little hard for me here.*
SPIKE LEE: I'm really telling you. I mean, they don't want to tell me that the script sucks because then they want to work with me somewhere down the line. This is very political. So they just don't want to make it. It's as simple as that.

CHARLIE ROSE: *And because obviously they didn't believe it was box office?*
SPIKE LEE: I guess they considered this a black baseball film, and . . .

CHARLIE ROSE: *And you considered it what?*
SPIKE LEE: I consider this a great American story.

CHARLIE ROSE: *Will it get made?*
SPIKE LEE: Yes.

CHARLIE ROSE: *You'll get the money.*
SPIKE LEE: We'll get the money.

CHARLIE ROSE: *And will you make it by 1997?*
SPIKE LEE: No. that's not going to happen, but we'll get the film made. Marvin Worth, the man who produced *Malcolm X*, it took him twenty years to try to get that film made. So, I'm not crying about it because this is the first time since I've been a filmmaker I've not got a film made that I wanted to make. So I've been very lucky, and we're on a roll. And it didn't work on Jackie Robinson, but this is the first time it's ever happened.

CHARLIE ROSE: *The Knickerbockers. What do you think about them this year?*
SPIKE LEE: Well, I was very happy when—on national television—the Knicks creamed the Bulls.

CHARLIE ROSE: *And your pal, Michael [Jordan].*
SPIKE LEE: My pal Michael, and I was glad that the Artist Known as Prince and his wife [Mayte Garcia] were my guests at that game.

CHARLIE ROSE: *Now, he does the sound. Does he do the music?*
SPIKE LEE: Yeah. He did all the music for *Girl 6.* The Knicks are going to beat Indiana tonight, and tomorrow my wife and I will be going to Chicago.

CHARLIE ROSE: *To watch them beat the Bulls.*
SPIKE LEE: They'll be without Scottie Pippen.

CHARLIE ROSE: *They'll be without Pippen and Rodman.*
SPIKE LEE: Yeah, both of them.

CHARLIE ROSE: *Well, I guess they could do it then.*
SPIKE LEE: Well, I don't know. Michael might pick up the slack so it's not going to be easy.

CHARLIE ROSE: *That's a lot of slack to pick up. What do you think about the new Knicks with the new coach [Jeff Van Gundy]?*
SPIKE LEE: Oh, I'm ready, you know. For a while, things looked very bleak, but I think that [Dave] Checketts and Ernie Grunfeld did the right thing by . . .

CHARLIE ROSE: *Getting rid of [Pat] Nelson.*
SPIKE LEE: Yeah. He had to go.

CHARLIE ROSE: *Why? The chemistry wasn't right with the players?*
SPIKE LEE: It wasn't right. And, you know, if the coach insults the main man, I mean, you have to be more . . .

CHARLIE ROSE: *Patrick [Ewing] being the main man.*
SPIKE LEE: Yeah. You have to be very diplomatic. I mean, if the coach doesn't have the main man, doesn't have his confidence, and the other players follow it up, you've lost the team.

CHARLIE ROSE: *Speaking of main men, how about John Thompson down at Georgetown Hoyas?*

SPIKE LEE: Yes. The boys love John Thompson, and I did a . . .

CHARLIE ROSE: *An HBO special . . .*
SPIKE LEE: *Real Sports . . .*

CHARLIE ROSE: *The sports magazine profile was terrific.*
SPIKE LEE: Yeah, I did that. That was fun.

CHARLIE ROSE: *You enjoyed doing that?*
SPIKE LEE: Very much. I'm going to do a couple more for them, and I'm looking forward to going down to Atlanta Saturday. My grandma lives in Atlanta. She's ninety-one. Spend the day with her, go to the Georgia Super-dome.

CHARLIE ROSE: *This is your dad's mother or your mother's mother?*
SPIKE LEE: My mother's mother. And going to see what really should be a national championship team. Georgetown against UMass. They both win Thursday night.

CHARLIE ROSE: *Can Georgetown beat UMass?*
SPIKE LEE: Yes.

CHARLIE ROSE: *Can Georgetown win it all?*
SPIKE LEE: Yes.

CHARLIE ROSE: *Because Allen Iverson, the MVP.*
SPIKE LEE: He will be if they win. It's going to take him playing like that, playing like an MVP, for Georgetown to win, and I hope they'll make it back to the Meadowlands.

CHARLIE ROSE: *What's next for you?*
SPIKE LEE: Well, I'm doing a film, Charlie. We start shooting April first.

CHARLIE ROSE: *On?*
SPIKE LEE: It's called *Get on the Bus,* and the film is about the Million Man March. It's about the journey of twenty African-American men who board a bus in Los Angeles and make the cross country trip to D.C. for the March,

and so, in seventy-two hours, you get to know every one of these guys on the bus and all the specific reasons why they're making this trip.

CHARLIE ROSE: *Did that Million Man March speak to you?*
SPIKE LEE: Yes. Yes, it did. You know Jesse [Jackson] wants to boycott . . .

CHARLIE ROSE: *He's going to protest out of the Oscars.*
SPIKE LEE: Yeah.

CHARLIE ROSE: *Why aren't you out there on the line with him?*
SPIKE LEE: I am Jesse's full support. But first of all, I can't be out there because it makes me look like sour grapes: I'm just out there because I didn't get nominated. But I think what's even better is that this film is being financed totally by fifteen African-American men: Johnnie Cochran, Bob . . .

CHARLIE ROSE: *Wesley Snipes.*
SPIKE LEE: Wesley Snipes, Danny Glover, Bob Johnson, who owns BET, Norm, Charles Smith, now of the San Antonio Spurs . . .

CHARLIE ROSE: *Late of the Knicks.*
SPIKE LEE: Knicks. All of us have come together and financed this film.

CHARLIE ROSE: *How about Michael Jordan?*
SPIKE LEE: Well, maybe he'll come in the next film. But Columbia Pictures picked up the distribution. And the film is going to come out October 16th, the one year anniversary of the March.

CHARLIE ROSE: *You are how old*
SPIKE LEE: Thirty-nine today.

CHARLIE ROSE: *Today's your birthday.*
SPIKE LEE: Yes. Thirty-nine.

CHARLIE ROSE: *How do you feel about thirty-nine?*
SPIKE LEE: You know, it's really no big thing, to be honest. I mean, maybe it'll hit me next year, the big 4-0. But you know, I'm getting ready to go to the game now to see the Knicks when they win.

CHARLIE ROSE: *Is your wife going to the game tonight?*
SPIKE LEE: Yes, she'll be right there with me.

CHARLIE ROSE: *Your wife is a young lawyer from Washington you met at Georgetown. Was she at Georgetown?*
SPIKE LEE: No. She was at UVA.

CHARLIE ROSE: *Good luck, my friend. Happy birthday.*
SPIKE LEE: Thank you.

CHARLIE ROSE: *Great to see you, as always.*

The Demystification of Spike Lee

ERICH LEON HARRIS / 1997

STARTING IN 1986 WITH THE release of *She's Gotta Have It,*
Spike Lee has made it his mission to provide work and apprenticeship to
young African-Americans trying to break into Hollywood, a process he calls
the "demystification of film." Yet over the course of the decade he's spent
deconstructing filmmaking myths, the press has gone about its own business, that of constructing a persona of near-mythic dimensions for Spike Lee
the man. Angry. Brilliant. Controversial. Outspoken. Maverick. Racist. These
are the words one encounters over and over again when reading about Lee.
Often left out of the discussion is the fact that he has become one of America's most gifted and prolific filmmakers.

On the day we met I found him to be quiet, unassuming, thoughtful, yet
somewhat guarded. Though his films are frequently peppered with exple-
tives, he uses none in conversation. In his spacious Brooklyn, NY offices our
conversation initially focused on his substantial body of work. But soon the
discussion extended to his persona, the press, and the future of African-
American cinema.

Published in *MovieMaker* 24 (March 1997). Reprinted by permission of *MovieMaker* (310) 234-
9234. This note, by Timothy Rhys, the Editor and Publisher of *MovieMaker,* appeared in the
Fall 2000 edition of *MovieMaker:* "On the morning of July 5, 2000, longtime staff writer and
actor Erich Leon Harris left his LA home on his way to an audition. Details are sketchy, but
he was evidently approached by a stranger and, in what may have been a robbery attempt,
was shot in the head and killed. Just like that. Gone forever."

ERICH LEON HARRIS (ELH): Get on the Bus *was your tenth film in ten years. What was it about this project that made you come on board?*
SPIKE LEE (SL) Bill Borden and Guy Rosenbush came up with the concept, and they got Rueben Cannon aboard, then the three of them called me. When they told me this story about these men on a bus going from L.A. to D.C. on the way to the Million Man March, it was intriguing. At the same time, I knew that we could not recreate the march. We felt that the journey was in a lot of ways more important than the destination, because everyone had seen the march on TV. The drama would come from what happens to this unique mix of individuals, this diversity of men who we feel represent African-Americans at this time. I still think that a lot of people think we're this monolithic group, but we chose to show this isn't the case.

ELH: *We see the breaking up and coming to terms of a gay relationship, and the mending of a relationship between an absent father and his son, to name just some of the characters. How important is it to you for voices like these to resonate through your film?*
SL: It's important that we try to be truthful. And we wanted everybody to have their say on this bus, because in a lot of ways each person has to stand for some ideology or some aspect of African-American men.

ELH: *Reggie Blythewood's screenplay was strong and complex, yet I understand that it came together very quickly.*
SL: Reggie has a TV background. He's the head writer on *New York Undercover.* I had worked with Reggie before. He had written a script for me that didn't get produced—but not because of the script; he's a fine writer. We needed someone with talent, but also someone who could really crank it out, and Reggie was the one who did that.

ELH: *Xavier, the UCLA film student, was played by Hill Harper. Manohla Dargis of the* LA Weekly *drew parallels between that character and yourself. Was that your intent?*
SL: No! It had nothing to do with me. She's off base. The line where Charles Dutton's character calls him Spike Lee, Jr. was something that Charles improvised. The line was funny, so we kept it in. The reason we had Xavier on the bus was because if he was a filmmaker and was shooting video, we could use the footage that he's shooting to give the film a different texture or look.

Also, since he's supposed to be doing a documentary, he can ask the guys directly why they are going to the march, and they can answer to the camera. To say that I was trying to hype myself up is just off base.

E L H :   *One thing I did notice was the development of Xavier's camerawork. At the beginning of the story it was all over the place, but by the end he was lining up his shots a lot better. He was developing his eye.*
S L :   That actually happened because the [video] you see in the film is stuff that Hill actually shot himself while we were shooting the movie. As we got further and further into the production, his operating got better.

E L H :   *Was this the first time you shot with Super 16?*
S L :   No, *She's Gotta Have It,* my very first film, was shot in Super 16. Duart Labs did the blowup for both. I think that only a trained eye could tell that it wasn't originally shot on 35 mm.

E L H :   *What was it like shooting in such a confined space?*
S L :   It was very difficult. A large part of the film was actually shot on that bus while it was moving. The small area was one of the reasons we elected to shoot with Super 16. I like to shoot two cameras at a time, but with two 35mm cameras in that space we would have been straining our necks. Super 16 gave us a lot more flexibility, and we wanted to experiment with a cinema verité style anyway. A lot of this film was shot hand-held, so when you add it up, it makes sense to go Super 16. The cameras were lighter.

E L H :   *There were a couple of sequences where the image looked grainy and almost sepia-toned.*
S L :   What we did there was to go to a different stock, a color-reversal stock. Then we did a cross-processing. The first time you see it is when the bus breaks down. We just felt that at certain times, when they get off of the bus, we wanted a different look. As if there was one world inside the bus and another outside.

E L H :   *One of my favorite sequences comes when De'aundre Bonds, who plays the estranged and shackled son, tries to escape into the woods. The sequence is backlit with smoke, and is very beautiful.*

SL: Elliot Davis did a very good job shooting this film, especially since he only had about two weeks of pre-production time.

ELH: *This whole effort was, in many ways, a return to your earlier way of shooting. With all of the budgetary and time constraints, did you expect it to be more or less difficult than it was?*

SL: I knew that it would be hard, but any film is hard. We had a certain amount of days to shoot, so we just had to get our pages every single day. The biggest problem was trying to get the same caliber of performance in such a short shooting schedule, because even though the film had a low budget we didn't want the acting to look that way. Everyone's aspirations were high in spite of the budget.

ELH: *This was the first time you got to work with Charles Dutton. How was that experience?*

SL: Charles and I have known each other for a long time. I saw him in *Ma Rainey's Black Bottom.* We've always talked about working together, but this was the first time that things clicked.

ELH: *You have a talent for finding brand new people that you may even have to Taft-Hartley, then bringing them together with talents like Ossie Davis and Charles Dutton. Is that by design?*

SL: I think that each film dictates who should be cast. But at the same time, I think about casting movies the same way the great General Managers think when they put together a ball club. You have to have the right mix of youth and experience, because the two feed off of each other and enhance each other. If you go too young, that could be too much like school where you have to learn too much on the job. If you use veterans all the time, they could be too stodgy or set in their ways.

ELH: *Who surprised you in the cast?*

SL: The only person who really surprised me was De'aundre. I had worked with him before (as executive producer on *Tales from the Hood*) and knew what he could do, but since he's a little flighty he was the wild card. But he came through with flying colors.

ELH: *Are you influenced by shots you have seen other directors use?*

S L : If there's a shot I like, the first thing I try to find out is how they did it. Then I see if there's a place in the story where the shot will make sense.

E L H : *One of your more interesting shots is a dolly shot that gives the effect of walking on a moving sidewalk.*
S L : The first time I used it was in *Mo' Better Blues* with my character Giant. To get that shot you have to lay dolly tracks. Then you put the camera on the dolly. Then you put the actors on the dolly also. Then you move the dolly along.

E L H : *Would you call that your signature shot? (Lee shrugs) I mean, Quentin Tarantino has that shot from the trunk of the car that—*
S L : Well, I think you have to have more than two movies before you can have a signature shot. You have to have more than two movies before you're Orson Welles, don't you think? (laughs)

E L H : *Starting with the book* Spike Lee's Gotta Have It, *and throughout your career, you have invited your viewers to read up on the making of your films.*
S L : The reason we do that is because we have always been about the demystification of film. There has always been this hocus-pocus or magical-mystical thing associated with the making of film that sort of psyches people out and makes them think that this cannot be done, that this is a craft that cannot be learned.

E L H : *Who are some of the people that helped you in the beginning of your process?*
S L : My process really began in film school after a former classmate of mine finished his first film a year out of NYU—when Jim Jarmusch released *Stranger Than Paradise.* Here was someone I knew, someone who went to the same school that I did, who now had a hit film. I worked in the equipment room as a TA and I had checked equipment out to him, and here was someone who had an international hit. To me, that's when it first became do-able. I owe a great deal to Jim Jarmusch. He showed me and everyone at NYU that we could do this.

E L H : *Do you feel your work was treated fairly at NYU?*

SL: I felt like I was treated fairly, but at the same time I realized that this world of NYU was not going to last forever. It was a three-year program, and the only thing that was going to count was what you had to show when you finished. Are you going to have a film that's going to be a calling card and get you meetings? I was fortunate enough to have *Joe's Bed-Stuy Barbershop*. That was my thesis film.

ELH: *It won you the student Academy Award. Did you think in that moment that your career would go right into high gear and there would be no more troubles for you?*
SL: I definitely did. I was naive. From the little acclaim that I did get, and with that award on my mantle, a couple of agents did call for me and I signed with one. I felt that I was on my way. But it didn't happen that way, and it didn't happen then. I graduated in 1982, so for the next three years I was just hell-bent on making a feature film. The first attempt was unsuccessful. It was a film called *Messenger,* about a bike messenger. That was the summer of '84. In the summer of '85 we shot twelve days in July for *She's Gotta Have It.* Finally at the end of that year it came out.

ELH: *The story of that $175,000 film is now legendary. It seems like a negligible budget now, but was it difficult to raise that money at the time?*
SL: That was the hardest money I ever had to try and raise. It was a struggle.

ELH: *Do you recommend that young filmmakers just starting out go to film school?*
SL: No. There's not one route. I think that you have to make or find a way. What's best for Spike Lee, or Quentin Tarantino, Robert Rodriguez or Joel and Ethan Coen may not be the best way for other would-be filmmakers.

ELH: *When you were courted to some extent by Hollywood—*
SL: I was never courted by Hollywood. I had confidence in my agent that he would find me work, but no work surfaced.

ELH: *So what do you say to other cats who think that getting the right agent is the key to their success?*
SL: You really can't rely on an agent for the most part. I don't want to make a blanket statement, but when you're a young filmmaker I think an agent

can only help you once you've established yourself. If you haven't directed a feature film yet, you basically have to do it yourself. Or try to align yourself with other people who are going in the same direction you're going.

E L H : *In your case there were people like Ernest Dickerson and Monty Ross, who were central figures.*
S L : Well, Monty's not with us anymore. His last film with us was *Girl 6*. He was very important. People may have read about Spike Lee, but it wasn't just me. It was Monty Ross, Ruth Carter in costume design, Robbi Reed was casting, Ernest Dickerson was shooting, Wynn Thomas was production design, my father (Bill Lee) was doing the score, Barry Brown was doing the cutting. This is a team we have.

E L H : *Which pictures stand out in your mind as your favorites?*
S L : *Do the Right Thing* and *Malcolm X*.

E L H : Malcolm X *was more than just another picture. Many things about it seemed more like a war.*
S L : Most films are like that, but it was heightened on *Malcolm X* because a lot was riding on it. I looked at it for the first time on laser disk last Friday night, and that film is going to hold up forever. But the thing that gets to me is when people like that idiot Todd Boyd writes in the *L.A. Times* that the only thing that *Malcolm X* is good for is to see Spike Lee lindy hop. I mean, that's just insane.

E L H : *My personal observation is that you are the one filmmaker that people, most of whom have never met you, have volumes of negative things to say about. Are you the one they love to hate, or the one they hate to love? Which is it Spike?*
S L : I don't know. I think that one of the reasons this happens is because I'm in my films—therefore people know my face—and most directors aren't. I also do a lot of things outside of filmmaking, like commercials and videos, so I have a different life outside my feature films. A lot of the time I'm just amazed when I read these reviews of my work, and the review isn't really about the work as much as it is whether they like or dislike Spike Lee. I was glad when you said before the interview that when it comes down to it, it's all about the work. I'm amazed at how often the work is never discussed.
    When you look at all of the films I've done, you realize a lot of people got

shortchanged. People rarely talk about the great cinematography Ernest Dickerson was doing, or Ruth Carter's costume design—although she did receive an Oscar nomination for *Malcolm X*. Barry Brown did a great job of cutting all my films. Robbi Reed's casting—look at *School Daze*, which is Tisha Campbell's first film, Jasmine Guy's first film, Darrell Bell's first film. *Do the Right Thing*, Rosie Perez's first film, Martin Lawrence's first film, Robin Harris's. Shall we go on? *Jungle Fever:* Halle Berry's first film, Lucinda Williams, Nick Turturro's first film. The list extends behind the scenes as well.

E L H :   *What's the biggest misconception that people have about Spike Lee?*
S L :   For white people—or should I say for white men—they have this misconception that I am a racist or an anti-Semitic.

E L H :   *What would you say has created this misconception?*
S L :   Some of my films deal with the touchy subject matter of racism, and a lot of people say that it indicts white America as the culprit. Therefore it's putting those people on the defensive.

E L H :   *When people look at films like* Do the Right Thing, Malcolm X *and* Jungle Fever, *you can see how they might reach that conclusion. But that's less than one third of your filmography, which includes themes involving music, love, sex—*
S L :   I think that's a fair assessment. People tend to focus on those three films and say those are my only interests or those are the only films I can make. I think my first decade as a filmmaker has covered a broad spectrum of stories. It has also covered the broad spectrum of the African-American community as a whole, and the different stories that we share.

E L H :   *Even at the beginning of your career you had to defend your work. Didn't you have to answer charges of misogyny with* She's Gotta Have It?
S L :   I think what I was guilty of early on was that my male characters were more fully developed than my female characters, as opposed to any hatred of women. So those charges that fault my filmic depiction of women are not as strong as they used to be.

E L H :   *Do you attribute that to your growth as a writer?*
S L :   Just my growth as an individual.

E L H :   *Was it your original intention to release a film a year?*

S L : No, but it was my intention to amass a body of work. The generation of filmmakers above me, people like Halle Guerima and Charles Burnett and individuals like that, it seemed like they spent so much time frantically trying to raise money. Sometimes it would take two or three years to raise that money. It was hard to do films back-to-back, but I really wanted to continue working.

E L H : *What draws you to a story so much that you begin to see it, write it, then direct and produce it?*
S L : I think that I usually have several different ideas I am thinking about, but the one that I keep thinking about is the one I always make. I've got to mull it over a while.

E L H : *In terms of the size or scope of a project, do you prefer to work on a smaller production with less people or budget, or with a larger crew?*
S L : No filmmaker is ever going to tell you honestly that they would rather work with less money than with more money. But the reality of this project was that we were raising the money ourselves. Even though we raised $2.4 million, it was not a cakewalk. I think that we really had a solid plan, and we told people that they could not lose money. We were going to make this film for "x" amount of dollars, and sell it to Columbia Pictures on a negative pick-up deal that will be in excess of what "x" was. The Thursday before the picture opened, all of the investors received a check for their original investment, plus eight percent interest—before the movie even opened.

E L H : *How did you do at the box office?*
S L : Terrible. Nobody went, or the word didn't get around.

E L H : *Why do you think the audience didn't support this film?*
S L : I don't know. Maybe the black audience didn't want to see a movie like this. Not now, I mean. They want to see shoot 'em up stuff. I think it was a combination of things. Some missteps were taken with the marketing. But I'm not going to put everything on Columbia Pictures. We could talk about this or talk about that, what Columbia should or shouldn't have done, but at the end of the day the African-American moviegoing audience did not support the film. It's as simple as that.

ELH: *Is it incumbent on you as a director to bring people into the tent? Or do you feel your job is done once the film is cut?*

SL: A lot of times I feel my job is just beginning after the film is done, because you have to get out there and promote it. A lot of the actors and I did everything we were asked to promote [*Get on the Bus*]. The African-American audience for the most part was unresponsive.

ELH: *Was it apathy?*

SL: That's a very complex question, but I think apathy has a lot to do with it. I was speaking to Branford Marsalis about this the other day, and he said that black folks think they know what they like, but they only like what they know.

ELH: *So if you try to do something different—*

SL: They don't want to hear it. And why people thought this was a documentary, I still don't understand. We took care to make sure with the TV commercials and radio spots that this was an entertaining picture and not some diatribe about "Let's uplift the black man!" and all of that kind of stuff. You have to look at the numbers. We've been out since October 16th, we've yet to crack $6 million. *Set It Off* is going to make $30 or $35 million. It's disturbing because studio heads are looking at these numbers, and the next time a black filmmaker tries to make a film with any substance, they'll say, "Well, the last time somebody tried a film like that was *Get on the Bus,* and nobody came. But you know, they sure did come to see *Set It Off,* so we've got to have more shoot 'em ups, more violent pieces." And those are the films that they'll continue to make. That's the sad part. But while all this is happening, black people will still be crying, "Oh, they never do us right in Hollywood, and we get hit with the same stereotypes again and again. Our image is not put on the screen." If you want something, you gotta bring something. It's as simple as that.

ELH: *I had a conversation with Carl Franklin, and he echoed some of your concerns.*

SL: About how more black people should have supported *Devil in a Blue Dress?* And that was with Denzel [Washington] in it. We didn't have a star. I'm not talking about the caliber of actor, I'm talking about movie stars.

ELH: *How important is having that movie star to the overall success of a project?*
SL: It's very important. Movie stars are what opens a film. That's why some of these bums are allowed to get $20 million for a movie.

ELH: *You've been a catalyst for the latest wave of African-American cinema. What changes in filmmaking have you seen that have impressed you?*
SL: Even though we didn't make the financial return we wished to with *Get on the Bus,* I think the way this film was financed was unique and can be used as a paradigm for other projects. I think that people shouldn't sleep on the fact that fifteen African-American men from diverse backgrounds can get together and invest in a film. Black people doing that? (laughs) Black people getting together to invest in anything? That's revolutionary.

ELH: *Do you want to talk about Jackie Robinson?*
SL: There's nothing to talk about. Ted Turner put it into turnaround, but I still hope to get that film made.

ELH: *What do you need to make it?*
SL: Forty million, to do it right.

ELH: *Forty million? Why is it in turnaround?*
SL: Forty million. (laughs) The scope of the story is epic.

ELH: *More epic than* Malcolm X?
SL: No. We won't be shooting in Mecca, South Africa and Egypt, but it's a period piece. We have to recreate Ebbets Field, the Polo grounds, Yankee Stadium, all those places.

ELH: *You have to take us back in time. Time is money . . .*
SL: Time is money, money is time. Forty million.

ELH: *Will the public support this type of film?*
SL: I think so, but what filmmaker truly knows in his heart of hearts whether the film is going to make money or not? You just don't know sometimes. Who would have thought that Mike Tyson would have lost to Evander Holyfield? Nobody. The first odds were twelve to one. I wish I'd had that bet.

ELH: *Where do you see yourself in five years?*

SL: We're going to executive produce a lot more films, and I hope to be established in television also. I'm doing a pilot with Brandon Tartikoff for ABC called *L.I.E.*, which is an acronym for *Long Island Expressway*. It's a half-hour drama. Hopefully we'll be shooting it this spring.

ELH: *Didn't you just get back from Indianapolis?*

SL: I shot a Nike spot with Reggie Miller. Before that, I directed a spot with Michael Jordan for the United Negro College Fund.

ELH: *Commercial work and videos, is that how you keep your eye sharp between features?*

SL: I consider it all filmmaking.

ELH: *What is history going to say about Spike Lee?*

SL: I can't answer that.

ELH: *What would you like to be remembered for?*

SL: All any artist can ask for is to be remembered by their work. That's all you leave behind anyway.

ELH: *Do you have any parting words for young filmmakers who want to follow in your footsteps?*

SL: A lot of times people come up to me and ask, "How have you done it?" and it's really hard for me to explain everything in a minute, right there where they've cornered me. I think that we put everything in that book, the one about *She's Gotta Have It*. That really tells it step-by-step, how to make a film with nothing. So the knowledge is out there. Robert Rodriquez wrote a book about *El Mariachi*. It's out there. You just have to go after it.

ELH: *You're a family man now. You have a daughter.*

SL: Yes, her name is Satchel. She was two in December.

ELH: *Would you encourage her to pursue a career in film?*

SL: Yes. I would want her to be behind the camera, not in front of the camera. That's where the power is.

An Interview with Spike Lee, Director of *4 Little Girls*

BRANDON JUDELL/1997

THE MOVE IS ON to get Spike Lee's *4 Little Girls* a Best Documentary Oscar nod. To help make this a certainty, his hard-working publicist, Jackie Bazan, is browbeating the media overtime so the acclaimed feature won't be forgotten by nomination time. Since we've always been slightly fond of Spike, we decided to share our chat together with you. The film, by the way, chronicles the bombing of the Sixteenth Street Baptist Church in Alabama on September 15, 1963, which left four young women dead.

4 Little Girls just finished a nine-city run Thanksgiving and will next be broadcast in February on HBO, the company that pulled together the project along with Lee's own 40 Acres and a Mule Filmworks.

indieWIRE: *Did you have any memories of the church bombing? You were only five at the time.*
SPIKE LEE: I have no remembrances of it all. I do remember the Kennedy assassination which occurred when I was eleven, but not the bombing of the church.

iW: *So when did that event first enter your consciousness?*
LEE: I really can't tell you. I heard about it from my parents. My father is from Alabama, though not Birmingham.

iW: *Frederick Douglass said, "We have to do with the past only as we can make it useful to the present and to the future." Is that your goal with this film?*

From *indieWIRE* (12 December 1997). Reprinted by permission of the author.

LEE: I think that there's a lot of young people, both black and white, that really don't know about the Civil Rights struggle and Civil Rights movement, and African-Americans in particular who today are bearing the fruits of everybody who had to sacrifice and struggle. They have no idea what happened, and they think it was always like this because they were always allowed to vote or go wherever they wanted. That wasn't the case at all. Afro-Americans somehow fear going back and revisiting painful parts of history, nevertheless we need to do it. All we have to do is look at our fellow Jewish brothers and sisters and see how much they revert back to the Holocaust. Most blacks don't even want to bring up slavery. Why bring that up? But that's our legacy. Even though I don't know how *Amistad,* Spielberg's film, is going to turn out, I hope it's good. I do hope the success of that film generates many more projects about that whole dark period in this country.

iW: *One person wrote of you that you have the misfortune to be the most prominent black director of this time. Because of this, you're given the responsibility to make the political films—or to the THE black spokesperson. Do you feel the weight of that when you make a film?*
LEE: No.

iW: *It's just a media thing?*
LEE: I have never, ever felt that I was a spokesperson for Afro-Americans in this country. I understand that the media is trying to pinpoint individuals that they do think speak for the masses or particular groups. It's not really the case now, but there was a time a couple of years ago when anytime something happened in the world concerning black people, the phone would ring in my office asking me for a comment. Being naive, I would comment. Now I guess I really consciously pick and choose sponsoring an issue that I want to talk about.

iW: *But many would say you have helped politicize film in this country more than any other director.*
LEE: Oliver Stone has done that, too. With *Nixon* and *JFK.* We're not the first. Also I think that when you make statements like that, you really have to look at whomever you are talking about. Look at their role by their work. I've done ten films. Not all the films are polemical about issues. I love that stuff but that's not necessarily the only thing that I do.

i w : *Just by putting blacks on film and not stereotyping them, you are being polit-ical.*

L E E : You're saying that just putting blacks on film is political?

i w : *Absolutely.*

L E E : (Laughs.) Okay. I've also heard it argued that just the absence of poli-tics in a film is political. Just the absence is a political move in itself also, so I won't argue with that.

i w : *Were you surprised when you heard that Birmingham, once the bastion of racism in the South, was also the only city in America to ban the "Ellen Comes Out of the Closet" episode?*

L E E : Not at all. When I read that was going to happen, I knew that Bir-mingham was one of the cities not going to run that episode. I was not sur-prised. They're just following their legacy.

i w : *Malcolm X once said, "South was south of the Canadian border." Is Bir-mingham just America intensified, or do you think it's a land unto itself?*

L E E : No, I'm not going to put everything on Birmingham. Malcolm said that when those people in those buses in Boston were being overturned and all that stuff. I think a lot of times the North is too quick to finger everything on the South. The midwest up to the northwest with all those militia people, that's the scary thing now. These militia groups. Neo-nazis and stuff like that. Most of that stuff is not even in the South. It's Oregon. Utah. Things like that.

i w : *Certain groups—gays, blacks, women—are finally getting the power to make their own films. You have said in previous interviews that you're not happy with some of the films and TV shows they're making. You thought* Booty Call *and* How to Be a Player *are degrading to African-Americans and doing little to improve their image. You said you wanted to break a TV set when you saw* Homeboys from Outer Space.

L E E : (Laughs.) I said all those things. There is nothing wrong with comedy. Nothing wrong with laughter or laughing. I'm talking about performers. I have problems with buffoons. Coonish type of humor. That's what my prob-lem is. I just was finding it disturbing why every show, not every show, 95% of the shows dealing with African-Americans are sitcoms. Why can't there be some dramas?

iW: *Do you sometimes think that throughout your whole career you'll always be—quote unquote—a black director?*

LEE: Yes, I have no problem with that. I have no problems with white America looking at me as a black man because I understand the mind-set and where we are in this country. I think the majority of white Americans are unable to look at somebody black and not the skin of their color first. That's just the reality. And if that's the reality, I'm not going to spend valuable time agonizing over that, getting ulcers or hypertension worrying about the fact that people can't see who I really am and see the skin of my color. We're not at that point in this country. This country is not mature enough to get beyond that point.

iW: *Addison Gayle Jr. wrote in* The New Black Voices: *"Perhaps to be sane in this society is the best evidence of insanity."*

LEE: I don't know exactly what that means.

iW: *Well, maybe you wouldn't be able to do what you're doing now twenty years ago. You'd have to be playing games and kissing ass in Hollywood.*

LEE: I have to do that also. (Laughs.) It just amounts to how much butt kissing.

iW: *Is it easier to be black now than it was anytime in the past?*

LEE: As far as working in corporate management or in the arts and movies? What do you mean?

iW: *In general.*

LEE: It really is a paradox because at the same time that there are more successful African-Americans than ever before, the black underclass is bigger than it's ever been. So the cup is half empty; the cup is half full. I think you can just move back to the 1950s where in a lot of states black people could not vote, could not buy clothes in stores downtown. They had to ride in the back of the bus. Public transportation. At the same time if you look at it, black businesses flourished back then. At the same time, look at the statistics. Black males weren't murdered at the rate we are now. We have this unbalance.

iW: *In your film, there are scenes of the young black girls' bodies, who were killed by the bomb, being laid out in the morgue. That's something I don't think I'll ever forget.*

LEE: The quick cuts.

IW: *Were you shocked when you discovered them?*
LEE: Very shocked. Here's the story. We were in this public library in Alabama, and we asked to see the morgue photos, not knowing that they had them. When the clerk called the photos out, we were startled and taken aback. You can imagine what twenty sticks of dynamite can do. But when you see the results, it literally brings tears to your eyes. I have to be honest with you, I was not 100% sure whether I should include those shots. The postmortem photographs. But I decided if we didn't linger on them, it would be tasteful. They reinforce the horror and the crime that was committed when those sticks of dynamite went off in the Sixteenth Street Baptist Church and killed the four little girls.

IW: *By the way, is your Jackie Robinson film getting any closer to reality?*
LEE: I hope so especially after the enormous press that the fiftieth anniversary of Jackie breaking the color barrier received. I hope that one or two studios will now be willing to open up their purse strings.

Hoops to Conquer

CHRIS NASHAWATY/1998

EVER SINCE 1986's *She's Gotta Have It,* Spike Lee has sported a rep as the quintessential straight-talking director. But in his courtside seats at Madison Square Garden, the 41-year-old auteur's rep is for trash talking—namely, with anyone who dares to show up his beloved New York Knicks. With the release of his latest joint, *He's Got Game* (which reunites Lee with the De Niro to his Scorsese, Denzel Washington), we sat down with him for a taste of both.

ENTERTAINMENT WEEKLY: *A lot of people thought you'd win the best documentary Oscar for* 4 Little Girls. *Were you disappointed?*
SPIKE LEE: No. Because one of the films was a Holocaust film [*The Long Way Home*]. I think 15 or 16 Holocaust films have won the short and feature-length categories. I'd rather be the Knicks playing the Bulls at the United Center down by 20 with 10 minutes left—those odds are better than going against a Holocaust film.

EW: *Did you like* Titanic?
LEE: It was all right . . . But I don't understand why [James Cameron] is upset it didn't get nominated for best screenplay. I think Mr. Cameron is a great technical director, unsurpassed, but he can't write, and he definitely can't write dialogue.

EW: *Compare Milwaukee Bucks guard Ray Allen [who plays* Game*'s high school phenom Jesus Shuttlesworth] with that other NBA actor, Shaquille O'Neal.*
LEE: What, you didn't like *Kazaam* I can't believe it. [Laughs] Shaq wants to be a superhero, which is fine. We definitely knew [the actor playing] Jesus had to be from the NBA. We didn't want someone who we had to cut away from every time the ball left his hands. Travis Best, Walter McCarty, Rick Fox—they all went out for the role, and Allen Iverson came in too. But Ray had a certain je ne sais quoi.

EW: *Did you have to keep the cameras rolling all day for Denzel Washington to make those baskets?*
LEE: No, Denzel can play. In the final scene, Jesus beats his father 11-0 in the script, but Denzel said, "F——that." Those five baskets he got are real.

EW: *The female characters in the film aren't very flattering.*
LEE: I think that if people really look at this film, everybody is trying to exploit Jesus. That's not based on gender or race. And because women . . . haven't had the opportunity to be in the same powerful positions [as men], historically they've had to use what they have. If you look at how these kids are exploited, it's cars, money, gold, and women.

EW: *How on earth did you get the idea to mix orchestral Aaron Copland music with heavy-duty Public Enemy?*
LEE: I know people think that's insane, but that's the music I listen to. I play Aaron Copland and Public Enemy and the Beatles and John Coltrane and Steely Dan and Busta Rhymes and Dinah Washington and Ella Fitzgerald and Patsy Cline. I don't make distinctions—just the music I love and the music I hate.

EW: *How come it took so long to make a movie about your passion for basketball?*
LEE: Well, [my] first sports film was supposed to be the Jackie Robinson story. I'm still hoping to get funding someday. Right now it's in limbo. . . . Nobody wants to make it.

EW: *Any chance you'll just make the movie on your own?*
LEE: [Smiles and pulls out his wallet] I don't think I got $50 million here.

Big Words: An Interview with Spike Lee

GEORGE KHOURY/1999

''I'M NOT GOING TO LIE,'' Spike Lee stresses. "There were times when I felt like quitting, but those thoughts were just leaking. I'm not a quitter and I hate to lose, so I just had to break through." True to his words, he broke barriers and pushed the film industry forward for all, especially for minorities. Yes, at times he's overexposed and outspoken, but his body of work, high-lighted by twelve features, demonstrates his endless quest to provoke audiences to stop and think about the world around them. "I just want people to come out talking, discussing, debating, fighting, and all that stuff; and hopefully they've been entertained at the same time."

He was born Shelton J. Lee on March 27, 1957 to Jacquelyn, a school teacher, and Bill Lee, a distinguished musician, in a household that was a center of artistic and liberal creativity. Encouraged to be observant and understanding by his mother, who planted Spike's love for cinema, he grew up in the '60s surrounded by the teachings of Malcolm X and Martin Luther King. As he matured, Lee began to understand that blacks lacked a voice within the powerful forum of cinema, which he knew had the power to transform and teach all audiences about the real African-American image. In 1984, Spike wrote in his journal, "I feel that there is a vast black audience out there that's been craving for an intelligent black film." Later in his life he would revise this hypothesis.

After Lee completed his studies at Morehouse University, he began to pur-

Published in *Creative Screenwriting* 6, no. 3 (May/June 1999): 38–42. Reprinted by permission of George Khoury.

sue his burning interest in film by entering NYU. He was one of only two black students enrolled in their film program at the time. "I never went to NYU expecting teachers to teach me," he logged into his journal, "I just wanted equipment so I could make films, and learn filmmaking by making films." His thesis film *The Answer* was a humorous story of a black man chosen by a major studio to direct a remake of *Birth of a Nation*. The thesis was met with great resentment and opposition by the NYU faculty, who had made *Birth of a Nation* an integral part of their teaching curriculum while ignoring its racist content for years. Lee defended his film adamantly.

He continued to establish himself with his subsequent short *Joe's Bed-Stuy Barbershop: We Cut Heads,* which was extremely well-received on the film festival circuit and won a student Academy Award. From there he began to work on what was supposed to be his first feature, *Messenger,* which had actor Laurence Fishburne attached. But the project quickly fell apart due to what has continually been a problem throughout his career—"Money." The financial and other obstacles left Lee devastated and disillusioned. Lee says, "What kept me going was that I knew that this could possibly be my one and only shot, and I could not be an old man wondering coulda, woulda, shoulda." It was that determination that forced Lee to pull himself together and write the script that would open all the doors, *She's Gotta Have It.*

Following upon the efforts of John Sayles, *She's Gotta Have It* provided Independent cinema with a stylistic push. Unlike the typical Independent art film of the day, *She's Gotta Have It* adopted a raw, take-no-prisoners approach that was surprisingly funny—an approach that is still a staple of Independent film. Critics embraced the film, and Lee quickly became a darling of the media and an inspiration to young filmmakers (including Kevin Smith). On being an influence, he says gleefully, "A lot of people might think it makes me feel old, but it makes me feel good. The first time I was in LA for the Los Angeles opening of *She's Gotta Have It,* this kid came up to me and said, 'I'm in high school and I'm gonna be a filmmaker just like you.' [laughs] And he did what he had to do to make that prediction come true. That kid was John Singleton."

The films that Lee made after *She's Gotta Have It* demonstrate an incredible range of human emotion while focusing on everyday African-American life. His script for *Do the Right Thing* challenged a nation to think about racial tension and earned a 1990 Academy Award nomination for best original screenplay (Lee would lose to Tom Schulman's *Dead Poets Society*). He has not limited himself to the big screen, making countless music videos, television commercials, and the 1998 Academy Award–nominated documentary *4 Little Girls*. One of the first to believe in Lee's skill was independent film producer/ guru John Pierson, who poignantly wrote in this book *Spike, Mike, Slackers, and Dykes*, "Spike Lee's career has been exemplary: hardworking, disciplined, inspired, experimental, rabble-rousing, committed, and marked by steady growth. He's stumbled occasionally, but even those imperfections seem to play an essential role in his process. He's far more evolutionary than revolutionary." But how did Lee's writing craft develop?

"I first wanted to be a filmmaker, but then I realized that the quickest way to become a filmmaker was to write—to become a hyphenate. I never took any classes or anything like that, I just learned by doing. I mean I can't explain it. When I write I'm not aware of the first, second, or third act and that stuff. It's there, but I'm not aware of it. Filmmaking is how I express myself. I really consider myself a storyteller, and I think that's what all great directors do—not to say I'm a great director—but that's something that I aspire to be and you have to tell a story. And the great storytellers use everything that they have to tell that story with. Whether it be the script, music, costume designs, the actors, the production designs . . . you have to utilize everything at your disposal that can help you tell the story."

Spike's method has evolved naturally over the years. In the beginning he was often influenced by films and other filmmakers like Martin Scorsese. Spike admits, "I get inspired, but I can't remember recently where a movie gave me inspiration to do one of my films." But the evolution comes with a price, that he becomes more restless with each film "because I know a lot more. I would say that on any film I do, I've, hopefully, matured since the last one. I'm not going to remain stagnant."

The screenwriting process always starts with an idea for Lee, either a characterization or a thematic message, and the script evolves from there. He wants the audience to identify with his characters and where they are coming from. When he's writing, he fights his way through the rough edges of his script, always exploring every possible angle and constantly tweaking the script until it reaches believability. He has no secret formulas for anyone, just hard work.

She's Gotta Have It rose from the ruins of what was to be Lee's first feature film, *Messenger*. "We were trying to do a film and keep open a production office. We had hired a staff and were doing all of this for eight weeks before things fell through. Out of those ashes, I came up with the idea for *She's Gotta Have It*. I needed to do a movie that would have very few characters, almost no locations, no sets or costumes, and could be made for almost no money, but—and this is important—could still be a commercial film, a good film. I came up with a script that could be done as cheaply as possible. I had to get my work out there. I couldn't spend four or five years of my life, my prime, trying to raise millions. I had to prove that I could turn things around and get things going, or else my career would have been over," Lee says.

In *Do the Right Thing*, Lee structured the film so that it seems anecdotal, but all the bits build to a point. "I didn't want people to see the plot, but it's there. The most important thing is for people to see how big a part the heat plays in all of this. The heat tests everybody's patience, and it builds from small incidents: If Radio Raheem had turned down the radio, nothing would have happened. If Sal had put up a black person's picture on his Wall of Fame, there wouldn't have been any static. But it all culminated in a tragedy."

His scripts immerse us into oppressive environments within the so-called land of the free. Spike once told *Boston Globe* writer Jay Carr, "The American dream is a lie. Ask the native American Indians." I ask him if it's fair to label his films as black films when they deal with universal emotions, dramas, and struggles. He tells me, "I've always felt that way, but we've not evolved into that place as a country . . . as a world. So I try not to let it bother me. There's still a lot of racism. That has not changed in the ten years since we've done *Do the Right Thing*. At the end of that film I wanted people to feel the horror."

Lee only directs screenplays he writes (or at least re-writes), and his vision has clashed with that of an original writer or lead actor on occasion—most notably with Lee's rewrite of Richard Price's screenplay *Clockers*. Price's novel and screenplay were written from the point of view of the cop, Rocco Klein. Lee redirected that focus to the ghetto kid Strike. Lee told Scott and Barbara Siegel from *Dramalogue*, "I think Harvey read the drafts that [Price] had written for Marty [Scorsese], so there was a lot more Rocco in those drafts than in the film I wanted to make. A lot of actors, you know, want more scenes and more dialogue. I had to assure Harvey that he was still an integral part of the film. Sometimes he felt that I was giving this movie completely over to Strike, but that wasn't the case. I was shifting the focus over to Strike's point of view, but Rocco was still a key figure in the film. That's where [the friction] might have come from."

For Spike, the most important part of his artistic independence is retaining final cut on his films. "I think John Sayles, now that's independent filmmaking!" Lee admits. "Me—I've said this so many times—I think that I have the best of both worlds. For the most part, I've gotten my finances and distributions in Hollywood but I've always had final cut, so I've always had creative control."

Until *He Got Game*, Spike hadn't written an original solo screenplay in eight years. During that time, he surrounded himself with many talented screenwriters and injected some of his idealism into them. What does Spike look for in other writers' scripts? "I look for original voices, people with something to say." Why did he move from directing his own material to working with other writers? He ponders and then responds, "Let me give you the area: I wrote *She's Gotta Have It, School Daze,* and *Mo' Better.* I wrote *Jungle Fever.* Now comes *Malcolm X.* The producer, Marvin Worth, had been trying to make this film for twenty years. Norman Jewison was slated to direct this film. I really had two options: I could write another original script from scratch, or I can read the six or seven scripts that had been done over a twenty year span in Marvin Worth's quest to get this film made. I figured, 'Maybe let's not reinvent the wheel, maybe there's a script that I can work on.' I read all the scripts. The best script was the first script that was written by James Baldwin and Arnold Perl. So I rewrote that one. The next film *Crooklyn* was an original screenplay by my brother Cinqué and my sister Joie. I worked with them on that. Then we had *Girl 6,* which was the very first screenplay by a very talented playwright Suzan-Lori Parks. Then I got this phone call to do this film about twelve men going cross-country on a bus to The Million Man March. And I had time to write that with a very fine writer Reggie Bythewood; he wrote that. And then this is where my beautiful wife Tonya stepped in, and she said, 'Spike, you need to write an original screenplay. I've missed your voice.' At first I said, 'What is she talking about?' And then I saw she was right as usual. I checked the top of my mind and saw that the last original screenplay I had written was *Jungle Fever*—which I did back in 1990. So it was like seven years since I had written an original screenplay. And that's how *He Got Game* came to be."

Lee has publicly criticized some cinematic depictions of African Americans: for example, he appeared on the television program *Nightline* to speak out about the injustice in Steven Spielberg's *Amistad.* Lee's problem with *Amistad* is the same complaint that some critics had about films like *Cry Free-*

dom, Mississippi Burning, and *Glory:* they turn the African-Americans' struggle into a subtext for white heroism. Lee felt that Spielberg committed a travesty by not going further into the slaves' struggle, and that he lost something far more emotional and powerful. "My problem with *Amistad* was that they left the good stuff on the cutting floor," he said firmly. "They chose to go with the usual, the other angle. Where the real story about *Amistad* is about the slaves, they wanted to focus on Matthew McConaughey and Anthony Hopkins."

The discussion about *Amistad* leads into another sore subject in Lee's mind. Quentin Tarantino. The two filmmakers have had a feud that has taken place through television, print, and even inspired an *MTV Celebrity Deathmatch* bout. "The problem with *Jackie Brown,*" he tells me. "I will say it again and again and again. I have a definite problem with Quentin Tarantino's excessive use of the N-word. And let the record state that I never said he can not use that word—I've used that word in many of my films—but I think something is wrong with him. You look at *Pulp Fiction, Reservoir Dogs,* and even that thing he did with Christian Slater, *True Romance.* It's just the N-word, the N-word, the N-word. He says he grew up on Blaxploitation films and that they were his favorite films but he has to realize that those films do not speak to the breadth of the entire African American experience. I mean the guy's just stupid. He [Tarantino] said that he and Ricki Lake were the two most revered white celebrities among the black community. Where did he get that from? Because Sam Jackson kisses his butt, that means black people love him? That's wrong. I am not the only African American in this world who has a problem with this excessive use of the N-word."

It is easy to see Lee's point in the Quentin-Spike feud. Tarantino's black characters speak like the stereotypical foul-mouthed black pimp and whore that we've seen too many times on television and film. Spike goes even further into the subject and reminds us that his crusade is not a two-way street, "I'm not going to say he's a bigot, but I'll go further than that, he's just stupid. Then he has to argue, 'Well, I'm an artist and I can do whatever I want.' Well, that might be the case, but I would state that Michael Jackson is a much greater artist than Quentin Tarantino. Quentin Tarantino will never be the artist that Michael Jackson has been over the last thirty years. And Michael was brought to his knees because of 'Jew me, sue me, kick me, kike me' in his song 'They Don't Care About Us.' He had to pull the record from the stores, redo the lyrics, and then make an apology to the Simon Wiesenthal Center. Now how is it that Michael Jackson has to do all that because of 'Jew me, sue me, kick me, kike me?' Even if we want to leave out [the rest of] Tarantino's body of work and just focus on *Pulp Fiction,* where he used the N-word thirty-eight times, why is it that Quentin Tarantino is an artist? And Michael Jackson is anti-Semitic? To me a slur is a slur, and I think we need to talk about this disparity. There's a different set of standards. I called up Harvey Weinstein, head of Miramax, and said, 'Harvey, if I brought you a script that had thirty-eight Jewish cocksuckers in it, thirty-eight kikes in it, would you make that script?' And he said, 'No.' And I think that if I went to any other executive in this business, they would say the same thing. But if you put 'nigger' in it, that's all right."

I point out a Tarantino appearance on Charlie Rose where he taunted Lee and suggested physical violence. "All he has to do is speak," Lee said, unfazed by Tarantino's tough talk. "And then Sam Jackson, for him to get up there and defend Quentin Tarantino: to me, it really smacked of 'House Negro' defending the master. Let's be realistic: Quentin Tarantino came off of *Pulp Fiction,* one of the most highly anticipated films of recent years. So Quentin Tarantino could have filmed whatever he wanted to do, and somebody was going to finance it. The guy's very talented. I'm not gonna knock him. I'm not gonna say anything about his film work. I'm just talking about his excessive use of the N-word. And I have to call out about that. Because a lot of people just don't see it. And the white media, they're not gonna say anything about it."

But even more than Quentin Tarantino's dialogue, Lee is concerned about the poor box office that most serious black films receive. He recalls a scenario that's happened often in his career, "On a film like *Get on the Bus,* the week it opened, people would come up to me and say, 'Hey, Spike, when is your next film coming out?' There was no awareness at all." But it isn't just white audiences that aren't showing up. As Lee pointed out in an October 13, 1998, *New York Times* article: "I cannot tell you why a large segment of African-Americans would rather see *Booty Call* than *Rosewood* or *He Got Game.* I just don't know."

If you ask Spike if he's had any regrets about his career, he'll quickly tell you, "The only thing I would like to do over is that rape scene in *She's Gotta Have It.*" The scene grows horrifying as Jamie, previously the most understanding and gentle of Nola's three lovers, reaches a boiling part and explains to her, "I'll fuck you, but I won't make love to you." He brutally demands to know, "Whose pussy is this?" The scene betrays the strong characterization that occurred in the pages prior to it. Nola's character is supposed to be sexually liberated and independent, exploring her sexuality when and how she wants to. But the great betrayal occurs when Nola announces that her body belongs to Jamie, who used violence to control her. At this moment, she announces the defeat of her individuality and beliefs. Had Nola said that her body belonged to her and her alone, she would have demonstrated strength and shown Jamie what power really is. Spike sought to correct this mistake in *Girl 6*, and succeeded in creating a strong female character who strives to live life by her own rules.

As bell hooks points out in her book *Reel to Real*, "[*She's Gotta Have It*] generated more discussion of the politics of rape and gender, of rape and violence against black women, than any feminist article or book on the subject at the time." The mistake in judgment might have been the result of Lee trying to get the greatest dramatic effect possible, but the script's climax seems concocted and unnatural. After the rape, Nola becomes celibate and tries to have a friendship with her rapist, Jamie. She has lost the strength and independence at the core of her character. But these faults don't lessen *She's Gotta Have It's* value: it remains an important and significant film.

In July Lee's new film, *Summer of Sam*, will be released by Touchstone Pictures. In this film Lee again returns to his role of re-writer/director, extensively reworking an original screenplay by actor/writers Victor Colicchio and Michael Imperioli, and Jeri Carroll. Based on the real life experiences of the two actors, *Summer of Sam* focuses on The Bronx, circa 1977, and relives the infamous summer when New York recoiled from the serial killer dubbed, "Son of Sam."

Presented the script by the two actors at the wrap party for *Girl 6*, Lee first intended to executive-produce the film with Imperioli directing. But as the project developed and the focus of the script was expanded, Imperioli began to have second thoughts. He told Ed Morales of *The Village Voice*, "it was kinda beyond someone who was going to direct for the first time. Besides, Spike is a New York Storyteller." Lee felt he could make the film, his first with an all-white cast, because he knew these characters. "I don't think there's anybody in this script that I haven't met or I'm not familiar with," Lee told Morales. But Lee is already anticipating the criticism. "There are still folks who, after *Do the Right Thing* and *Jungle Fever*, think I don't have white characters in my films," Lee said. "Then the African Americans are going to say I'm a sellout because the movie doesn't have a black theme."

Focusing not on the grisly murders, but on the hot summer heat and flames of fear, paranoia, and intolerance the murders fanned, *Summer of Sam* may be a worthy bookend for Lee's *Do the Right Thing*.

The past few years Lee has also been developing a half-hour drama called *L.I.E.*, a television show that would have focused on the hardships of interracial friendships. But after the death of Brandon Tartikoff, the project was put on hold. Spike said softly, "It's still a blow how he's not here anymore." Another project, which could be the most important film of his career is a cinematic biography of Jackie Robinson, who is perhaps the single most powerful symbol of civil rights within twentieth-century U.S. history. But Lee has always had a problem securing a decent budget from any film studio. For example, financial contributions were required from various black celebrities to complete *Malcolm X*. As to whether *Jackie Robinson* will ever be made, Lee sadly said, "I hope so. We've always had a script, we just don't have the money."

Spike Lee has proven to be one of cinema's most important visionaries within the last fifteen years. He has resisted the temptation to make formula Hollywood films and has fought for the artistic freedom to make the films he chooses. He understands that most studio executives and the media have labeled him as difficult, to which he wrote in Fireside Books' *Do the Right Thing*, "Any black man who is intelligent, opinionated and who doesn't smile 'ha-ha, chee-chee' is continuously branded as difficult. I'm not difficult, I just know exactly what I want."

Despite a perceived lack of recognition fro the Academy, and AFI's failure to include *Do the Right Thing* within its top one-hundred American films, Lee's work has had a tremendous impact on American filmmaking. The depth and breadth of his footprint can be seen in minority filmmakers like F. Gary Gray, John Singleton, Kasi Lemmons, and the Hughes brothers who have followed his lead and told their own stories. Lee has made being black not incidental but a privilege, and helped usher in a film renaissance that makes our whole society richer.

Spike Lee's Seventies Flashback

STEPHEN PIZZELLO/1999

OVER THE COURSE of his career Spike Lee has excelled at capturing the urban experience on screen. After exploding onto the scene with the sexually charged, ultra-low-budget comedy *She's Gotta Have It* (1986), the director has injected a vibrant sense of life into a variety of cinematic cityscapes. *Do the Right Thing* (1989) made a powerful statement about interracial relationships in a neighborhood threatening to explode; *Mo' Better Blues* (1990) captured the moody ambience of a jazz musician's life; *Malcolm X* (1992) tracked the rise of the titular figure from street hustler to savvy statesman; *Crooklyn* (1994) contrasted the edginess of inner-city life with the comforts of the suburbs; *Clockers* (1995) explored the hazardous lifestyle of crack dealers; and *He Got Game* (1998) set father against son on asphalt basketball courts.

With his latest film, *Summer of Sam,* Lee chose to revisit an epochal moment in the history of New York City: the middle months of 1977, when various events and trends converged to create a memorable mosaic of the world's most volatile metropolis.

Lee recently took time out of his frenetic schedule to answer *AC's* questions about his latest picture for "joint," in the director's playful parlance).

AMERICAN CINEMATOGRAPHER: *Why did you choose this particular topic and time frame—the Son of Sam killer, and the summer of 1977 in New York City—as the basis for a film?*

Published in *American Cinematographer* 80, no. 6 (June 1999): 50–52. Reprinted courtesy of *American Cinematographer* magazine.

SPIKE LEE: I grew up in New York, and I found that whole summer to be significant. What I really want to try to emphasize to people is that this film is not just about the Son of Sam—David Berkowitz. This film is more about how the Son of Sam killings affected and changed the lives of eight million New Yorkers during that particular summer. The summer of the killings was also one of the hottest ever on record in New York, which consequently caused a big blackout; Studio 54 had just opened, and disco was at its peak; Plato's Retreat was in full swing, so to speak, with that whole sex thing going on; the punk scene was happening at CBGB's; and in addition, it was Reggie Jackson's first year with the Yankees.

Also, I came home from school that summer. I had just finished my sophomore year in Atlanta, Georgia at Morehouse College, and I couldn't find a job. I had gotten a Super 8 camera, so I spent the whole summer just going around New York City and filming stuff. That was really when I decided that I wanted to be a filmmaker.

AC: *Back then, did you immediately think that the Son of Sam story would make a good film, or did that idea come along later?*
LEE: That idea occurred to me much later, but I'm still trying to find my Super 8 footage so I can cut it into the movie. I've looked all over the place, but I can't find it! [Laughs.]

AC: *How did this project develop?*
LEE: I was approached by Michael Imperioli, a very fine actor who's been in several of my films, as well as a few of Martin Scorcese's. He also has a lead role in that great new TV series *The Sopranos*. He came to be and said that he and his friend Victor Colicchio had a really good story about Son of Sam and that whole summer. They knew I had a development deal, and I told them I'd read it. I loved the script, and I told them I wanted to get it made. My first intention was to serve as executive producer on it, so we made a wish list of actors and directors, but we couldn't get any of our top choices to commit. I wasn't really satisfied with the people we *could* get to commit, so I eventually decided to do a rewrite and open the story up a bit. It was a great script as it was, but I felt that we needed to incorporate more of New York City instead of just setting the story in this one Italian neighborhood in the Bronx. Once I finished my rewrite, I decided that I wanted to direct it.

A C : *What kind of research did you do in preparation for the film?*

L E E : We did a ton of research. I tried to read everything I could about psychopaths and serial killers. I also wanted to see all of the news reports and commercials that were airing during that period, and to dig into the whole music scene as well. I was driving various researchers mad!

A C : *Even though the film is set in the seventies, it seems that you managed to resist satirizing that period.*

L E E : A lot of times when people go back and do period films about the seventies, they make fun of that era—the hair, the clothes, the dancing, the music. When you do that, it's almost as if you think that the subject matter isn't serious or worthy, and I think that comes across in the movie. I let everyone on the film know that I didn't consider the period of the film to be a joking matter. I had lived through that era, and I had worn those clothes; back then, I thought I looked great, and everyone else felt that way about themselves too. I didn't want our movie to have a condescending attitude. That can be hard to resist, because it's very easy to make a quick joke about bellbottoms or polyester shirts, but we wanted to do more than that with this film.

A C : *You have a small role in the film as a TV reporter, and it seems as if you wanted to emphasize the media's presentation and distortion of the Summer of Sam story.*

L E E : I think that's a very important point. The New York media really played up the frenzy, and the circulation of the *Daily News* and the *Post* doubled while Berkowitz was killing people. Every day there was a new headline. I know the reporters were just doing their jobs, but I think they also contributed to the frenzy and the mayhem that was gripping the city at the time.

A C : *It's ironic, because that type of coverage can both spur a killer on and simultaneously lead to his capture.*

L E E : That's true. I mean, Son of Sam started writing letter to Jimmy Breslin that were published in the papers. I actually gave Jimmy a cameo in the film. His opinion of Berkowitz was short and sweet—he called him a sick f***. [Laughs.]

A C : *Along with Martin Scorsese and Woody Allen, you're one of the country's most prominent New York–based filmmakers. How familiar were you with the neighborhoods presented in* Summer of Sam?

L E E :   To tell you the truth, I wasn't really too familiar with the Bronx before I made this film. The only time I ever went to the Bronx was when I went to Yankee Stadium. In saying that, I don't mean any disrespect to that part of town, but if you live in Brooklyn, you just don't really go the Bronx! To a New Yorker, those places are like the two opposite ends of the world.

A C :   *Many of your past films have been set in African-American neighborhoods, but this one takes place in an area that's predominantly Italian.*

L E E :   Well, this is not specifically an African-American story, it's more of a story about New York as a whole. Most of my films have been set in New York, so I felt more at ease telling this particular story. I've done other stories with Italian-American characters—*Jungle Fever, Do the Right Thing, Clockers*— and I think one thing that helps me in that regard is that I'm a good listener. If I don't know about something firsthand, I ask! It's as simple as that.

I know it sounds stupid to say, but I have a lot of Italian-American friends [laughs], so I felt very comfortable dealing with that aspect of the story.

A C :   *What kind of coaching did you give to the actors in this picture?*

L E E :   The cast members were all very fine, trained and talented people, so I didn't have to do much coaching. I just wanted them to be authentic, and since they were mostly Italian-American actors, they knew what I was after. I needed them to be 'in the moment' at that particular point in time, during the summer of 1977.

A C :   *Your director of photography, Ellen Kuras, ASC, demonstrated that she really knew the 1970s New York scene in* I Shot Andy Warhol. *She's also shot 4* Little Girls *for you, as well as numerous commercials and music videos. What makes the two of you click so well?*

L E E :   Ellen is not only a great person, but she's a listener who tries to be flexible and adaptable. So often when you work with people, they're set in their ways—in this business, you've got to be flexible. Also, Ellen comes from a documentary background, which I feel is a great asset. If I say, "Ellen, let's not use a light here," she's fine with it. I think a lot of cinematographers light not for the movie, but for their fellow directors of photography. They're more concerned about what their peers are going to say. That approach might be all right for them, but it might not be what's best for the film.

Ellen is also very aware of the actors. I've worked with cinematographers who will set up a light right in an actor's face, without caring about the discomfort it causes—that type of director of photography only cares that the shot looks good.

A C : *What did you and Ellen talk about during prep?*
L E E : We discussed using a lot of different stocks. A lot of the story is told through the media, so we wanted to use video and shoot stuff off of TV screens. We also used some reversal stock and cross-processed it, as I'd previously done on *Clockers*. We basically just kept our minds open to every possibility, because I thought the script called for a lot of different looks.

Ellen and I tried to plan all of the visual elements during preproduction, but she sat next to me every day in dailies, and we made some adjustments here and there. When I got to the set every day, everyone would gather around me—the gaffer, the grip, the AD and Ellen—and we'd go over what we were going to do.

A C : *Did you improvise much on the set?*
L E E : Sometimes everything was planned out, and other times we'd have to do some blocking. Nothing on this film was storyboarded, though. I storyboard very little. I don't mean that I just show up on the set and make things up, but I feel that storyboarding can sometimes lock you in too much. If you're trying to get something very specific, or if you only have one or two takes, or if it's a big, big shot, then storyboards can be helpful. The riot sequence in *Do the Right Thing* is an example of a situation where storyboards were very useful. I also used boards for the assassination sequence in *Malcolm X*. All of that stuff was very involved.

A C : *I noticed several times that you used your favorite technique of placing actors on cranes and dollies to create an unusual floating sense of movement.*
L E E : Yeah, the famous "Spike Lee dolly shot." [Laughs.] In this film, we basically used that for scenes where characters were in various mental states caused by their use of uppers, downers, cocaine, and so on.

We also used the Steadicam for five or six days. [Operator] Larry McConkey did a few shots where the actors were standing on a Titan crane; the camera rode along with them as the crane was lowered to the ground, and then Larry followed them along as they walked off it.

A C : *Did you use two cameras for dialogue scenes, as you generally have in the past?*

L E E : I always shoot with two cameras simultaneously, because it makes a great difference to the actors. Actors will eventually be spent if they keep giving their all while reading lines offscreen. If you shoot the actors at the same time, they can avoid stepping on each other's lines.

On this film, we had some long dialogue scenes involving four or five people, and those were the situations that I found to be the toughest. We always had two dollies covering the action, and we had to keep them from running into each other.

A C : *What kind of pace do you maintain on the set?*

L E E : I work very fast. I don't like to wait around, and it's always been that way. I shot *She's Gotta Have It* in twelve days.

A C : *Almost all of this film was shot on location. Do you generally prefer real settings to studio work?*

L E E : I don't really like shooting on stages. When you shoot at a real location, it's not fabricated, and you get that extra flavor of being there. I don't really mind if we have to make some adjustments because it's a real location. It would be hard for me to go to the same stage every single day. That would drive me up the wall.

Delroy Lindo on Spike Lee

DELROY LINDO/1999

D ELROY L INDO : *The first things, Spike, that I'm interested in are your influences.*

SPIKE LEE; Well, growing up, I had no idea I wanted to be a filmmaker. And I would say that most filmmakers found out at an early age that this is what they want to do: they saw a film that changed their lives. I had no idea I wanted to be a filmmaker. In fact, I didn't know people made movies. You know, you just went to the movie theater and they were there. So it wasn't until I was in film school, a graduate student at NYU film school, that I really started to study, not to become a filmmaker, but to study cinema. And so I'll say Martin Scorsese's been a big influence, and the master, Kurosawa. In fact, *Rashomon* was sort of like a blueprint for my first film, *She's Gotta Have It*. My mother, my parents, were a great influence on myself and my siblings, as far as encouraging us in the arts. My father's a jazz musician, so I grew up seeing him play in the Beer Inn and the Village Gate, all those places, going up to the Newport Jazz Festival, and my mother was dragging my brother Chris and I to Broadway plays and movies.

LINDO : *And your parents introduced you to Broadway plays; they would take you to Broadway plays?*

LEE : Not my father, he wasn't going, but my mother did.

LINDO : *[Laughs] Okay.*

LEE: And then there's another group—not so much by their work—but pioneer African American directors, people like Oscar Micheaux and Spencer Williams, people that opened it all up, like Ossie Davis.

LINDO: *Can you just expand on what it was exactly about their work that influenced you, and how that affected you?*
LEE: I think that as an artist, you really have to understand, whether you're black or white or whatever, that you're not the first person there. There were many people before you that were doing things. They went through a lot of shit, whatever the circumstances were, so you, so I could be in the position I was.

LINDO: *Did you ever entertain the thought of doing any other career?*
LEE: Well, really, I thought I was going to be an athlete, but that was . . .

LINDO: *As in what?*
LEE: A baseball player, playing second base for the Mets. But, when I went to Morehouse, I said I had no idea what I wanted to do. I mean, it was expected I'd go to college. I knew that was a given, because my father went to Morehouse and my grandfather went to Morehouse, and my mother went to Spelman and my grandma went to Spelman, which is across the street. There was a time at the end of my sophomore year, when I had used up all my electives, because I hadn't declared a major, and I finally decided upon mass communications. I'd deal with film, radio, print journalism. And I really got pushed by a teacher, Dr. Herb Eichelberg, who's still there. He really took a deep interest in me. And so, when I graduated from Morehouse, I knew I still had to further my education. The only way you can become a filmmaker, I think, is by making films. You don't have to necessarily go to film school, but for me, the best route was to go to film school. So, then I went from there to NYU.

LINDO: *How did you get into NYU?*
LEE: I was lucky, because to get into NYU back then, you did not have to take the GRE. I also applied to UCLA and USC, and you needed the GRE and you needed the astronomical score on the GRE, and I didn't get it. Lucky for me, you didn't have to do that for NYU. You just had to submit a creative portfolio. It was at NYU where Ernest Dickerson and I hooked up. And it was

interesting that we were both products of predominantly black schools. Ernest had graduated from Howard University, and so going in Ernest and I knew that we had to be ten times better than our fellow white classmates. That's the way it is.

LINDO: *You connection with Ernest: it wasn't just that you were black students in the same program?*
LEE: That had a lot to do with it, though. I mean, we had similar tastes, we both loved cinema. But we were like the only two black people there that made it from our class, that made it throughout the whole three years. Ernest and I just naturally hooked up.

LINDO: *When you speak about the pressure that is on black filmmakers—every film must answer all of the questions.*
LEE: But it's not as bad as it used to be. *She's Gotta Have It,* in 1986, was really like the only black film that came out. Because of that, Nola Darling had to represent every single African American woman.

LINDO: *All black womanhood.*
LEE: And no role can do that.

LINDO: *Describe for me the first day on the set of the very first film you ever made and then describe for me the first day on the set of* Summer of Sam.
LEE: I don't remember.

LINDO: *She's Gotta Have It.*
LEE: I don't remember. We shot *She's Gotta Have It* in twelve days and it was a blur. It was like the twelve worst days of my life.

LINDO: *Why do you say that?*
LEE: We were shooting sixteen, seventeen hours a day. I had never worked with real actors before, you're under tremendous pressure. You know, it was do or die. I had no money at all, but I was the caterer—I mean, I had to worry about everything, including the costumes.

LINDO: *So you were worrying about communicating with the actors, the catering—making sure everybody gets fed.*

LEE: The location manager, all that stuff. On *Summer of Sam,* all I know is, it was in the Bronx. I cannot tell you what we shot the first day.

LINDO: *You said you didn't have the vocabulary to communicate with the actors, yet you got the performances on film. Did they come from the actors? How did that evolve, how did that happen?*
LEE: To be honest, we just wanted to get image on film.

LINDO: *[Laughs] Okay.*
LEE: Because earlier, the summer before, I tried to do a film called *Messenger,* and that was a fiasco. And it never happened, and my name was mud. So literally, this was like my last shot, you know, a twelve day shoot. We only got one or two takes per shot. I mean, I wasn't doing that much directing. My part of being a filmmaker came in the editing process, because that was the first and only film that I edited myself. So, it's not the way to make a film.

LINDO: *When I asked you about your influences, one of the things you spoke about was the circumstances that the filmmakers were up against and that suggested to me something about your social stance as a filmmaker. Can you expand a little bit on what you meant by that and how that has influenced you?*
LEE: Not too many people get to make films. Number one, it costs so much money. And I think that that's the reason why, as a people, we haven't made the great inroads we've made [laughs] in the other arts. Because no money was needed for us to pick up a trumpet or whatever that instrument was. In filmmaking, it takes money. We have not produced our Duke Ellingtons yet, or [Romare] Beardens, Jacob Lawrences, or Toni Morrisons. I'm talking about, as far as coming out of cinema. It's going to happen. We're really in the infancy stage, as a people, I feel. I just always felt that there were people before me, pioneers that set the path, that have shown us a way this could be done, and then if I could learn from their victories and also where they might have made some mistakes, you know, it would be to my advantage.

LINDO: *I've watched a number of your films back to back to back to back, and the thing that occurs to me is that you have great love for African people, for African American people, and your films explore different aspects of what that experience is. Did you have, at the beginning of your career, some specific plan in which you wanted to investigate those kinds of things, or is it more on a film by film basis?*

L E E :   It was a combination of both things. I think that when I decided I wanted to be a filmmaker, I wanted to attempt to capture the richness of African American culture that I can see, just standing on the corner, or looking out my window every day, and try to get that on screen. And then I also made a conscious effort not to fall into this whole positive-negative trick bag which a lot of African American artists get caught up in. The fact that we have been dogged out for so hard and for so long in films, television, and stuff. You have a faction of people who, in response to that, want every image of African Americans to be a hundred percent pristine—God-like and Christ-like [laughs]. And I said, I don't want to do that. Number one, it's not truthful. Number two, it's not interesting either. In *She's Gotta Have It,* you know, I'm perpetuating the myth of the black woman being loose and that kind of stuff. And in *School Daze,* it's the so-called petty differences that keep African Americans from being a more unified people, differences based upon skin complexion and class and hair texture, whether you have "good hair" or "bad hair." Black people tell me, "Oh, now white people going to know." White people [laughs] have been knowing that. In fact, they were the ones that put that whole practice in place, when we were brought over on the slave ships. It's documented: they did not put everybody speaking the same language chained together. If you spoke one dialect, your ass was over here, and if you were another tribe, you ass was on the other end of the ship, because they knew that if they put everybody together, it was going to be mutiny, you know, it'd be their ass.

L I N D O :   *You made* She's Gotta Have It, *and that makes a splash, and then you make* School Daze, *which makes less of a splash.*
L E E :   A lot less.

L I N D O :   *Okay, you said it. How disappointed were you with regard to the reception of* School Daze, *and to what extent did that affect you going in to* Do the Right Thing?
L E E :   I really wasn't disappointed with the reception of *School Daze,* because, you have to remember, when *She's Gotta Have It* came out, the whole hype—which was nothing of my doing—had people trying to put me in as "a black Woody Allen." And then when they see my next film, it's a semi-musical

about a predominantly black college. Well, a lot of these people wouldn't even know that predominantly black colleges existed [laughs]. I had to take their reaction with a grain of salt. It was because of the various stagings of the musical sequences in *School Daze* that I was able to direct the riot sequences, and work with a lot of people, which I'd never done before. So, everything was a process, you know, preparing me for the next show.

LINDO: *Do you consider* Do the Right Thing *a kind of milestone in your career?*
LEE: Well, I mean, when I'm walking down the street, that's what everybody keeps saying: *Do the Right Thing.* And any time people want me to do commercials, I always try to stick that in there: "Do the right thing." *Do the Right Thing* came about from me just reading the newspapers about three African American men. They were in the Howard Beach section of Queens, and they're chased out of a pizzeria by a gang of bat-wielding young Italian Americans. One of the men runs across the BQE [Brooklyn-Queens Expressway], whatever the thing up there, and he gets hit by a car. So, when I read about that, I said, you know, I'm going to make the setting for *Do the Right Thing* this pizzeria and I'm going to put it in a predominantly black neighborhood.

LINDO: *A Spike Lee set is like no other set in the world, simply by virtue of the fact there are so many black people working. The number of opportunities that you're creating behind the camera, was that part of your idea?*
LEE: Oh definitely. Once the door was opened up a little bit, you know, we had to try and get as many people as we could in with us. And so that was a struggle, because we had to fight with the unions.

LINDO: *What was the content of that fight?*
LEE: The unions historically are just set up for white males. And so any time you want to bring people in, they say, "Well, they're not in the union." But we always knew that if we wanted to do something we'd have to go through the unions, because that's the stranglehold.

LINDO: *I wanted you to talk a little bit about where that kind of ethic comes from, in you?*
LEE: I think it really just comes from sports. You've got to have a team. You have a team, and everybody comes together. I mean, film is a collaborative

effort and you've got to have a core. Now, you're going to fill in different spots, but you're still going to have your core, and the core has always been Wynn Thomas, production design; Robi Reed was casting; Ruth Carter was costumes. Ruth went on to do *Amistad,* where she got nominated, and then we started hiring her assistant, Sandra Hernandez. And my father had been doing the scores. And Ernest Dickerson, up to *Malcolm X,* was the DP. After Ernest, we had to find another DP. When you think about it, that was the hardest thing to replace, because it's a very special relationship between the director and DP. And then I worked with Malik [Sayeed] for *Clockers, Girl 6,* and *He Got Game.*

LINDO: *How did you arrive at Malik Sayeed?*
LEE: Malik was an electric on *Malcolm X.*

LINDO: *I know that. When I got on* Clockers, *and Malik was the DP, I was like,* "Well, okay."
LEE: Malik always wanted . . . he was training to be a DP. He was doing commercials and stuff before *Clockers. Clockers* was his first feature.

LINDO: *And this is a major job, his first feature.*
LEE: He said, "Let me in on it. I might get my neck cut, but let me take a shot."

LINDO: *Did Malik come to you or did you go to him?*
LEE: No, I went to him. Because I understand, it's a difficult situation, because it might have been another five or six years before Malik would get another opportunity to shoot a feature. It's a delicate balance: you want to give people opportunities, but at the same time, you don't want to jeopardize the film.

LINDO: *What I remember about* Clockers *is that it was his* [Malik Sayeed's] *look.*
LEE: He uses a different stock. It was his idea to start using the cross processor: that's his look.

LINDO: *That's his signature.*

LEE: That's his signature. And we used it more on *Girl 6,* and a lot on *He Got Game* too.

LINDO: *Did it take you a minute to embrace that?*
LEE: Yeah, because when we were on pre-production for *Girl 6,* he wanted to shoot the whole film on tape, on videotape, and transfer to film [laughs]. And I said, "Nah, we ain't doin' that."

LINDO: *What effect was he going after?*
LEE: Something that looked different.

LINDO: *Okay, okay.*
LEE: [Laughs] I said, "We're going out, but not that out!"
[laughs] But to finish the answer, I think that I've always felt the responsibility, that if I was able to get through, then I would have to—not because I'm in the Salvation Army or the welfare system or anything—give talented, young, hungry people opportunities.

LINDO: *I want to ask you about how you use actors. You have an extended ensemble of actors that you work with. Are you writing for those actors when you're putting a piece of work together?*
LEE: Some parts have been written for people. I wrote *He Got Game* for Denzel, wrote *Mo' Better Blues* for Denzel. Other parts, you don't know. You could be surprised to find somebody who fits, who you hadn't thought of. I've received a lot of criticism because some people think I use the same actors all the time. But it's not like it's the same actors playing the same role in five of my films.

LINDO: *That's right.*
LEE: Each time they come back, it's a different part, and they're showing something different too.

LINDO: *In terms of the films that I saw, I think about John Turturro. John's had an incredible range of parts.*
LEE: He's been in seven.

LINDO: *Bill Nunn, in the early works, Giancarlo [Esposito], Sam Jackson: an incredible range of opportunities that you're providing for actors.*

LEE: You go through the films: *School Daze,* that was a lot of people's first film. It was Jasmine Guy's first film, and Tisha Campbell's. *Do the Right Thing* was Rosie Perez's first film, Martin Lawrence's first film. *Jungle Fever* was Halle Berry's first film. *Clockers* was Mekhi Phifer's first film. He's really turned himself into a fine young actor now.

LINDO: *What about Sam and Halle in* Jungle Fever? *Brilliant performances.*
LEE: I'd first like to talk about Halle. When people see *Jungle Fever,* they still don't realize that that's Halle Berry, because she doesn't look like Halle Berry, and I think that there are not too many women who look like Halle who would've gone through that transformation or look.

LINDO: *What about in terms of what they were bringing and how you dealt with them in the rehearsal process and on the set?*
LEE: Oh, they worked a lot together, because he was taking her around the places in Harlem, stuff like that, because Halle had lived in Ohio. She grew up in Cleveland, and then she lived in L.A. She didn't know New York, so Sam took her around, and they rehearsed. We all rehearsed together, but I think they did a lot of work by themselves then. So that's why it was as good as it was.

LINDO: *For me, the whole thing was really well acted, sensitively acted.*
LEE: The thing about *Jungle Fever* was, I think a lot of people got tripped up into the whole interracial thing, but for me, that wasn't even the most important part of the story. For me, the thing was the devastation that crack is afflicting upon families, and generations and generations just being wiped out.

LINDO: *You see, I didn't know that, because I thought that in making* Jungle Fever, *you were making a film about an interracial relationship.*
LEE: That was the hook, but for me, that really wasn't the most important thing.

LINDO: *That's not what the story was.*
LEE: Ossie Davis, the Good Reverend Doctor, killing his own son: we took that from Marvin Gaye, Sr. shooting Marvin Gaye, Jr. There's something biblical about it, you might say, a father taking the life of his own son.

LINDO: *Was that in the script originally?*
LEE: Yes.

LINDO: *Okay.*
LEE: With the scope of *Malcolm X* that we wanted, it would not have gotten made without Denzel, and there were times when we were shooting *Malcolm X* that we all had to pinch ourselves collectively, because we thought we were seeing the reincarnation of Malcolm. And Denzel always said, "Spike, I cannot be Malcolm X. But if I put myself in the right place, I'll be open, so the spirit of Malcolm can come through." We could not go anywhere without black people telling us, "Don't mess up Malcolm." Denzel and I used to joke that we had to keep our passports handy if we had to slip out of the country.

LINDO: *Might have to skip town, right?*
LEE: Yeah, we've got to slip out of the United States of America under the cover of darkness while we still could.

LINDO: *Do you remember when we shot the scene at the SRO?*
LEE: Yes, I remember, we had talked about West Indian Archie [Lindo's character in the film], that he had a stroke but we hadn't discussed how severe it was going to be. You surprised me. I mean, the thing was all broke down. I say, "Ooh," and Denzel's like, "Damn" [laughs].

LINDO: *The process of the work felt really good, very focused. There was a lot of incredible energy, all focused in the same direction on this film, it seemed to me, and without it being spoken.*
LEE: You could feel it. And people knew what this film was about, who Malcolm was, and that they had to come in their "A" game, as simple as that. That's why I have to really give it to actors because, you do your work and then you just leave. But you could do good work, see your scene, and then the filmmakers don't even use the right takes or whatever. It's like a complete act of faith. I can never act. That's why I've got to direct, because you have control.

LINDO: *It's nothing to do with you. But it's happened to me a few times.*
LEE: That's tough.

LINDO: *If I had* Crooklyn *to do again, I would have worked more with the fear that I felt. I was afraid of those children, and I think that what I did was put a lot of that energy into the whole thing about playing the piano. And ultimately, I was somewhat disappointed with my work in* Crooklyn, *especially after West Indian Archie. Then you came along and you offered me* Clockers.

LEE: I was not disappointed in your work at all. I think you did a wonderful job. I think that what makes great actors is that they're versatile and just like an athlete. The great athletes, the great artists, have to have the total game: they have range and you have that. And so I had no qualms, no hesitation, knowing that you'd be able to bring that terror to *Clockers.*

LINDO: *You have given me, and I've observed that you give other actors, a latitude, room to work.*

LEE: Well, I don't do that with everybody. I think that as a director, you've got to know—same thing as a coach does in sports—you've got to know what people's limitations are. You have to play to people's strengths. That's really just what it is.

LINDO: *You remember what you said to me, when you called me about* Clockers?

LEE: What'd I say?

LINDO: *You said that you wanted to put the nail in the coffin on this kind of film.*

LEE: Well, we were unsuccessful. [both laugh]. Still making those.

LINDO: *That was my next question.*

LEE: We're still making those [laughs]. I mean that the film's very good, but they still keep making those ghetto-shoot-em--ups.

LINDO: *But what did you think about your achievement with* Clockers, *from the point of view of what you wanted to do?*

LEE: Number one, I really think that we demystified this whole romantic vision of gangsters, drugs, hip-hop, you know, shoot-em-up. It really tried to establish that this is a dead end. It's interesting that it was not an original project of mine. It was Richard Price, a very fine novelist, he wrote the novel, *Clockers,* and Martin Scorsese was supposed to direct it and Rocco was going to be played by Robert De Niro. Marty decided he wanted to do *Casino* instead, so he said, "Spike, I want you to direct it, and I'll executive produce." At first I was very resistant, because, like I said before, I had not wanted to make another hip-hop gangster shoot-em-up film. And then also the script that Richard Price wrote for Scorsese to direct was really a star vehicle for De Niro. So, I pitched my deal, where I really wanted to tell it through the viewpoint of this young African American male drug dealer who's caught between the proverbial rock and a hard place, and they said, "Okay." And that's where we found Mekhi Phifer to play Strike. So we changed up everything after that.

LINDO: 4 Little Girls: *can you tell me why you wanted to make that film?*
LEE: I've always wanted to do a feature length documentary and this subject matter was just calling out to be done. *4 Little Girls* tells the story of the bombing of the 16th Street Baptist Church, which was blown up in Birmingham, Alabama. I wanted to go back and try to bring to life these four girls, who they were, and also what they might've become, by talking to their parents and relatives, and put it within the context of that pivotal moment in American history, you know, the Civil Rights movement, and Birmingham was the focal point. I wanted the people who were there, who were right up in it. No one could tell us better than the people who were there.

LINDO: *The fact that you have become a parent, did that have any bearing one way or the other?*
LEE: It really only affected me while—not before, not in the decision to do the film—but while we were doing it. Because when you interview these parents and they talk about the loss of a child, then if you're a parent, you definitely think about your child and how would you react if your child was murdered in a heinous crime like that. You cannot duplicate what a parent is going to say as she pulls out her daughter's dress or her report card or her Girl Scout banner and all those things that they've kept as reminders of their children, no longer here.

LINDO: *When we were speaking about Malik Sayeed, you talked about Malik having developed a signature. Do you feel like you have a signature?*
LEE: I think that they could probably tell, if you take the credit off it, you could still probably tell a film I directed. I do one shot, you know, where a

scene's like people walking down, floating down a block. People might say that's the signature shot.

LINDO: *Tell me about how you use your music. How is that a part of your creative process?*

LEE: My use of music and my understanding of music—I have to give all the credit to my father, because he introduced me to music—jazz, as he would say, the only real music—at a very early age. I grew up in a household where music was played all the time. We give the same respect to music, pay the same attention to music, that we pay to the actors, to the costume design, to the production design. It is an integral part of filmmaking.

LINDO: *And to somebody who says, "Well, there was too much music in the film, it kind of was taking away from the acting, I couldn't follow because there was too much music in the thing." What do you say to them?*

LEE: I think that the human brain is a very wonderful thing. And one can talk on the phone and watch television at the same time. The human brain allows you to do many things at the same time. I think that maybe if they say it was a little too loud, they might be right, but I just like to have music, where you really hear it. That's the taste thing.

LINDO: *When I saw* He Got Game, *your use of Aaron Copland's music worked for me. But, you know, Aaron Copland . . . who would've thought?*

LEE: Not only Aaron Copland, but Aaron Copland and Public Enemy, back to back.

LINDO: *I could see Public Enemy.*

LEE: Yeah, you could see Public Enemy, but could you see Public Enemy and Aaron Copland played side by side? When I was writing *He Got Game,* I was listening to Aaron Copland. I knew Aaron Copland would be right for this film.

LINDO: *Why?*

LEE: Aaron Copland is one of the American composers and basketball is an American game. And I just felt that the largeness and the scope of his sound, when you hear it, really, is always . . . Forget about *He Got Game.* When you hear "Appalachian Springs" or "Fanfare for the Common Man," you hear

America. It's the bigness and vastness, and I thought that the combination of the two [Copland and PE] would work. I love that "Lincoln Portrait" was used for the climactic game between Denzel's character and Ray Allen's character. I went through all of his works, with the great cooperation of the Aaron Copland estate. They were very enthusiastic about this project and they felt that this really would reach people who had no idea who Aaron Copland was.

L I N D O : *What's your favorite part of filmmaking process?*
L E E : To me, the favorite is the whole post-production, after the actors are out of there. Not just actors. It's the crew as much as the actors.

L I N D O : *[Laughs] Okay.*
L E E : But people don't really understand, unless you become a director, how intense it is during the actual production; it's just physically and mentally taxing. So, my favorite part is just being alone with the editor. I've been very fortunate to work with only really two editors, Barry Brown and Sam Pollard. And we have a great relationship and it's just you and the editorial staff. You have hundreds and hundreds of thousand feet of film and you try to shape and mold, put some type of . . .

L I N D O : *Cohesion.*
L E E : [Laughs] Try to make it cohesive.

L I N D O : *With regard to Sam Pollard and Barry Brown, can you tell me about their different styles of working, if any, and how their styles of working impact your work?*
L E E : The biggest similarity between both those guys, besides them being great editors, is that they both come from the documentary field background. Sam was one of the producers on *Eyes on the Prize*. He's got this new one coming out, *Make Me a World*. Barry, his first film got nominated for an Oscar; it was called *The War at Home*, which is about the anti–Vietnam War movement here in the United States of America.

L I N D O : *Oh, I didn't know that, Barry did that.*
L E E : Barry gave me my first job in film. I was in NYU and Barry was one of the owners of this small American independent distribution company called

First Run Features. I was the inventory person, so I cleaned the films, shipped them out, ran errands.

L I N D O : *I asked you about the first day of shooting on* Summer of Sam *and you said, "I don't remember, but it was in the Bronx" [laughs].*
L E E : [Laughs] We shot the whole film in the Bronx. The only time I ever go to Bronx is to see the Yankees. I mean, it's funny, because if you live in Brooklyn, you don't go to the Bronx, and if you live in the Bronx, you don't go to Brooklyn. It's like neither one knows about the other borough. Michael Imperioli and Victor Colicchio came to me and said, "Spike, we got this great script for a movie, it's about the Son of Sam." The summer of '77, New York was crazy, and I remember, at that time, I said, "Fine." And I loved the script and, you know, I wanted to executive produce it.

L I N D O : *You didn't want to direct this one?*
L E E : I didn't want to direct it at first. We couldn't find a director, and I looked at it again and said, "This is something I'd like to direct." But at the same time, I felt the story was a little too small because their draft only stayed within this small Italian American community, and I wanted to open it up and try to show the blacks and Puerto Ricans who were also living in New York City at the time. Before we began, there was some controversy from some of the parents of people who were victims of David Berkowitz, the Son of Sam—they objected to the film.

L I N D O : *Did you feel an obligation to explain what the film would be about?*
L E E : We didn't do that, and we felt that there's no way you're going to win talking to a parent whose daughter was murdered by the Son of Sam.

L I N D O : *What were they saying? "Don't make this film?"*
L E E : They didn't want the film made at all. If you look at *The Boston Strangler,* you know, there have been films like this based on . . .

L I N D O : *Serial killers or whatever . . .*
L E E : . . . real events, and in no way, shape, or form did we feel it was an exploitation of the victims of Son of Sam. For me, the film was really about New York City that summer. It was crazy hot that summer of '77; conse-

quently, that's why we had the blackout. The Yankees were going great, they went on to win the World Series, Reggie Jackson had three homers in game six against the Dodgers. You had the whole disco thing, in '77 Studio 54 opened, Plato's Retreat [the club in the film] was that.

LINDO: *This is an encyclopedia.*
LEE: And the whole punk rock scene, you know, we have scenes shot in CBGB's. So, it was really about that summer and how the Son of Sam affected everybody and how crazy New York City was. Another thing that's going to be strange about this film—well, no, strange is not the word, interesting to see—is that this is going to be my first film where it's not really an African American theme, since the film was predominantly Italian American.

LINDO: *Are you feeling any response, any whatever, about the film?*
LEE: No. I anticipate there are going to be some black people saying, "You know what, you're not black anymore. What's the matter?"

LINDO: *"You're abandoning your people?"*
LEE: Yeah, "You're abandoning your people." You're trying to do crossover, but it's none of that. I think that this is a great story, and I'm in New York, and this is a New York story.

LINDO: *Where do you feel you have evolved to as a filmmaker, at this point in your career?*
LEE: Well, number one, I hope that I'll continue to be given the chance to make films until I don't want to make them any more. And I also say my prayers every night, that I've been very fortunate to have amassed the body of work I've done, in a relatively short time.

LINDO: *I'm just glad, and I appreciate the fact you took the time to come down and talk to me.*
LEE: No, thank you.

LINDO: *I saw* Malcolm X *about a week and a half after it had opened and Aretha singing, "Some Day We'll All Be Free" just took me through the roof. It just was right.*

LEE: That wasn't my idea. That was Eric Martin's idea.

LINDO: *Well, it worked brother. I appreciate your honesty, but it worked.*
LEE: But you know what I'm going to say though. I'm going to say, when you were just saying, "A song . . . ," I thought you were going to say another song.

LINDO: *That's the moment I recall from* Malcolm.
LEE: I know, but I have to disagree. The best use of a song in *Malcolm X* is the Sam Cooke song.

LINDO: *No, I'm not arguing that. I mean, what all I'm telling you is what I recall from my experience of seeing* Malcolm *was that moment right there.*
LEE: More than "A Change Is Gonna Come" when he's about to get assassinated?

LINDO: *No, not more [laughs]. I'm just saying it worked. But we're getting off the subject here.*

Summer of Sam: An Interview with Spike Lee

PRAIRIE MILLER / 1999

S PIKE L EE MAY HAVE a fascination in his movies with the way dramatic conflict heats up with the temperature, but on this hot summer day Lee strode into the room looking cool and collected. Dressed sleekly in black with a diamond stud gleaming from his left ear, the outspoken moviemaker was more than ready to butt heads with the press over his latest controversial film touching on a very hot topic, *Summer of Sam.*

PRAIRIE MILLER: *What convinced you to make this movie?*
SPIKE LEE: Well, it's a very interesting script. I felt it had characters that are real. And the story talked about all the things that I remembered in that summer.

PM: *What do you remember about the summer of '77?*
SL: It was a great period in the history of New York City, with good and bad. So those were the things that drew me to the project.

PM: *What was good?*
SL: Oh, I remember the heat, the Yankees, disco . . .

PM: *This script was brought to you. Did you expand on the original material?*
SL: Yeah. We all shared. I did a rewrite. And I share screenwriting credits with Victor Colicchio. And Michael Imperioli. He's one of the stars now of *The Sopranos.*

Published in *All Movie Guide* (1999). Reprinted by permission of the author.

P M : *What did you add to the script?*

S L : Well, I just wanted to keep the thing intact because it was fine. But I wanted to expand and just come out of the neighborhood. So . . .

P M : *You seem to have a thing in your movies for hot weather. Do you see a connection between temperatures rising and drama or destiny?*

S L : After ninety-five degrees in New York City, things definitely change! Like homicide rates, domestic violence, and traffic accidents. That's been well documented.

P M : *What about the way personal lives intertwine with the temperature in* Summer of Sam?

S L : Everybody reacts differently, and things just become more strained and hectic as the temperature rises. Especially in a place like New York City, where everybody's living on top of each other.

P M : *Talk about your own character in the movie, the newscaster. I hear he's based on an actual reporter.*

S L : Nah. It's not in any way, shape or form John Johnson, no. You know, if I wanted John Johnson, he would have gotten to play himself.

P M : *Talk about David Berkowitz and the whole serial killer thing as a source of stress for everybody.*

S L : Well I think it's very simple. This film is not about David Berkowitz. It's not about Son of Sam. This film is about his evil energy that affected eight million New Yorkers. And I think that was the way it was portrayed in the film too.

P M : *How did you intend the movie to deal with people turning against each other in a crisis situation?*

S L : It could be anything. It could be Emmett Till in Mississippi, it could be Jews during the Holocaust. Whoever is the scapegoat.

It could be Marilyn Manson now, who's being blamed for what happened in Colorado. You know, things happen, and people want a scapegoat. It could be Oliver Stone, along with Warner Bros., who are being sued because some idiot saw *Natural Born Killers*. Now they're being blamed because they went out and killed people.

Now TV is being held the scapegoat for the violence in America. But the same scrutiny is not being brought upon guns and the NRA.

P M :   *What is the movie suggesting about human anxiety against outsiders?*
S L :   I think that anybody, if you have that village mentality and somebody comes in as an outsider or is deemed strange, you're going to get treated like that.

P M :   *The vigilante justice we see in the movie, did that really happen?*
S L :   That happened. A lot of people get hurt. And particularly in that neighborhood, the Country Club section of the Bronx. A lot of this film is true. And it didn't really matter to those vigilante mobs whether the guy was Son of Sam or not. They were going to get somebody. And with the police, it was like, we're going to collar somebody.

P M :   *Why do you tend to look at Italian Americans when you're focusing on white people in your movies?*
S L :   First of all, I think that you have to look at the body of my work. I've done twelve films. There are only three out of the twelve where I do that: *Do the Right Thing, Jungle Fever* and this one. *Summer of Sam* really is not my doing. I mean, it wasn't my original idea. The original story came from Michael Imperioli and Victor Colicchio. They're Italian Americans, and this event took place in this Italian American neighborhood.

In the other two movies, I was trying to deal with the dynamics. There's so much strained dynamics over the years between the African-American community and the Italian-American community here in New York City. *Do the Right Thing* was based upon the incident that happened in Howard Beach, and *Jungle Fever* was about the incident when Yusuf Hawkins was murdered by Joey Fama's gang in Bensonhurst. So those are the two incidents that were the impetus for both of those films.

P M :   *How about the role of the media in stoking up things in* Summer of Sam?
S L :   Well number one, they had the responsibility to report what was happening. But at the same time I felt that they knew they could sell a lot more papers too. So it was not a surprise that the *New York Post* and the *Daily News* doubled their circulation during that time.

And Jimmy Breslin once told me that Rupert Murdoch, who had just

bought the *Post,* was furious that Son of Sam was writing letters to Jimmy
Breslin who was a columnist at the *Daily News.* So the *Daily News* had an
exclusive that the *Post* could do nothing about. And they would try to outdo
each other with their headlines. The headlines you see in the film, we didn't
make those up. Those are original headlines from that summer.

P M :   *Jimmy Breslin kind of became a character in that whole drama.*
s L :   Unwillingly!

P M :   *That was great, the way you bring Breslin into the movie. Did he let you in
on any surprising stuff about those events?*
s L :   No. But any time Jimmy speaks, it's interesting. You just show up and
listen. Because he's a storyteller, and he's, for me, one of the truly originals.

P M :   *Why did you put him in the movie?*
s L :   Because to me he symbolizes New York. Just the way he talks, and the
way he writes and sees things. You know, we've become friends over the
years. And I thought that he needed to be a part of this film. There are going
to be a lot of young people who were born after 1977, and I think that he'll
be a great introduction to try to put all this into an historical context. And
to wrap it up at the end.

P M :   *What did you see in John Leguizamo that made you feel he was right for the
starring role?*
s L :   He's a great actor. I mean, people just get sidetracked by thinking, oh
he does comedies. But when you're doing a one man show on Broadway and
you're playing fifty something characters, that's acting. And it's also showing
he has a range, that he's versatile. A Derek Jeter range!

P M :   *Which character did you feel most connected to?*
s L :   You know, when I'm a director of a film, I think it's dangerous to
become attached to one character or another. You can't do that. I know I
don't do it.

P M :   *Talking about blame, what about that guy Calvin Johnson from Georgia,
who spent sixteen years in jail for rape and was just found innocent because of new
DNA evidence? I hear you went to school with him.*

SL: Yeah. I'll have to look in my yearbook because I don't remember what he looks like.

PM: *Is there anything else coming up for you?*
SL: Not that I could talk about! Not right now.

PM: *Oh, all right! Hey, what about Harvey, that talking dog in* Summer of Sam. *Who was that doing the talking?*
SL: John Turturro.

PM: *How's that for non-traditional casting! So how old were you and what were you up to when Son of Sam was on the loose?*
SL: I was twenty. It was very spooky. Everybody was scared then, you know?

PM: *How about you?*
SL: Not me. Son of Sam wasn't coming into Fort Greene. He wasn't coming into Bed-Stuy or Harlem. So it wasn't the heightened fear that you had elsewhere. People of color were alarmed up to the point where they found out he was white. And that's why I put that in the film. Because we were all scared that like if this guy's black, we're all gonna catch hell for this.

PM: *Why did you decide to keep the Son of Sam and his story in the background?*
SL: Because this is the movie we wanted to make. Our intention was never to do a film about a serial killer. Our intention was never to do a film about Son of Sam or David Berkowitz. Our intention was never to go into the mind of a psychopath, and to follow him. That's not the film we wanted to make, and that's not the film we made.

PM: *And yet you did include him in some way. So what was his purpose in being there? Was there some kind of combustibility factor at work?*
SL: He's an evil presence. An evil cloud hovering over eight million New Yorkers.

PM: *What kind of presence was the music of the time for you?*
SL: Well, it was not just the music. It was the whole age. People were just starting to come down with AIDS too. And the whole drug experimentation

thing was going out. Reagan was coming in. So the whole swing of the country was reversed. Elvis died. That had a huge effect on white America.

P M : *In a couple of words, what's your response to the controversy surrounding* Summer of Sam?

S L : What we are just really trying to do is stress the fact that this is not a film about a serial killer. It's not a film about David Berkowitz. It's a film about what happened during that very strange and peculiar summer. And how a madman changed the lives of eight million people. You know, how they had to alter the way they lived.

By Any Means Necessary: Spike Lee on Video's Viability

STEVE GOLDSTEIN / 2000

W HEN S PIKE L EE CAME UP with the idea of making a movie about a fictional TV show featuring black performers in blackface, it probably didn't take him long to realize that he wasn't about to set off any kind of bidding war.

Lee has always known how to get his movies made—by any means necessary—and the means at his disposal when he shot *Bamboozled* in September 1999 was digital video. This complex project—which would cast backward glances at other caustic takes on show business and the media like *A Face in the Crowd, Network, Ace in the Hole* and even *The Front* and *Jailhouse Rock*—promised great financial rewards to no one, but became viable once Lee made the decision to shoot it on video.

"We decided to shoot in DV early on, as the script was written," Lee says. "We knew that getting this film made would be a very hard task. Ellen Kuras—who's one of the best DPs working and who shot *Summer of Sam* for me and *4 Little Girls*—and I did a lot of tests of different cameras and different formats of video."

Lee and Kuras didn't like the look of Beta, DigiBeta or high definition, and went with miniDV, using a battery of Sony VX1000 cameras. "With this film it makes sense because it was about a television show," Lee says. "And we also had a 132-page script and not a lot of days. We had to run, and with the cameras just this big [holding his hands about six inches apart], there's a lot of flexibility. We were able to shoot eight, nine, ten cameras at a time. And

Published in *RES* 3, no. 4 (Fall 2000): 49. Reprinted by permission of Steve Goldstein.

it enabled us to put in the run-and-gun offense. So we were able to just shoot."

Lee elected to shoot the television show itself, *The New Millennium Minstrel Show,* in Super 16mm film to give it a different look from the rest of the movie. The bulk of *Bamboozled* manages to combine the gunslinging camera moves and relaxed, layered performances that are among DV's hallmarks with the dense writing and plotting found in *A Face in the Crowd* and *Network.* In fact, Lee dedicated *Bamboozled* to Budd Schulberg, the writer of *A Face in the Crowd* as well as of *On the Waterfront* and the great Hollywood novel, *What Makes Sammy Run.* In terms of content that dedication makes perfect sense, but in terms of form, a secondary dedication to DV pioneer Thomas Vinterberg wouldn't have been inappropriate. "*The Celebration* was the film that showed me that this could be done," Lee says. "Ellen and I had seen it before, but before shooting we screened it together."

Trumpeted as a technological breakthrough that opens the doors for all kinds of cinematic voices, DV can also be perceived as a new cog in an industry that Lee views with equal doses of love and contempt. "With *Bamboozled* we really wanted to focus on media and its misuses and its abuses of people," Lee says. "And on the people that get co-opted and go along and fall for the okeydoke. As artists we all have to make choices. And there are consequences of those choices. This film is much more lenient with the generation of actors that includes Bill Bojangles [Robinson], Hattie McDaniel, Stepin Fetchit, Mantan Moreland, Willie Best, Bert Williams—they didn't really have a choice in the roles they were getting. Nowadays we have choices. Everybody has to do what he or she feels they have to do, but at the end of the day, what you do is not going away. Because whether it's a movie or a song or a TV show, that thing is out there in the universe, and it'll be there 'til infinity."

With *Bamboozled,* Lee makes it clear that in the early twenty-first century it is possible for a black TV producer to reach the heights of success, that black performers can become rich, famous, egotistical and paranoid just like anyone else. He also shows us that, armed with inexpensive DV cameras, a filmmaker like Spike Lee can make a movie like *Bamboozled.* But Lee makes it clear that people of color have virtually no more power in the entertainment industry than they did in the days of D. W. Griffith and *The Birth of a Nation.*

"Will's getting $20 million, Chris Tucker's getting $20 million, Martin's getting $17 million on his next film," Lee says. "We're all happy for that, but let's not be bamboozled. The gatekeepers—these are the people that decide what goes on television, what movies are made, what gets heard on the radio, what's getting written in the magazines—I can tell you those are all exclusively white males. These are the guys making the choices for all of Western Civilization. There are seven or eight guys, and they decide, boom, this is what we're gonna do. And we've got to get in those positions. And that's when you'll start to see some change."

Spike's Minstrel Show

ALLISON SAMUELS / 2000

BAMBOOZLED, WHICH STARS Damon Wayans and Jada Pinkett
Smith, follows the life of a black television writer who, under pressure to
drive up ratings, creates a black minstrel show. Convinced the show will
offend everyone and not make it on air, he instead watches the show take
off. The movie lurches from satire to melodrama, with overlapping plot lines
and confusing characterizations, and though some of Lee's criticisms are
unclear, they are sure to spark heated debate. *Newsweek's* Allison Samuels sat
down with Lee.

ALLISON SAMUELS: *Why did you make* Bamboozled?
SPIKE LEE: I wanted to do something about the images of black people for
a long time, and the NAACP's push last year [to have more blacks represented
on TV] just happened to occur at the same time. I think a lot of the white
people in Hollywood are convinced that they know black people better than
anyone. That's why I have a white character say in the film to a black writer,
"I know niggers better than you."

AS: *The center of the film is a minstrel show. The characters on the ads for the
film are of very degrading images of black people. Why go to such extremes?*
SL: I don't think these things should be swept under a rug just because they
are offensive. The *New York Times* shouldn't not run them because they're

offensive. They're real. And this is what the film is about. A minstrel show could happen again. The networks will do just about anything to get ratings.

AS: *Can we assume that you're saying UPN and the WB don't help the images of blacks?*

SL: I was watching the show *Girlfriends* last week, and I mean, is the only thing black women can talk about is getting f——ked? And then the show had black men holding their johnsons and looking into the camera smiling. What white show has white men grabbing their nuts and smiling into the camera? And why do all the black people have to sing and dance in the opening sequence? The subtext is, "Lord, we're so happy we on TV."

AS: *What does Hollywood say to someone like you?*

SL: They throw things like BET in your face. Then all you can do is shut the f——k up because all BET does is show videos 24/7.

AS: *But* Bamboozled *isn't just harsh on the white media. It's tough on blacks as well.*

SL: My people have to wake up and realize what's going on and our responsibility in it. I mean, back in the day we didn't have a choice. Hattie McDaniel and Bojangles didn't have a choice. Nowadays we don't have to do this stuff. So anything you do is on you.

AS: *You take pretty big shots at actors Ving Rhames and Cuba Gooding Jr. in the film for the way they accepted their awards. [Rhames gave his Golden Globe to veteran Jack Lemmon; Gooding did a back flip at the Oscars.] That bothered you a lot?*

SL: When you give your award to a man you never met in your life, what do you expect? That sent chills down my spine, to see him do that to an award he earned. The same with Cuba spinning on his head. What was that? But you notice neither has stopped working since. That kind of entertainment will keep you working.

AS: *You've been fighting and saying these things a long time. Does it get frustrating?*

SL: You know what's frustrating? Ignorance. Like white people asking, why does Spike hate white people? That's ignorant to me. My films deal with the problems blacks have as well, but it always comes back to the silly notion of me hating white people no matter what I do.

Black like Spike

MICHAEL SRAGOW / 2000

''As the most prominent black director in the American movie industry," critic Terrence Rafferty once wrote about Spike Lee, "he probably feels as if he were sprinting downcourt with no one to pass to and about five hundred towering white guys between him and the basket." This was in 1989, at the time of *Do the Right Thing*. A dozen years later, Lee hasn't tamped down his provocative public blend of cockiness and earnestness. Yet he has displayed new sides to his creative personality.

He checked his tendency to showboat and extended his powers of empathy for the heartbreaking 1997 documentary *4 Little Girls,* about the Civil Rights–era bombing of a black church in Alabama. And a gift for expressing undiluted joy suffused his 1997 book *Best Seat in the House: A Basketball Memoir* (written with Ralph Wiley) and exploded on-screen in his hit comedy-concert film, *The Original Kings of Comedy.* In that film, four black comics— Steve Harvey, D. L. Hughley, Cedric the Entertainer, and Bernie Mac—take the stage in spiffy ties and jackets and prove that grass-roots comedy can be devastating when presented with old-fashioned style. The movie builds to multiple crescendos of earthy parody and farce. It climaxes with Bernie Mac's audacious chronicle about life with his sister's disruptive kids: Everything that W. C. Fields suggested about the horrors of living with children Mac makes painfully and uproariously explicit. Along the way, these four musketeers don't just entertain two sold-out crowds at the Charlotte Coliseum— they involve them in riffs, ad-libs, and entire musical numbers.

From *Salon.com* (26 October 2000). Copyright © 2001 Salon.com. Reprinted by permission.

The absence of that organic connection between performer and audience is part of what Lee bemoans in his prickly new movie. *Bamboozled* takes place in the lily-white corporate halls of our mainstream media. It begins with Damon Wayans reading a dictionary definition of satire and ends with a montage of black and white minstrelsy from the dawn of Hollywood through its heyday. The title comes from a Malcolm X speech: "You've been had. You've been took. You've been hoodwinked, bamboozled, led astray, run amok." Wayans plays Pierre Delacroix, the one black executive in a fledging, WB-like network. Jada Pinkett Smith plays his smart, well-meaning assistant, and Michael Rapaport his repulsively crude boss. The network chief orders him to deliver a show as black as *Amos 'n' Andy*; Delacroix decides to produce the most monumental racial throwback he can think of—*Mantan: The New Millennium Minstrel Show*, starring tap-dance wonder Savion Glover and comic veteran Tommy Davidson as a pair of prancing plantation darkies named Mantan and Sleep 'N' Eat. Delacroix hopes that he will be fired and the show will be a cautionary flop. Instead it boomerangs into a hit—and wounds the soul of every character.

Bamboozled has received wildly diverse reviews, and I thought it far more effective as a conversation piece than as a movie. Luckily, Lee was visiting San Francisco and willing to talk all about it—even when I admitted that the movie lost me. A couple of days after we spoke, Lee announced that he had made a deal with Studios USA (the company behind the enduring hit *Law and Order*) to develop TV series of his own.

M S : *It's fascinating that you've had* The Original Kings of Comedy *and* Bamboozled *coming out so quick.*
S L : Back to back!

M S : *Were issues surrounding black entertainers percolating in your mind, or is it just happenstance that the films came out this way?*
S L : *The Original Kings of Comedy* fell out of the sky. We had shot *Bamboozled* already and I was approached by Walter Latham and David Gale/MTV Films, who asked me: Would you want to direct this?

M S : Bamboozled *protests the paucity of blacks in mainstream media, while* The Original Kings of Comedy *shows that talented black performers can operate beneath the radar of mainstream media and still be huge.*

S L : The gatekeepers were not paying attention. I mean, the Original Kings of Comedy were selling out arenas, not little dumpy comedy clubs; they were filling 20,000 seats. And they still weren't even being reviewed. They were totally ignored.

M S : *But isn't that a hopeful thing? You watch the movie with this incredible parade of talents and part of the fun is that the audience has come to embrace them and share in the act—literally when they join in with the comics' singing. It makes you feel that audiences don't have to be attracted with big studio or big network hype.*
S L : Well, nothing stopped their tour, which is the all-time top grossing comedy tour ever.

M S : *How conscious were you of these guys before you made* The Original Kings of Comedy?
S L : I knew about them. But every time they came to New York I was shooting so I didn't get to see them. The first time I saw them live was when we were taping them, in Charlotte, N.C.

M S : *Had you worked much with stand-up comedians?*
S L : *Do the Right Thing* was Martin Lawrence's first film, and [the late, great] Robin Harris was in that movie too.

M S : *When Paul Mooney appears in* Bamboozled *as the antihero's father, a nightclub comedian named Junebug, he seems to have stepped out of* The Original Kings of Comedy.
S L : Well, to me, Paul Mooney is really playing himself. You know, he wrote a lot of Richard Pryor's standup material. He's a great talent who could've maybe had a much bigger career, but just wouldn't play along. He wouldn't play the Hollywood game. And that's who Junebug was.

M S : *And is he bitter about that?*
S L : He's not bitter: he's happy. He has his dignity. He has his self-esteem.

M S : *And the guys in* The Original Kings of Comedy *carry themselves like, well, kings.*

SL: But what's really interesting—and I say this very respectfully—is to look at what they do on television and then look at what they do in stand-up. It's like night and day. You know, they're not writing that TV stuff. You only get the real them when they do their own material and it's not filtered.

MS: *Do you relate to them when they talk about being from the "old school" in style and music, loving romantic songs from, say, Marvin Gaye, that get all the men and women in the audience to sing along?*
SL: Oh yeah. The funny thing about that was, the hip-hop kids thought it was funny too.

MS: The Original Kings of Comedy *gets you high and keeps you high;* Bamboozled *starts out in a comic mode then takes radical shifts.*
SL: Three-quarters of the way in, there is a tonal shift and it was deliberate. We wanted to change it up; we wanted the laughs to stop and get serious. And we felt it was time, you know, to pay the piper—let's see what happens. What are the consequences going to be for the choices that people have made connected with this show?

MS: *And I have to say, I have a problem with that—not just in this movie, but in* A Face in the Crowd *[the scorching 1957 Elia Kazan satire on TV stardom] and* Network *and other, similar films. I guess I feel that if you grab audiences with comedy, you take them to other places by modulating the comedy, not detouring into whole other dramatic or melodramatic areas.*
SL: But I love films where you mix it up—where a film doesn't really even keep the same rhythm, the same tone all the way through. I mean, it's hard to do, but when it's successful I think it works very well.

MS: *You took on the subject of* Bamboozled *because it's become so woefully apparent that the African-American presence in the decision-making halls of network TV is minimal.*
SL: And it's the same for the studios. There is not one African-American executive in Hollywood that can green-light a picture. I'm not talking about Wesley [Snipes] or Will [Smith], or Denzel [Washington] or Chris Tucker or Chris Rock. I'm talking about suits. These are the people who are called the "gatekeepers." I think we have to gain access to those positions.

M S : *So then you decided on a strategy for combining that cause with your knowledge of movie history and the African-American part of our film heritage. And you came up with what I would call an industrial-strength satire.*
S L : I got to write that down; can I steal that from you?

M S : *Sure. I took it from some commercial.*
S L : What was that, Mr. Clean? I remember that, or something just like it, labeled "industrial strength"—it came in a plastic drum.

M S : *Do you think that Damon Wayans's character, Pierre Delacroix—someone educated beyond any natural reflexes or connection to his heritage—is unique to the black experience? Or can he be compared to cultural bureaucrats from other racial and ethnic groups?*
S L : What makes Damon's character unique is that Pierre Delacroix has a lot of self-hatred. Here's someone who's never been comfortable with his blackness: hence the name change and the diction and that type of stuff.

M S : *He seems to have stylized himself into a parody of white cultivation. How specifically did you and Damon work that out?*
S L : We talked about it. It was Damon's idea for the diction. First he came up with a Cockney accent; we made a couple of changes on that until we agreed on what you hear in the film.

M S : *Was there a real-life model for Delacroix?*
S L : Yeah. Damon never told me the guy's name, but it's an African-American TV writer in Hollywood today. The sad thing about Delacroix is that he doesn't gain knowledge of self until he's getting ready to buy the farm. And that is something people haven't really picked up on: We took the device from one of the great masters, Billy Wilder. It's from *Sunset Boulevard,* where William Holden is floating in that pool and you hear his voice and it's not until the end of the movie that you realize the voiceover is coming from a dead guy. In this movie, all the voiceover of Delacroix comes from after he's gone to the "upper room."

M S : *Well, I got that. But I'm not sure I picked up on every beat in Delacroix's progress. I understood his opening tactic. Responding to the order to deliver what the top suit considers a real black show, he decides to develop the most awful stereo-*

typical program he can think of—a blackface minstrel show. He wants to get fired.
But after that the transitions got hazy for me.

SL: Well, see, once they decide to do the show, he's trying to make the best
out of it. He knows that if this type of material falls into the wrong hands,
he'll definitely become a Dr. Frankenstein. So the film then becomes a struggle between Delacroix and [the white network boss] Dunwitty. Delacroix gets
tricked into thinking he has some power on the show. And then once the
show becomes a hit, he gets intoxicated like everybody else and therefore
becomes protective of it. That's the point when the downward spiral really
begins.

MS: *For a portion of that descent, I thought Delacroix was sincere when he tried*
to make a post-modern, post-whatever argument: as if he believes he's so ironic
about this blackface stuff that he feels he's a pioneer.

SL: He's trying to convince himself of that. It's the standard defense for that
type of stuff.

MS: *But in your mind there's no validity to it?*

SL: No, I don't think we can justify what he does. I don't think we make
any alibis for that.

MS: *The initial response of the TV studio audience to the minstrel show . . .*

SL: It's the same response we get in the audience of people watching the
film.

MS: *Right. And that, I think, is totally accurate. I imagined you throwing people*
into the seats of the TV studio set and watching them go into shock during the
minstrel show.

SL: They weren't acting. Not everybody knew that Tommy [Davidson] and
Savion [Glover] were gonna come out there in blackface. And we did that
live. By live, I mean we had cameras on the audience and the performers at
the same time.

MS: *Again, I understood the initial discomfort and disbelief of the audience*
within the film. But, for me, the build into audiences buying this TV show was
blurry. How did you want us to respond to audiences ultimately going wild for it?

s L : I think the initial break comes when the black people start to applaud. I
know you remember the shot where there are a couple of white people looking around like, "Oh . . ." and seeing whether it was OK to clap. Now, mind,
if the black guy next to them is clapping, they feel it's OK to clap—and then
we see the applause signs and people respond and it just catches fire. I mean,
who knew that *Survivor* or *Who Wants to Be a Millionaire* would catch fire?
You can't plan that stuff. So in the world I created, we made blackface the
rage. You know, it just [slap] catches fire and takes off.

M S : *Which is also what happens to the country singer's TV show in* A Face in
the Crowd. *And I see you dedicated this film to that film's writer, Budd Schulberg.*
s L : Budd Schulberg and Elia, they had the crystal ball on this. Even the
sponsor of the show in that film, Vitajex—what's Vitajex but Viagra? And
Budd wrote this back in 1956. The jingle went "Vitajex, what you doin' to
me?"—they really had the crystal ball on that, too. Budd told me a story that
before *Network,* [screenwriter] Paddy Chayefsky called him up and said,
"Look, we're gonna try to leap-frog what you did with *A Face in the Crowd.*
Crowd. That's another film I've always liked. And that's what Paddy told
Budd.

M S : *So at that point in* Bamboozled, *blackface becomes part of a media steam-
roller.*
s L : Television is the opiate. The Opie-ate.

M S : *When you have the white people looking to the black people in the audience
to see how to react, you also seem to be making an analogy to the way suburban
white kids, looking for cutting-edge pop culture, go for hip-hop and gangsta rap and
all that.*
s L : Yeah, and they might be looking in the wrong places. I think I've said
this before: Culture is for everybody to enjoy. But if these young white kids
want to emulate black people—I think there are better things that they could
take from hip-hop than wearing their pants below their ass and calling each
other "nigga." You know, "Whassup, my nigga?" I mean, I don't condemn
all of hip-hop; I've used a lot of it in my films starting, back in '89 with *Do
the Right Thing* and Public Enemy. But I do feel gangsta rap has evolved to a
modern day minstrel show, especially if you look at the videos. You ever
watch BET?

M S :   *I confess, I don't watch a lot of music videos on TV.*

S L :   When you get an hour, just turn on BET and watch these gangsta rap videos, for your own education. It's sad.

M S :   *When you make a movie like* Bamboozled, *are you particularly intent on addressing the African-American audience?*

S L :   It's for everybody. It's for everybody. I think this film deals with our shared history. Earlier you used the word "heritage." I mean, people can sing "Hooray for Hollywood" and talk about the "Golden Age of Television" all they want. But a large part of that stuff is what we put in the final montage of this film. Every year at the Academy Awards they have this guy Chuck Workman do these little [compilation] films. I say, at this year's Academy Awards, get rid of Chuck: Show the final montage from *Bamboozled* instead. A lot of people don't want to deal with the images in this montage. But we're showing them. And we're showing that these images didn't just spring from the warped mind of D. W. Griffith, but reflected accepted behavior. Judy Garland, Mickey Rooney, Bing Crosby, they all did the black minstrel thing. This was accepted behavior. And people don't want to deal with this as part of the legacy of these two powerful mediums—television and film. In both, people were doing this from the beginning—from the very beginning.

M S :   *One of the most effective scenes in the movie comes when Mantan and Sleep 'N' Eat are at their minstrel peak. They do a bit where they anticipate each other's moves without saying anything, and it's so beautifully worked out between the two of them that you really do laugh, despite this terrible context. Even when you watch your montage at the end, you feel that there are these immense talents that are . . .*

S L :   Marginalized.

M S :   *And I've always felt there should be a way of appreciating the artistry of black movie actors who had to play subservient characters or buffoons.*

S L :   Yes. And what's been great about this film for me, personally, is that I have a greater understanding of those giants, people I might have just totally dismissed as Uncle Toms. This film made me realize—I hope not too late— that they were great talents and they were doing the best of what was being offered to them at the time.

On one hand, we should have a greater understanding for those people in the past. On the other hand, it made me focus with much more scrutiny on my generation and the stuff we're doing. Because we have choices—a lot more than they had.

M S : *In that vein, I was thinking about your credits and wondering what happened to Wesley Snipes, who worked for you twice [in* Mo' Better Blues *and* Jungle Fever*] and was consistently pretty wonderful ten years ago; now he's become this action figure.*

S L : That's what he wanted to be. Even when we were doing *Jungle Fever* and *Mo' Better Blues,* Wesley told me himself, he wanted to be the black *Schwarzenegger.* It's not like someone pressured him to do that. He's doing what he set out to do—to be a black action hero. But I love Wesley. I want to work with him again.

M S : *Because* Bamboozled *is so stylized, some viewers might think every character stands in for a whole social group. Dunwitty, for example, who's so obnoxious, feels he can say whatever he wants about race because he's in a mixed-race marriage.*

S L : Yeah, well, I really can't do nothing about that. If someone's gonna think that Spike Lee is saying all white males who are married to black women feel they can use the word "nigger" freely, that's just idiotic to me.

M S : *Are you more ambivalent toward characters like those kamikaze rappers, the Mau Maus? They do react with proper outrage to the minstrel show, even though they're clueless.*

S L : They're definitely confused, but they think they're profound. That's the scene where they're having a discussion about "how we're gonna spell the word 'black' " and it's like a discussion of the theory of relativity or something. "B-L-A-K. Yes, let's just drop the C." You know, it's crazy. And then they definitely do the wrong thing when they decide that they can play God and take a life.

M S : *In the movie, as Delacroix gets further and further into his minstrel show, he accumulates more and more of these "black collectibles." I've read that you collect them, too.*

S L : A lot of that stuff in the film was from my own collection. It's a reminder to me. It's a reminder. In fact, when I was writing the script to *Bamboozled,* on my desk in my office I had my Aunt Jemima cookie jar to my left and my Jolly Nigger bank to the right. Every time I see that stuff I think about the depths of the sickness and the hatred behind it.

M S :   *What's up next?*
S L :   Got to hit the frontier of television; got to try to get something done in television.

M S :   *Any definite ideas?*
S L :   No sitcoms!

M S :   *But is that what networks still want?*
S L :   The same with cinema: What do you got? You got another *Scary Movie?* I mean, what was this summer about: *The Klumps, Big Momma's House,* and, in a different way, *The Original Kings of Comedy.* Let's keep it funny and light. What I want to do is a dramatic series.

M S :   *Well, when black groups protested how few African-Americans appeared in last year's new shows, you suddenly saw black characters in series like* The West Wing. *Is this something you can build on?*
S L :   Wait and see. I've got that wait and see attitude.

M S :   *Do you have any expectations for tonight's third debate you'd like to share? Will you be watching?*
S L :   What sane, red-blooded American would miss Game Six between the Yankees and Mariners to determine if there's gonna be a subway series?! Miss that for the debate? Sheee . . . hell, no! I know who I'm gonna vote for. I'm watchin' the game. If I was in New York, I'd be there.

Interview with Spike Lee

KAM WILLIAMS / 2000

W HETHER BY DESIGN or coincidence, Spike Lee can always be
found in a swirl of controversy. Since the 1986 debut of *She's Gotta Have It*,
the two-time Oscar-nominee (for *Do the Right Thing* and *4 Little Girls*) has
never been one to shy away from speaking his mind. Over the years, the
actor/director has felt the heat for taking unpopular political stances, for
making debatable aesthetic choices and for a shameless display of towel-
waving fanaticism at NY Knick games. Such honest, if suicidal tendencies,
are unknown in Hollywood, where most publicists pressure their stars to
avoid any controversy at all costs. So, in an industry full of phonies who
work hard at being all things to all people, Spike is refreshingly rare. Just last
month, for instance, he publicly criticized Mel Gibson's new movie, *The
Patriot*, for its inaccuracies. Last summer it was Mr. Lee who was attacked for
his patently anti-Italian *Summer of Sam*. Prior to that, there was his openly
race-based lobbying to direct *Malcolm X* and other incendiary issues. So it
would be a relief, or so I foolishly expected, to interview Lee about his new
concert film, *The Original Kings of Comedy*. Other than its presumptuous title,
how could there be any tension around a movie of four comedians doing
their stand-up act? You'd figure that all Spike had to do was point a camera
at the stage and take a seat. Figure some more. My separate interviews with
Lee and with stars Steve Harvey, D. L. Hughley, Cedric the Entertainer, and
Bernie Mac revealed some interesting issues simmering just beneath the sur-
face of smiles.

Published as "Spike Lee: The Interview with Kam Williams" in *Black Talent News* (21 December 2000). Reprinted by permission of the author.

K A M : *Bernie Mac dogged you, telling me that you're riding on his train. He seems to be upset that you're making more than he is on this film.*
S P I K E : Well, Bernie and I have been going at it for a long time, with his being a Chicago Bulls fan. (Chuckles) Since Jordan's retired, Bernie has hit on hard times, so he tries to take a whack at me whenever he can.

K A M : *What made you want to do this film?*
S P I K E : A chance to work with Bernie again, after *Get on the Bus,* and to work with the other guys for the first time.

K A M : *But why a concert film?*
S P I K E : I had made John Lequizamo's one-man Broadway show *Freak* for HBO. Before I decided to do this one, I went back to take another look at Eddie Murphy's *Raw* and *Delirious,* and Richard Pryor's *Live on the Sunset Strip.* And I welcomed the challenge.

K A M : *These comedians had already toured together. Did you do much more than set up cameras?*
S P I K E : I set up fifteen cameras, but I wasn't brought on to rewrite the show. It had been a success for two years, so I wasn't there to change stuff. I was hired to document something that was essentially already done.

K A M : *What's unique about this stand-up movie?*
S P I K E : I try not to hang myself with claims like, "This has never been done before in the history of cinema!"

K A M : *Steve Harvey told me he was upset about some of his act that was edited out.*
S P I K E : There was a lot that was great that was left on the cutting room floor. Thank god we have DVDs now. That stuff will make it back into the DVD edition.

K A M : *What's up next for you?*
S P I K E : *Bamboozled* is coming out in October with Damon Wayans and Jada Pinkett Smith. It's a satire about the TV and film industries.

K A M : *Why didn't you like* The Patriot?
S P I K E : Did you read my letter published in the *Hollywood Reporter?*

KAM: *I only heard about it.*

SPIKE: My wife and I went to see it, and came out of the theater furious. I wrote a letter to the *New York Times* because they had done an article the previous Sunday asking why Hollywood had made so few American Revolution Era films. I wrote them a letter saying the real question was why *The Patriot* was so historically incorrect. They wouldn't print it, so I faxed it to the *Hollywood Reporter* who put it on the front page.

KAM: *Why did you do this film in association with MTV instead of BET?*

SPIKE: As quiet as it's kept, Bob Johnson (Black Entertainment Television Chairman) wouldn't give up any money. We wanted to be paid with more than sodas and subs.

Thinking about the Power of Images:
An Interview with Spike Lee

GARY CROWDUS AND
DAN GEORGAKAS / 2001

SPIKE LEE IS JUSTLY FAMED for raising important social issues in all of his films. His latest, *Bamboozled,* is no exception. As the Critical Symposium in this issue makes clear, *Bamboozled* explores the relationship of popular culture and racial mythology in an emotionally and intellectually provocative manner. Despite the film's bold and decidedly controversial subject matter, however, *Bamboozled* did not fare well during its theatrical release. Its scheduled April release in home video formats—including a special edition DVD, which, among other features, will include a commentary track by Lee and a documentary on the background and motivations of the filmmakers—will hopefully enable the film to reach a wider viewing audience.

Cineaste felt it was important—as we did in our comprehensive coverage of *Malcolm X* in 1993—to supplement the Critical Symposium on *Bamboozled* with an interview with Spike Lee. *Cineaste* Editors Gary Crowdus and Dan Georgakas met the writer/director in his New York office in January to discuss the social and artistic aspects of his film, a conversation which turned into a broader consideration of race in the movies, past and present.

CINEASTE: *Was there a direct inspiration for* Bamboozled?
SPIKE LEE: My first film at New York University was called *The Answer.* It's a twenty-minute, black-and-white film about a young African-American screenwriter who's hired to direct a big, multimillion-dollar Hollywood

Published in *Cineaste* 26, no. 2 (January 2001): 4–9. Reprinted by permission of *Cineaste.*

remake of *The Birth of a Nation*. I used clips from *The Birth of a Nation* in it. That's really the germ of the idea, so it's been a long time coming.

CINEASTE: *What sort of research did you do for the film?*
LEE: An important piece was Melvin Van Peebles's documentary, *Classified X*, a history of black images in the cinema. I was amazed by the imagery, so I contacted the film's researcher, Judy Aley, since she'd done a lot of the work already, and she was able to get us a lot of this material. During the rehearsal period, we spent very little time going over the script, because we were reading and looking at clips most of the time. None of us had seen this material. For example, I had never seen Bugs Bunny in blackface! Unfortunately Time Warner would not allow us to use that clip because Bugs Bunny is too valuable a commodity to them, and they didn't want the world to see that.

We produced some animation, which you see at the beginning of the TV show, where you see "Massa" Charlie shooting at Mantan and Sleep 'n' Eat. That is really taken from the Bugs Bunny cartoon—it's Yosemite Sam shooting at Bugs Bunny. I'm telling you, there's a whole lot of Walt Disney stuff that they don't want out either!

CINEASTE: *You dedicated* Bamboozled *to Budd Schulberg, which we are sure surprised a lot of people. What was your motivation for that?*
LEE: Budd is one of my dear friends. I could not have done *Bamboozled* without him having written *A Face in the Crowd*. In fact, Budd told me that Paddy Chayevsky called him before *Network* came out and said that he couldn't have written *Network* if it hadn't been for *A Face in the Crowd*. I think it's one of those seminal movies which Kazan and Budd did in the late fifties. They had a crystal ball. I mean, what's Vitajex? It's Viagra! Everything that we know now about the power of the media, of television and film, on society, was all there in *A Face in the Crowd*. By the way, Budd and I were talking about this recently, his film didn't fare too well at the box office, either [*laughs*], so we shared the same fate.

CINEASTE: *That's a film that still holds up today.*
LEE: Yes, and only time will tell, but I think the same will hold true for *Bamboozled*. Budd and I and Burt Sugar are currently collaborating on a script about Joe Louis and Max Schmeling. That'll be an epic—more epic than *Malcolm X*.

CINEASTE: *We wondered whether the fact that Schulberg had run the Watts Writers Workshop, and had tried to cultivate good black writers, was involved in your dedication.*

LEE: That's something a lot of people don't know about, but no, it's really for *A Face in the Crowd* and for being a good friend, for introducing me to Kazan, and coming to speak to my graduate film class at NYU. My students had seen *On the Waterfront,* but they had never heard of *A Face in the Crowd.* I made sure they got his scripts and Budd came and spent three hours with the class and they were amazed. There are a lot of older guys around who have a wealth of information and most of them will gladly part with it. They're so glad that people know who they are and recognize the great body of work that they've achieved.

CINEASTE: Bamboozled *also obviously references* Network. *You seem to be saying that all of Chayevsky's nightmare visions have come true. Do you think that television is even worse than the cinema in perpetuating negative images of African Americans?*

LEE: No, television is just as bad as cinema, but to me it's not important which has been worse. They've both been guilty.

CINEASTE: *Do you think that blacks in particular have been badly portrayed, or do you think the whole culture is collapsing?*

LEE: You see the same thing with the portrayal of women that you see with the portrayal of people of color or of other minorities. What we wanted to do in *Bamboozled*—and I think we were successful—was to show that from their birth these two great mediums, film and television, have promoted negative racial images. Look at three of the earliest so-called "landmark" American films—*The Birth of a Nation, The Jazz Singer,* and *Gone with the Wind.* It's not a coincidence. You have to understand that these mediums are not separate from society. Racism is woven into the very fabric of American society, and it just makes sense that it's going to be reflected in sports, in movies, in television, in business, and so on. These aren't just islands. People come from somewhere and they bring stuff with them. I think *Bamboozled* demonstrates how interwoven racism—or let's just say race—has been in this country, but people still want to deny it, or not deal with it.

CINEASTE: *A lot of Hollywood movies today feature characters that are por-*

trayed by black actors but their race is not particularly acknowledged. Do you think that's healthy or is that denial?

LEE: That doesn't bother me. What really bothers me is this new phenomenon of the "magical nigger" that you see in films such as *The Green Mile, The Family Man, The Legend of Bagger Vance,* and *What Dreams May Come.* These films all have these magical, mystical Negroes who show up as some sort of spirit or angel but only to benefit the white characters. I mean, Michael Clarke Duncan gave a good performance in *The Green Mile,* but when I saw that movie I knew he was going to get an Academy Award nomination. The Academy just loves roles like that because it makes them feel so liberal. But if this character has such magical powers that he can touch Tom Hanks and cure him of his urinary tract infection, why can't he use those gifts to walk out of prison?

CINEASTE: *Or hire a good lawyer?*

LEE: Right. Johnny Cochran. I mean, he tongue-kisses cancer out of a white woman and cures her. And in the end Tom Hanks offers to set him free, but guess what? He refuses to leave Death Row. He'd rather die with Tom Hanks looking on. Get the fuck outta here! That's that old grateful slave shit.

And what about *The Legend of Bagger Vance*? No disrespect to Will Smith because I really put this more on Robert Redford, the director, but this is a film set in early 1930s, Depression-era Georgia. Georgia has always been one of the roughest states for black people, a lot of Negroes were castrated, lynched and whatnot in Georgia. So this is sick—they didn't even have black caddies! And if this magical black caddy has all these powers, why isn't he using them to try and stop some of the other brothers from being lynched and castrated? Why is he fucking around with Matt Damon and trying to teach him a golf swing? I don't understand this! That is insane. What world was that?! Please tell me.

The Family Man is the same thing. Don Cheadle is a great actor, but it's this same magical nigger mystique—magical Negroes who appear out of nowhere and have these great powers but who can't use them to help themselves or their own people but only for the benefit of the white stars of the movies.

CINEASTE: *It's Chingachgook, and Tonto, and . . .*

LEE: This is what we talk about in *Bamboozled,* in the scene where Sleep 'n' Eat breaks up with Mantan, and he says, "Look, it's the same old stuff we're doing. They dress it up, they're slicker about it, it's much more sophisticated, but when you analyze it, it's the same old shit."

CINEASTE: *Among the white characters in* Bamboozled, *Dunwitty, the TV executive, is offensive, the white guy in the Mau Maus is pathetic, but the scariest part is the white people in the TV audience who put on blackface and say, "I'm a nigger." It's scary because it's plausible. What do you think about the 'wigger' phenomenon of white suburban kids who emulate black gangsta rappers?*
LEE: Well, as I've said in the past, and I'll continue to say it, culture is for everybody. Culture should be appreciated by everybody, but for me there is a distinction between *appreciation* of a culture and *appropriation* of a culture. People like Dunwitty are dangerous because they appropriate black culture and put a spin on it as if they are the originators of it. There's a big difference. This sort of thing is so powerful, though, that for many years I thought Bob Marley had covered Eric Clapton on "I Shot the Sheriff," when it was really the other way around!

If these young white suburban kids like rap, that's fine, but I don't think they should try to emulate the so-called gangsta mystique. There's a difference between appreciating the music and taking it beyond that by trying to live out what is a fantasy life even for the rap artists themselves—they're not real gangsters, either.

CINEASTE: Bamboozled *seems very clear about that aspect of black culture, because the Mau Maus are critiqued as much as any of the white characters. You obviously don't have any respect for the ludicrous excesses of gangsta rap.*
LEE: I think their intentions are honorable, but they're misguided. I think a lot of this is because they don't read. If you don't read, then you're going to be ignorant, and you're just going to be making up stuff as you go along. I like rap music but I'm not a fan of a lot of gangsta rap. I think it's obsessed with the "bling bling," with the gold chains and diamonds and Bentleys and all the other trappings—you know, the titties and the butts shaking and jigging into the camera. I don't think that's uplifting, not at all. It's all about massive amounts of consumption.

CINEASTE: *In regards to some of the stereotypical black roles in film and televi-*

sion, performers such as Hattie McDaniel and Stepin Fetchit didn't have many options, but do you see any differences among them? On The Jack Benny Show, *for example, Rochester would occasionally tell off his boss.*

LEE: What was really beneficial for me in doing the research for *Bamboozled* was gaining a greater understanding of that generation of Negro performers. In the past I've said such ignorant things about these people—that they were Uncle Toms and Mammies—but saying that without a full understanding that that was the only choice they had. As Hattie McDaniel said, "It's better to play a maid than to be a maid." While this film gave me a greater understanding of what they had to go through, at the same time it's made me much more critical of the roles that African-American entertainers or athletes choose to play today. If we don't take a demeaning role, we're not reduced to cleaning up somebody's house. I'm not saying there's a wealth of opportunities available to black performers today, but no one is going to the poor house if they turn down some of this stuff. Otherwise, I think we betray those performers who came before and who played those roles so we wouldn't have to do them now in the twenty-first century.

I mean, if you look at a lot of these magical Negro roles in current movies, or especially some of the shows on television—on WB, UPN, that type of stuff—they're borderline minstrel shows. I don't think we have to do a lot of the things we're doing. Look at some of the recording artists. I know record companies put pressure on their artists, but when Lil' Kim says she's an example of the empowerment of women, that's hard for me to understand.

CINEASTE: *There's one scene, during the broadcast of* Mantan: The New Millennium Minstrel Show, *where the Mau Maus are shown watching it, and one of them cracks up, and the others turn on him and ask, "What are you laughing at?" What was your intention with that scene?*
LEE: Well, I think that one of the reasons the film works is that a lot of that stuff is funny.

CINEASTE: *So you acknowledge some ambiguity in the response to this kind of humor.*
LEE: Yes, there is. We wanted to put the moviegoing audience in the same position as the TV audience in the movie. It's funny, but they're thinking, "Wait a minute. Should I be laughing at this?" That's why we have that scene with the white couple. The first time the performers come out in blackface,

the white people look around them to see if black people are laughing, because if they are, then it's sanctioned, and it's OK for them to laugh, too.

If you look at a lot of this material, even some of the scenes in the montage at the end of the movie, some of that stuff—despite how much hatred is behind it, and despite how painful it can be—*is* funny, and the reason it's funny is because of the genius of the artists, of the performers who are able to make it funny even within that context. That's the irony—that these artists were so great that they could take a dehumanizing form and still make it somewhat humanistic.

CINEASTE: *You're walking through a minefield here . . .*
LEE: Yes, we knew. The reality of black people putting this stuff on their face was devastating for Tommy Davidson and Savion Glover. It took away part of their soul, it took away part of their manhood, and it made us think of Bert Williams. Tommy and Savion did it for a couple of weeks, but Williams had to do that his entire career.

CINEASTE: *In* Bamboozled, *Sloan seems to be the most principled character. She seems to understand things better than anybody else. Is it coincidental that this character is a woman or was that a specific choice?*
LEE: I felt a woman should play that role. I'm married to a very intelligent woman—she's a lawyer—and since we've been married I've made a concerted effort to have a better understanding of female characters. In terms of the criticism of my earlier films, that's one thing that was true, that the female characters were not as multilayered as the male characters. So it was a definite choice to have Jada Pinkett Smith's character, Sloan, be the most sympathetic and the most intelligent. At the same time, her hands are bloodied, too, but she knows there is blood on her hands, whereas most of the other characters are in denial or just too stupid to know it.

CINEASTE: *Do you think the revelation that she had sexual relations with Pierre in any way compromises her integrity?*
LEE: No, I don't believe that! I truly feel that she did not use her sexuality to get the job. As she explains in her argument with Manray, people work long hours together, there is an attraction, and shit happens. But she didn't open up her legs to get that job. As she says, "Why is it that every attractive woman who's successful, people always think that she slept with somebody

to advance her career? I'm smart, I have drive, I worked my ass off, and that's how I got into that position. Did I go to bed with Pierre? Yes, I did. It was a mistake, we did it one time, and that was it. But that had nothing to do with me getting into the position that I'm in."

CINEASTE: *So you're just nuancing the character.*
LEE: I think the more layers you add, the more complex it becomes, and it makes the film better on repeat viewings.

CINEASTE: *Does your treatment of this character imply that you think black women are more insightful than black men about the social impact of media images?*
LEE: I would say that because circumstances are often more difficult for African-American women than for black males—in other words, because they're black and they're women, too—that might make them more perceptive.

CINEASTE: *Speaking of character development, in one scene you sketch Pierre's relationship with his father.*
LEE: Yes, I wanted to reveal the fact that they're disappointed in each other. The father, Junebug, feels his son has no integrity, and at this point Pierre feels that his father is a great talent but that he's wasting it. He feels that if he'd stop trying to be so noble, and a fighter and a warrior, and would instead just go with the flow and go along to get along, then he wouldn't be on this chitlin' circuit. He'd be on Jay Leno and David Letterman, he'd have his HBO Comedy Special.

CINEASTE: *Some of Junebug's comedy routines, as well as some of those in* The Original Kings of Comedy, *are not that much different from what we see in* Bamboozled.
LEE: Oh, I disagree. The material those guys do is stand-up in the tradition of black comics like Bill Cosby, Richard Pryor, Redd Foxx, Dick Gregory, and Eddie Murphy. To me that is totally different than stereotypical sitcom stuff.

CINEASTE: *Some of the material is pretty vulgar or sexist, like the routine about blow jobs.*

LEE: Yeah, but I don't know if that makes it buffoonish.

CINEASTE: *You take great pains in the opening scene of* Bamboozled *to define the film's approach. You even use a dictionary definition of satire. Were you concerned about making your intent obvious to critics as well as the average moviegoer?*
LEE: Yes, because it amazes me how intelligent critics are with a lot of filmmakers, but when it comes to my work, there's a total misrepresentation. For example, Lisa Schwarzbaum, who writes for *Entertainment Weekly,* said in her review of *Summer of Sam* that by introducing Italian guys carrying baseball bats, I was alluding to Howard Beach. Now do you see that in Scorsese's films or in *The Sopranos?* Yes, of course! They use baseball bats. But when I show it, I'm a race baiter. In Stephen Hunter's review of *Bamboozled* in the *Washington Post,* he literally says that I hate white people. No examples, no back-up, no nothing. Just writes that lie like it's the truth. Like the sky is blue, water is wet, fire burns.

I'm not saying I'm above criticism. I can take it. But these kinds of reviews are not talking about the films but about the critic's perceptions of me. In the Stephen Hunter review, for example, he writes about what he calls Spike's dilemma—"to have a revolution and to keep his courtside seats at the Garden for Knicks games." I'm tired of reading movie reviews that include references to me being courtside at Knicks games. Woody Allen has been sitting in courtside seats twice as long as me. And what about Jack Nicholson? I mean, what are we talking about here? Let's talk about what's on the screen.

CINEASTE: *In a way you might consider such comments a sort of backhanded compliment in that your films have addressed some very difficult, sensitive issues and resorting to an ad hominen critical approach is a convenient way to avoid dealing with those issues.*
LEE: I've read so many reviews of *Bamboozled* that talk about everything except what the film is about. They do not want to deal with the historical debasement of a people through film and television. I don't know how you can look at this film and not talk about the power of that montage at the end. I mean, we all know what D. W. Griffith did, but when you see Judy Garland, Mickey Rooney, and Bing Crosby putting on blackface . . . well, the critics didn't want to deal with that.

CINEASTE: *It reminds us of the Marx Brothers movie,* A Day at the Races.

Whenever it's shown on TV, they always cut the blackface scene at the end because they're embarrassed about it today.

LEE: I'm of that school that thinks we should show that stuff. I'm not one of those people who think that *Huckleberry Finn*—one of the great works of American literature—should not be taught in schools because it uses the word "nigger." That's insane.

I think African American artists are held to a different standard. Bruce Springsteen, for example, has made more money from "Born in the U.S.A." than I'll ever make in my life, but he's still considered a pillar of the working class. Now I've been going to Knicks games since I was a little kid, sitting in the blue nosebleed seats, but now I'm fortunate—thank you, God!—to have a little money so I can indulge myself by sitting courtside. But what does that have to do with the cinema?

CINEASTE: *We've never seen a review of a Budd Schulberg movie criticize him for having sat ringside at boxing matches since he was thirteen years old.*

LEE: I'm not crying over spilt milk, but I think there's been a great misrepresentation critically of my work.

CINEASTE: *You've often mentioned that you think a major problem is the lack of African-American executives in either the television or film industries . . .*

LEE: I use the word "gatekeepers."

CINEASTE: *But isn't it somewhat naïve to think that even the presence of African Americans in key decision-making positions at the studios or the networks would make a significant difference?*

LEE: I don't believe that. If you look at television and film today and the number of women executives that are working in the industry, I do think there's much more sensitivity to the depiction of women than there was twenty years ago when it was male dominated. If you had a black executive at UPN, for example, he would have told them, "You know what, this idea for a sitcom about slavery, *The Secret Diary of Desmond Pfeiffer*, this is not a good idea. You cannot make light of slavery, you cannot make a sitcom about this holocaust." There was no one in those meetings to bring that up. I understand what you're saying. I'm not naïve enough to think that things are going to change overnight, but you need to have a voice in there saying, wait a minute, this is wrong.

CINEASTE: *So you think you're going to get a media-style Colin Powell instead of Clarence Thomas?*

LEE: [*Laughs*] Well, let's not talk about Clarence Thomas. He's going to have a terrible legacy to live down.

CINEASTE: *Even if there were a key black executive at one of the Hollywood studios, wouldn't he or she likely bend over backwards to avoid greenlighting a film that would be too controversial, too political?*

LEE: It really depends on the individual—just like Clarence Thomas is not the same as Colin Powell. Charles Rangel is not J. C. Watts. I do think there is some way to operate within the system. That's something I've been able to do, even though I'm on the fringes of it. *Bamboozled,* believe it or not, was made through a Hollywood studio. I mean, thank God for New Line—even though we feel they botched the release—because no one else wanted to finance this film.

CINEASTE: *You believe that not just a single black executive, but a critical mass of a number of black executives over the course of time would ameliorate the situation?*

LEE: Yes, because look at the number of women in the film industry now— Amy Pascal is running Sony, you have Sherry Lansing at Paramount, and Stacey Snider at Universal—and twenty years ago there were no women heads of studios. This is a gradual process.

CINEASTE: *In what ways did New Line "botch" the distribution of* Bamboozled?

LEE: I don't think they ever really understood the film or who the audience was. At the time they were going through a very serious financial situation, so there were a lot of restraints about how much money would be spent.

CINEASTE: *Did they understand that it was a crossover film?*

LEE: They never knew exactly what they had. They approach these things on precedent. You know, "Well, this is the way *Menace II Society* was marketed." But *Bamboozled* was not like *Menace II Society* or *Set It Off* or *Friday.* They tried to do niche marketing but our film is a hybrid.

CINEASTE: *Did you have any real-life models for Pierre Delacroix, Dunwitty, or Myrna Goldfarb?*

LEE: Damon Wayans knows someone, a black TV writer, who he patterned Pierre Delacroix after. He never told me the guy's name. He was a good writer but he was frustrated because he was trying to write his best stuff but was continually beat down. When that happens, you just give up and write shit.

Dunwitty? *[laughs]* You see people like that in film and TV, but the majority of Dunwittys are in rap music. They're the guys who will tell you they know black people better than you.

CINEASTE: *And Myrna Goldfarb, the Jewish media consultant?*
LEE: There was an article in either *Vanity Fair* or *New York* magazine about these young Jewish women publicists for the Wu-Tang Clan, and she was sort of patterned after them. That's another thing, getting back to what we were talking about before, I'm supposed to be anti-Semitic. Because *Bamboozled* has a publicist named Myrna Goldfarb, that's another example of my anti-Semitism! That's what Amy Taubin said in the *Village Voice.*

CINEASTE: *A lot of critics attacked you for the portrayal of the white club owners in* Mo' Better Blues.
LEE: The easiest way to discredit the work of a filmmaker whose subject matter is race is to call him a racist. Simple. There is an unwritten code, especially if you're not Jewish, that if you have a Jewish character who is not positive, you're automatically considered anti-Semitic. But I'm not going to be handcuffed like that or be forced to falsify a situation. You mean to tell me that in the history of the music industry there have never been any white managers who deliberately exploited black artists? That in *Bamboozled,* while I can have rappers going around smoking herb, drinking malt liquor, and killing people, I can't have a Jewish publicist whose character might be a little shaky?

CINEASTE: Godfather II *or* The Sopranos, *both of which feature negative Jewish characters, have never been attacked as anti-Semitic.*
LEE: Let me give you another example. I could never appear in a scene where I'm seated in the back of a cab and talking to the driver about my wife—let's say she's Jewish or whatever—and I say stuff like, "Did you ever see what a .44 does to a Jewish pussy?" If I'd have done that scene that Marty Scorsese did in *Taxi Driver . . .*

CINEASTE: *They'd be coming after you with a rope!*
LEE: *[Laughs]* Exactly. Now, Marty's my dear friend. He's a humanitarian, not a racist at all, but why is it that he cannot only direct that film, but also play that character, and critics are able to distinguish between Martin Scorsese and the character he plays, whereas in my films—even when I'm not playing a character in a scene—critics assume that those are my thoughts, my beliefs, and not those of the characters?

CINEASTE: *When you were casting* Bamboozled, *did any performers turn it down because they felt it was too controversial?*
LEE: Will Smith turned it down. It was either *Bagger Vance* or *Bamboozled*.

CINEASTE: *Bigger paycheck?*
LEE: I don't know if Will understood the material as well as Damon, because if you understood what *Bamboozled* is about, you don't do *The Legend of Bagger Vance*. But Jada was working on him. She wanted him to do this one and they've been looking to do something together. But we're elated with Damon's performance.

CINEASTE: *Were some of the performers a little nervous because* Bamboozled *clearly critiques contemporary black actors who take demeaning roles?*
LEE: No, I mean Damon's a comic anyway. There was a line in the song, "Blak iz Blak," where MC Serch says "it's like giving a rap Grammy to Will Smith," and I said, "No, we can't do that, we gotta change it to Liz Smith." I mean, we're not going to disrespect Will or Jada like that. But, yes, people have asked me, "Have you heard from Ving Rhames? Have you heard from Cuba Gooding?" You remember when Ving Rhames gave his award to Jack Lemmon? That's where we got our scene from, when Pierre gives his award to Matthew Modine, and, as the character says, he "hasn't stopped working since then."

CINEASTE: Bamboozled *takes a violent turn at the end and becomes very melodramatic. We feel that took away some of the sting of the surreal images and replaces the psychic violence with more conventional physical violence.*
LEE: People keep asking, "Why does it turn so violent at the end?" We felt that it was time to pay the piper. When people put out something that pow-

erful, it has to be . . . I mean, Peter Finch's character went down in a hail of bullets at the end of *Network*. I do not feel it's melodramatic.

CINEASTE: *You have a police assassination, essentially, of the Mau Maus . . .*
LEE: That's believable . . . NYPD.

CINEASTE: *You also have the execution of Manray, and then Sloan shoots Pierre, so it's a crescendo of violence.*
LEE: We knew that some people would think that's too much, but we felt it was appropriate for everything that had transpired up to that point. You watch, one day there will be Pay Per View executions on TV, and they'll go back to *Bamboozled* and say, "Hey, he said it right there."

CINEASTE: *You opted for an over-the-top, melodramatic ending, whereas you could have gone for a psychically violent ending, where everybody is traumatized. The best comeuppance for Pierre might have been for him to be forced to live with the success of his show.*
LEE: That wasn't the way we thought about this, because another of the influences on this film was *Sunset Boulevard*, where you have this voiceover at the beginning of the film, and at the end you learn the guy is dead. We wanted to do the same thing with Pierre Delacroix.

CINEASTE: *It's another homage?*
LEE: Oh yeah, Billy Wilder is one of my favorite directors.

CINEASTE: *Do you think the critical response to the film was appropriate?*
LEE: Well, we really can't say what's appropriate, but we knew going in that people were either going to love it or hate it. But, again, my problem with critics is that it seems they don't review the films because they can't get past the so-called persona of Spike Lee. This was really perplexing to me, so after Woody Allen went through this whole thing with Mia Farrow, I made a point of reading every review of his next film, and there was no mention of any of that personal stuff. So I just wish critics would review what's on the screen and not write about who they think I am. Otherwise I think they do a disservice to their readers.

CINEASTE: *Even when a distributor is not behind a film or they botch the adver-*

tising campaign, sometimes good word of mouth can make the difference. Have you
tried to figure out why the film didn't get the kind of audience response you were
looking for?
LEE: Well, number one, it doesn't help when reviews are published which
state that "Spike Lee hates white people." That doesn't encourage moviegoers, and I've heard that sort of thing about me ever since *Do the Right Thing.*
I can show you reviews of that film by people like Joe Klein and David Denby
who said it would cause race riots. And one critic who really has it out for
me, it seems on a personal basis, is Armond White, but I don't even know
the man.

As for word of mouth, some films don't roll out like gangbusters, they
build very slowly. The film also dealt with a subject very painful for the African-American community. I don't think it's a gross generalization to say that
black people are not going to come out in big numbers to support anything
that smells of slavery—with the exception of *Roots*—or anything that has to
do with the pain of being African Americans in this country. I mean, look at
John Singleton's *Rosewood,* for example.

CINEASTE: *Your final montage is pretty painful to watch.*
LEE: So is the footage from the Auschwitz concentration camp, but you
have to look at it. This stuff cannot be swept under the rug.

CINEASTE: *We understand that a lot of the black collectibles seen in the film*
are from your own collection. What accounts for your fascination with them?
LEE: There are a lot of people, both black and white, who collect these
things. For me, it's a reminder of how we were viewed in the past and possibly still are today. You have to understand the hatred. When you look at the
film's end credits sequence, where we show all that stuff, you have to wonder
what type of mind it takes to turn that hatred into a wind-up toy.

CINEASTE: *Why do you think white audiences didn't turn out? Do you think*
it's the attitude that we're beyond all that?
LEE: I wouldn't distinguish between black and white. I think there's a feeling that we—black and white together—are beyond this. You know,
"Nobody goes around in blackface anymore, so why are you bringing this
up?" I was very disappointed in Roger Ebert's review. He's been kind to me
in the past, but he totally misread this film. Of course, no one uses blackface

any more. It's gotten more sophisticated. Gangsta rap videos, a lot of the TV shows on UPN and WB—a lot of us are still acting as buffoons and coons.

CINEASTE: *What, finally, would you like viewers to take away from* Bamboozled?

LEE: I want people to think about the power of images, not just in terms of race, but how imagery is used and what sort of social impact it has—how it influences how we talk, how we think, how we view one another. In particular, I want them to see how film and television have historically, from the birth of both mediums, produced and perpetuated distorted images. Film and television started out that way, and here we are, at the dawn of a new century, and a lot of that madness is still with us today.

INDEX

Conversations with Filmmakers Series

Peter Brunette, General Editor

The collected interviews with notable modern directors, including

Robert Altman / Theo Angelopolous / Bernardo Bertolucci / Jane Campion / George Cukor / Clint Eastwood / John Ford / Jean-Luc Godard / Peter Greenaway / John Huston / Jim Jarmusch / Elia Kazan / Stanley Kubrick / Mike Leigh / George Lucas / John Sayles / Martin Scorsese / Steven Soderbergh / Steven Spielberg / Oliver Stone / Quentin Tarantino / Orson Welles / Billy Wilder / Zhang Yimou